ABOUT THE AUTHOR

Lev Parikian is a writer, conductor and keen birdwatcher. He is the author of *Into the Tangled Bank* and *Music to Eat Cake By*. He lives in south London with his family, who are getting used to his increasing enthusiasm for nature. As a birdwatcher, his most prized sightings are a golden oriole in the Alpujarras and a black redstart at Dungeness Power Station.

LEV PARIKIAN

Why Do Birds Suddenly Disappear?

200 birds. 12 months. 1 lapsed birdwatcher.

unbound

First published in 2018
This paperback edition first published in 2021

Unbound
Level 1, Devonshire House, One Mayfair Place, London W1J 8AJ
www.unbound.com

Goldcrest illustration by Alan Harris, www.alanharrisbirdartist.co.uk

Text Design by PDQ

A CIP record for this book is available from the British Library

ISBN 978-1-80018-021-5 (trade pbk)
ISBN 978-1-78352-483-9 (trade hbk)
ISBN 978-1-78352-482-2 (ebook)
ISBN 978-1-78352-484-6 (limited edition)

Printed in Great Britain by Clays Ltd, Elcograf S.p.A.

1 3 5 7 9 8 6 4 2

To Tessa and Oliver, twin pillars of tolerance

JUNE 2012

It's not the teapot it once was. White china, with a pretty floral pattern in relief, it's longer than it is wide and has a certain faded elegance. But there are cracks and chips all over, and dark patches where it has been mended and the glue has seeped out. It has been used, and dropped. But someone has bothered to mend it. It's a terrible pourer, so often the downfall of a promising pot. But we don't know that yet.

It sits on the kitchen table of my mother's last house, the crest of a wave in a surging sea of teapots. My mother was a keeper of stuff, a collector of objects. This made for a childhood founded on curiosity. What's this? And why is it? And let's keep it so we can look at it. My father too was a collector, an annotator, a curator of lists. Miniature glass hats, wine labels, a notebook with details of every concert he ever played.

Mostly, I am grateful for these habits. I've inherited them, and they allow for occasional moments of heady nostalgia, afternoons spent knee-deep in old photographs. But right now, as we wade our way through the detritus of a life of accumulation, they feel like a monumental pain in the arse. The teapots are ranged before us on the table. Also in the kitchen are three dozen china toast racks, twenty-one pairs of glasses, nine keys, half a dozen unfinished Post-it pads with things like 'Call plumber' scrawled on them, and a small colourful plastic bird that makes an irritating tweeting sound when it rocks, which it does often.

Our friend Annie, also latterly my mother's friend, surveys the scene. She's devastated but efficient.

'What are we doing with the toast racks?' she says.

'Dunno. Know any toast-rack collectors?'

'Why so many?'

'It was an accidental collection.'

'Accidental?'

'They both thought the other collected them. Neither of them did. After a few birthdays it turned out they both did after all.'

Annie contemplates them in silence. This is her business. It's what she does. She's not just a house clearer – she's brilliant at helping people decide what to get rid of. But I can tell she's far from chuffed at the prospect of the toast racks.

'Well, I can try them at car boots, but don't expect anything. What about the teapots?'

'How many does anyone need? Get rid.'

'Oxfam. I'll just check inside them.' I give her a look, but Annie doesn't quail easily, one of the reasons she was friends with my mother. 'People put things in teapots.'

Indeed they do.

There are two pieces of paper, folded together. On the first the handwriting is scrawly and unfamiliar.

Manoug,

With thanks and congratulations on a fine performance.

RVW

The second, smaller, flimsier, has my mother's handwriting on it.

Teapot given to M by R Vaughan Williams. KEEP!

I turn to Annie.

'I think we might keep this.'

And my head brims full with the sound of my father's violin, silent these twenty-five years, the silver chain of music soaring upwards, higher and higher and higher, into the boundless sky, just as RVW intended.

JUNE 2013

It starts, like so many things in my life, with an idiotic mistake.

Chris is an affable chap, thin, with bright eyes and a ruddy complexion. Overtly outdoorsy in a way I will never be. He moved from the north-east to the Isle of Wight forty years ago, and has kept the accent. He's working on the walls. We're holidaying.

Tea is being had.

The weather is glorious in the way only a summer day near the sea can be. Bright and sunny, plenty warm enough to spend the day outside in perfect comfort, but with a fresh breeze coming in from the coast half a mile away. Being British, we're making polite conversation. Being British, we start with the weather.

'Glorious today,' I say.

'Oh aye.'

He appears happy to leave it at that. I don't feel I've quite done my bit.

'Lovely yesterday, too.'

'Aye.'

Progress, of sorts.

'We've been pretty lucky so far this year.'

'Yup.'

I am so bad at this.

'Were you working yesterday?'

'No, actually... we went up to the downs for some birding.'

This is music to my ears. I'm in a conversation with a workman and I have an opportunity to discuss something I know a bit about. This is rare. I place people who can fix things on a pedestal. I look up to them, in awe of their mysterious talents, and terrified that a stray comment will expose my ignorance. Chris, as a professional thing-fixer, is akin to a god in my eyes. So any way in is welcome. I pounce.

'Oh, are you a birdwatcher?'

'Oh aye. The Isle of Wight's grand for birding.'

'I can imagine.' I weigh up whether to reveal my interest. Oh, go on then. 'I loved birdwatching as a kid. I don't have so much time for it any more, but I still love it.'

Anything to stay in the conversation.

'Oh aye?'

He's polite but non-committal.

'So what do you get on the Isle of Wight? Lots of seabirds, I'd imagine.'

The words 'It's an island, you idiot – of course there are seabirds' seem to tremble on Chris's lips, but he's kind enough to suppress them.

'That's right. And loads of migrants at the right time of year. Diverse habitats, see. Estuaries, cliffs, mudflats, downs, woods, farmland.'

'Fantastic. See much yesterday?'

Here it comes.

'We had the first nightingale of the year. Gorgeous. Pretty rare these days.'

I have options. I could say nothing. I could make polite gosh-how-lovely noises. I could change the subject, talk about art, go-karting, nuclear physics. Anything. But I have to show that I can keep up.

'Oh, I saw one too.'

4

Idiot.

Chris is surprised, politely dubious.

'Really?'

'Oh yes. It was up...'

It hits me.

Not a nightingale. Of course not a nightingale. Never a nightingale.

Small brown bird, yes. Nondescript plumage, certainly. Known for its song, absolutely. But never a nightingale.

Slivers of old knowledge seep back.

You don't see nightingales. Or at least you have to work quite hard to. They're secretive, fond of pouring out their liquid song from the depths of a bush merely for the fun of seeing hapless birders in a state of delirium.

What they don't do is go up to the top of the downs where there isn't a tree or a bush or a hedge in sight, and, to rejig the poet Shelley, pour from their full heart profuse strains of unpremeditated art while higher still and higher springing from the earth like a cloud of fire.

Nightingales don't do that. Skylarks do.

Chris is waiting for me to finish my sentence.

All I need to do is this: 'Gah, silly me, not a nightingale. A skylark. I saw a skylark. Ha ha ha! What a mirthful moment has unintentionally resulted from my idiocy! Do tell me, an ignoramus, about the nightingale.'

But I can't. I can't admit I'm wrong. I'm a conductor. We don't do 'wrong'.

So I leave it there, like a turd in the middle of the carpet, and ignore it, even though I know I'm an idiot, Chris knows I'm an idiot, the whole world knows I'm an idiot.

I blather on for a bit, pretending I can't remember where I saw this mythical nightingale, and the conversation staggers on.

Chris drains his cup and gets back to work, pausing at the

door for a second. He seems on the verge of saying something, but he's an affable chap, as I may have mentioned. The moment passes and we each get on with our day.

After Chris has gone I sit looking out across the countryside and beyond it to the sea. Large black birds wheel and turn behind me, cawing and grawing, communicating in a language that to my ears is harsh and grating, but to them is conversation.

Carrion crows. Or are they rooks?

I used to know this stuff. I really did. Well, some of it.

I turn to look over the road. This part of the island is known as The Undercliff, and the land banks sharply up behind the house.

More snippets of knowledge return. The birds are circling a group of tall trees. That's a rookery, isn't it? So they must be rooks, not carrion crows, although I'm still none the wiser about how you distinguish one from the other.

They're acrobatic, tumbling down then soaring on an updraught, describing a broad arc before coming in to land, branches trampolining under their weight.

A movement to my left. A bird, flying across the road and landing on the wall in front of me, its direct flight a rebuke to the rooks' meandering. It's purposeful, a piebald flash with a purple-green gloss in its tail.

My mother's voice in my head, the words on my lips.

'Hello Mr Magpie, how's your lady wife?' Then spit three times.

Not actual spitting. More of a quick 'ttht'. A habit inherited from my mum, vestige of an old country superstition. And obligatory when you see a magpie. Magpies are harbingers of death. Good job I said hello to it, then. That'll stop it, the murdering bastard. A group of crows is called a 'murder', I recall, and while these thoughts waft through my head I'm suddenly aware that the place is full of birds I only partly recognise.

A bunch of sparrows jazzing around in the tree just over the wall. Definitely sparrows. But which kind? House? Tree? Hedge? They're in a tree. Must be tree sparrows then. Or hedge. Is that the one also called a dunnock?

I can't remember. And for some reason this upsets me. Why? I don't mind not knowing the name of the tree. I don't do trees. Never have. My dad did, even planting some in the field next to our house a couple of years before he died. They'll be all grown up by now. I picture them as they were, whippy saplings kept on the straight and narrow with restraining girdles, like the braces on my teeth. Oliver will be that age soon. I hope he doesn't have to endure what I did, teeth-wise.

I replay the earlier conversation in my head, the habitual practice of the paranoid. I'm struck by the irony of my mistake. Skylarks were part of my childhood, a regular spectacle over the field by the bus stop at the end of the lane. Once, I walked the quarter mile home, the larks' song lingering in my head, replaced as I approached the house by the sound of my father's violin as he practised *The Lark Ascending*, composed by the owner of a certain teapot. A satisfying conjunction of nature and art.

Confusing a skylark with a nightingale is an understandable slip of a rusty brain, a conflation of two brown songbirds. But still. It's like confusing Schumann and Schubert. No, worse, it's like confusing Schumann and Manfred Mann.

I try to dismiss it with a shake of the head, and am glad to be distracted. Oliver is approaching, cricket ball in hand.

'Catching practice, Dad?'

Catching practice it is. Sod birds. They're not for me.

JANUARY 2016

New Year. New hope. New plans.

Same old, same old.

The year 2016 begins with resolutions, mostly abandoned within a fortnight, according to long custom.

I claim not to make resolutions, knowing they're pointless. But like many who make that bold statement, I compile an informal and secret list in my head. Writing it down and sharing it would only lead to later remorse. It takes shape nonetheless, item by item.

More exercise, obviously.

Less booze, obviously.

I could lose some weight.

Some flexibility would be nice. My toes seem further away than they used to be. I'd like to be able to touch them when I'm seventy.

If I'm seventy.

Ah yes, that reminds me: find a way of silencing the little voice that pops up daily and reminds me I'm going to die.

I add two words to the list: INNER CALM.

I have a yoga app on my iPad. It's almost invasively peaceful. Inoffensive music meanders in the background while lithe people contort themselves into positions I can only dream of; a soothing voice accompanies the routine.

After five minutes I want to hurl the iPad out of the window.

But I do the yoga. And the mere fact of doing it makes me

feel better. Perhaps the devotion of time to yoga-like activity is the key rather than the yoga itself. Maybe a ten-minute nap on a purple foam mat every morning will provide all the rejuvenation I need.

Flushed with this early success, and eager not to be the guy who gives up within a week, I research local classes. I soon find my ideal. A Monday-morning session in a bright loft space ten minutes' walk from home. Our teacher, a tall and cheerful Californian called Gingi, has a way of making you feel that turning up is itself an achievement. This I can relate to.

'Slide your hands below your knees, maybe to your shins. Perhaps even your ankles. Don't overreach, just put yourself in a place of challenge.'

I grab my feet. No challenge at all. I'm brilliant at this. At some level I'm aware that being brilliant isn't the point, but still. Yay me.

When it comes to the sitting postures, my composure evaporates.

Sitting on the floor and I are uneasy bedfellows. I become aware of stiffness in my legs. I assume the starting posture with difficulty. And when Gingi rocks smoothly forwards, his weight transferring over his feet to crouch on all fours, inner calm has never seemed more remote.

'Ungainly' is one word you could use to describe my movements. 'Catastrophically awkward' are two more.

I'm rubbish at this. Woe is me.

Gingi's voice elbows its way through the defeatist noise in my head.

'Don't worry about what you can and can't do. Do what you can.'

Talk about timing.

Maybe he's telepathic. It doesn't matter if I can't do it. That's the point.

By the end of the session I've connected breath with movement and put myself in a place of challenge but not stress. No matter that I've spent an hour exhaling when I should have been inhaling and vice versa. That will come with practice.

I emerge feeling calm and purposeful. I have the rest of the morning to myself. There's work to be done, but I'm a freelance conductor, familiar with the internal dialogue between boss and employee.

Just going for a walk.

You going to learn that Strauss later?

Of course.

OK then. Twenty-five minutes. Forty, tops.

See you this afternoon.

Fine.

The park is a mile away. A couple of laps then home for lunch. Health, energy, vitality. Perhaps it's something to do with being fifty and born into a family with a history of heart disease on the male side. Perhaps it's because, for the first time in my life, the scales are beginning to nudge 80 kg, regardless of my efforts to stand on them more lightly. I used to vow never to let my weight go over 78. Now look at me, all chins and paunches and clothes that feel one notch too tight.

The park is familiar territory, patrolled by dog walkers, yummy mummies and joggers, their peaceful morning occasionally disturbed by a marauding cyclist or park vehicle. I stride through the gates, listening to a fascinating podcast about Thucydides, the details of which will leave my head fifteen seconds after it's finished. Sun. Sky. Frost. I ponder nothing more urgent than whether to take the left or right fork to skirt the boating lake.

A brouhaha from behind the trees makes the decision for me.

Eight Canada geese in a mood to party are difficult to ignore. I hear them clamouring, cackling, honking. This is what they're known for. Noise and poo and general unpleasantness.

11

Their ubiquity, dominance and brazenness combine to make them almost universally unpopular among those who frequent public spaces. Shit-squirters, honking bullies, bastards.

I get all that.

But as I turn the corner and the lake comes into view, they're a magnificent sight. A squadron of eight birds, organising themselves into formation, calling to each other in fervid excitement, a frenzy of organised chaos coming together at the last second as the final goose slots into place. They churn the water and the air, sending their fellow waterfowl scuttling for cover.

They come right at me, wings straining, so low I could almost reach out and touch their undercarriage. The air is full of their honking and flapping, the geometry of their formation kaleidoscoping – Escher brought to life as they heave themselves up. The displaced air wafts over me, a reminder of the weight and difficulty of flight.

As they deliver noisy chaos to another part of genteel Dulwich, I'm struck by the everyday beauty of the spectacle. A common bird flying from one place to another in a group. It's what they do. Maybe it's just the thrill of that movement and noise so close above me that stirs the blood. Or the timing of it, as if they were calling to me from behind the trees and assembled for my benefit, knowing the pram-pushers and mutt-draggers would dismiss them as mere background to modern city life. Maybe I'm just in a heightened state of post-yoga awareness, liable to wonder at anything. Hello birds, hello sky.

Whatever, they stay with me all the way home, those geese, the images of that magical minute looping in the cinema of my mind.

And they trigger something, a long-forgotten interest, a hidden memory buried deep under three decades of other stuff. There have been moments when it's resurfaced, but they've been fleeting. Noticing the swifts' return every year; getting and filling a bird feeder when we moved and acquired an accessible garden; rescuing a live woodpigeon from the jaws of the cat. But for each flicker of interest there's been a subconscious tamping down, as if to say, 'That's enough now. You're too busy for such fripperies.'

Now it comes surging to the surface, elbowing other thoughts aside. On the way home I not only notice the birds, I seek them out. There's another little park over the road. Why not go that way? Perhaps there'll be a moorhen or two. And sure enough, there they are, black corks bobbing on the water, distinguished from their coot cousins by the red blob on their forehead.

And that little ball of fluff on an ice-lolly stick. Long-tailed tit, no? Yes? No? Not sure. Not a wagtail. Too small. Sweet little thing, anyway.

A blackbird on the grass, head cocked, listening out for the movement of a worm. Robins, blue tits, great tits, magpies, crows, pigeons. The air is suddenly thick with them. Where have they been all these years?

I go home and revisit my past.

It's a handsome book, hardback, coffee-table-ish, with a striking portrait of a tawny owl, all feathers, eyes and talons, on the front. *The Reader's Digest Book of British Birds*. It sat on the shelf in our Oxfordshire home alongside *Grove's Dictionary of Music and Musicians*, *The Shorter Oxford English Dictionary*, and art books of glossy beauty.

Ours was a household of books: antiquarian ones my mother's trade, Armenian ones my father's hobby. They filled the shelves and every available surface. Old and new, read and unread, pristine and trashed. Thrillers, biography, humour; Jane Austen, Dick Francis, Ruth Rendell; *War and Peace, Tintin, Our Man in Havana*.

Both my parents read widely. I read a lot, but preferred the intense repetition method – devouring and redevouring my favourites, the emphasis on simplicity and comfort. I adored *Peanuts* from an early age and well into my teens, the deceptive simplicity of the drawings attractive to my lazy brain, their familiarity bringing solace when everything else was too much work. Laura Ingalls Wilder I read over and over and over again – something about the wildness and romance of a world far removed from my own somehow speaking to me. Then there was Roald Dahl, who magically knew what it was like to be me, and constructed his worlds according to my desires. Later I would appreciate the wit of P. G. Wodehouse, the acerbity of Evelyn Waugh, the mind-bending brilliance of Douglas Adams. But early on my tastes were straightforward. They remain with me still.

More than narrative, though, I loved lists, facts, graphs and charts. *Wisden*, the cricketing bible, was pored over, the Records section obsessively read and reread.

So the listing of birds, for a tragic eleven-year-old with long summer holidays to fill, was a logical enough activity.

Interesting, that use of the word 'tragic'; the assumption being that solitude equates to loneliness, that having an interest outside the norm is necessarily to be pitied. And the moment that interest tips over into what's regarded as unnatural expertise, we lay ourselves open to mockery.

Spod. Saddo. Geek.

And that's the widespread image of the birdwatcher. Bit of a nerd, maybe socially inept, prone to wearing drab clothes.

I was blissfully unaware of this. I just loved the birds.

It comes back to me as I leaf through the book. I place myself in the shoes of eleven-year-old me, lured by the fascination of the avian world. Each page is dominated by a fine colour illustration of a bird in a dramatic, if not always realistic, pose. So the hawfinch, shy and secretive, is shown eyeballing the reader – its proximity a far cry from the likely reality – and the relative hugeness of its bill diminished by foreshortening. The red-throated diver, mightily averse to land, seems to be hopping from foot to foot as if on hot coals. These striking illustrations were my gateway drug to the intoxicating world of bird guides.

If the illustrations were the marijuana, the distribution maps were the crack cocaine. Each bird had its own. The chaffinch, available in a nearby tree regardless of geography or season, had a map completely shaded with a delicate green probably known to posh paint suppliers as Splunge or Desperate Chameleon. Fieldfares, abundant winter visitors from Scandinavia, were afforded similar treatment, but in a light hue of Blotting Paper.

Most fascinating were the birds with narrow distribution, the rarer and more remote the better. When *The Reader's Digest Book of British Birds* was published in 1969, the red-backed shrike, once abundant and widespread throughout England and Wales, was down to about 150 pairs and fading fast. The perky-looking Dartford warbler was found nowhere near Dartford but only in Hampshire and Dorset. Nearly wiped out by the harsh winter of 1962–63, it was down to just ten pairs. The golden eagle, proud and wild and impossibly romantic, inhabited the Scottish Highlands, as remote as the moon. As I look at it now I relive my boyhood longing to see one in the flesh.

While the maps and illustrations had a magnetic allure, the text went largely unread. It was all about habitat and breeding and so on, and although it sustained my interest to a certain point, I was fuzzy on the finer details. I'd skimmed it enough to know that, despite the map's assertion that the redshank was widely distributed across the country, I wasn't going to see one at the bird table any time soon. And if we saw a bird of prey hovering by the side of the road, my knowledge of wing shape and likely behaviour were enough for me to holler 'kestrel!' without hesitation.

I suppose my parents bought this book for their own use, as part of a general interest in the countryside to which they'd moved when I was expected in 1965. But I remember it as 'my' book, and it bears unmistakable evidence of its provenance. Biro scrawlings, chocolate stains, a slight separation of the front cover from its binding.

I go through it at random, alighting on birds familiar and unknown. Collared dove, great skua, wryneck. Quail, scaup, red-necked phalarope. The names, as fascinating as the birds themselves, are known to me in a way that the names of butterflies or insects aren't. They surge back into my head as if they've never been away.

At the front there's a ten-page pictorial index of all the birds, over 200 of them. They're pictured side by side for handy comparison, grouped by colour, many with a tick in biro against their name to indicate that I saw them.

As I read, I'm swamped with outrage at the sins of my youth.

First is the blackbird. The tick against it is confident, and with good reason. We've all seen a blackbird. It's barely possible not to.

Next, the starling. Again, I'm on safe ground. In the 1970s there were loads of starlings everywhere, ubiquitous as air.

And now the shocker.

Black redstart.

Its tick has a shaky, apologetic air, as if deep down I knew it would return to haunt me.

I didn't see a black redstart.

How do I know?

Well, for one thing it's a relatively scarce bird. For another it favours rubble-strewn wasteland and nuclear power stations. And for another, I just know I didn't. I would remember.

Memory is a funny thing. Even at forty years' distance I retain a perfect image of my bedroom, its shape, size and smell embedded in my brain through daily familiarity over two decades: the sash windows through which I would hear my father mowing the lawn on summer evenings after I'd gone to bed; the fluorescent stars and moon stuck to the ceiling; the bookshelf, tall, unstable, books falling off it daily; the electric fire over which I warmed my school shirt on cold winter mornings; the gramophone in the corner, through which I became familiar with words and music – Beethoven, Mozart, Abba, Queen, Victor Borge, Flanders and Swann; my safe, a small metallic green box in which I kept bits of change, the occasional pound note and a fragment of rock my friend David swore had been brought back to earth from the moon landing.

There are the vague memories, too, impressions of a mood or feeling. The sense of tranquillity as the sun set on another endless summer day in which I'd done nothing except patrol the garden with a cricket bat and ball, or the engulfing tedium of rainy Sunday afternoons, all my books reread a dozen times and sod all on the telly.

And there are specific moments, occasions of high drama or comedy. The day I nearly made my father drop his Stradivarius; the time my mother called the milkman the rudest word in the English language; the Terrible Stereo Wire-Cutting Incident.

In this mass of memories, the sighting of a black redstart would have taken pride of place near the top.

The black redstart is just the beginning. As I work my way through the list, I don't know whether to be appalled or impressed by my sheer chutzpah. To place a tick against a bird, your identification must be certain. The chances of my fledgling ornithological eyes distinguishing the Arctic and common terns at a hundred paces were as slim as a stick insect on a diet. And if I saw a quail ('shy and secretive, usually only forced into flight by gun-dogs') then it could only have been on a plate, accompanied by game chips and a half bottle of Château Beychevelle '72.

As the list of imaginary birds lengthens, I sit back and review my childhood. It's an uncomfortable experience.

Obviously we all lie sometimes. Doctors and dentists know this. How often do you floss? Er, well... How much do you drink? Oh, right, I mean, yes, definitely within the guidelines... whatever they are.

If you say you've never lied, you're a liar.

But it's a question of scale. And here was incontrovertible evidence that I was washed through with mendacity.

Harsh? Possibly. But I had previous. The memory of my most extravagant bout of lying rises unbidden, wakening like the kraken, and just as fearsome.

My father couldn't swim. Never learned. My mother could but did so rarely. My brother, though, took to it with ease. I have memories of him scything through the water, a veritable Mark Spitz to my awestruck eyes. He could do the butterfly. The butterfly! Nobody can do the butterfly apart from ridiculous water babies with waists as narrow as a cotton reel and shoulders the size of Kent. My brother Step could.

My swimming, though. Feeble. I flangled around in the shallow end, crying whenever anyone splashed my face and keeping as much of my torso out of the water as possible.

After a while my inability even to float successfully became an embarrassment. I joined the ranks of the sinkers, the jetsam of society, destined no doubt for bitter, unfulfilled lives, our rancid discontent fuelled by our childhood inability to swim more than two feet without sinking to the bottom of the pool.

The orange inflatable armbands and chipped polystyrene floatboards – I needed three just to avoid drowning – were the final humiliation. I had to learn to swim.

Or I could just lie.

In a carefully planned campaign, I came home from school over a period of two weeks with reports of my growing prowess. I reckoned that by the time I was called on to prove my new-found powers of swimmery, I'd have had plenty of time to learn the essentials.

I told a story of ever-increasing bravado. I had, I informed my mother one evening, passed my 'width', a test which entailed, unsurprisingly, swimming one width of the pool without touching the bottom or sides. Then my 'two widths'. Then, thrillingly, the 'length'. Thrillingly, because it meant I'd ventured into the deep end, albeit with the constant ministrations of the PE teacher, who walked alongside the pool with a long hook in one hand, ready to fish me out. In his other hand he probably carried a medicine ball, because you weren't a PE teacher in the 1970s unless you had one of those permanently about your person should the need arise to throw it unexpectedly at the spindliest boy in the class.

In truth I was still floundering six inches from the edge, ready to cling to it the moment a drop of water came near my face.

The breaking point came. Two weeks after the last of my grand tales of natatorial derring-do, my bluff was called. We would, my mum said, be visiting her sister that weekend. What an opportunity for me to display my swimming skills in her beautiful temperature-controlled pool, didn't I agree?

Up to a point, Lord Copper.

Of all the tears in my life, none were more bitterly shed than at bedtime that evening. The whole story came out in a bubbling snotfest unprecedented in Oxfordshire. My mum, sympathetic but with a keen sense of the comically absurd, must have been hard-pushed to bite back the laughter.

Sadly, to judge by the disgraceful litany of falsehoods before me, this comeuppance doesn't appear to have changed my behaviour at all.

I do a quick stocktake. According to the markings in the book, I compiled a list of 133 birds in my childhood. Of these, it seems at least 30 per cent were fictional. Deep down, I'm not surprised. Memories of my habitual birdwatching activities float to the surface.

There's a flock of gulls over there. Herring gull. Tick. Black-headed.

19

Of course. Lesser black-backed. Probably. Bound to be a great black-backed in there too. Let's throw in common as well, why not? And a kittiwake for good measure.

I ask myself why I didn't pursue a career in politics.

These invented sightings have a whiff of Mitty-esque fantasy, but also remind me of Snoopy, the best beagle ever. Some of my favourite *Peanuts* strips were those in which Snoopy sat on his dog kennel fighting the accursed Red Baron. The habitual commentary, 'Here's the World War I fighter pilot...' later extended to other spheres, in particular his repeated attempts to achieve publication ('Here's the world-famous author...'), and reached a zenith with, 'Here's the world-famous checkout clerk.' Looking back from the safety of thirty-odd years, I can picture myself striding around the garden, binoculars at the ready. 'Here's the world-famous birdwatcher...'

I put the book away. In the real world there are things to do. Tessa will be back soon, in need of sustenance after a morning of singing at three-year-olds. I have emails to answer, procrastination to perfect. And at some stage I really must do some work. Easy as it is to assume that conductors merely wave their arms in time to whatever music the orchestra chooses to play, some pieces require serious study.

Birdwatching? It's for the birds.

But as I make myself a cup of coffee, a silly thought pops into my head.

Why not start again? Why not go out and look for birds? Why not make it this year's project?

There's my resolution, right there.

More exercise? I would get it hunting down a bittern in the reed beds of Suffolk. Inner calm? Almost inevitable when you're sitting in a hide waiting for a water rail to show its head. Improving the mind? Learn the difference between the plumages of a chiffchaff and a willow warbler and get back to me.

As the idea takes root, I look out of the window. A blue tit is at the feeder, ferreting around for seeds and then bouncing off on a secret blue tit mission.

It starts here.

One.

As well as a rich history of lying, I boast a decent inventory of abandoned projects. There's a pattern to them. A flurry of enthusiasm, a cooling-off period, a 'just-get-on-with-it' phase, a lull as real life intrudes, neglect as the project dies an early death, a brief resurrection as I revisit my grandiose plans weeks later, the gentle ebbing of interest as I realise it was a stupid idea, the quiet and unlamented death. It's been like that all my life. R.I.P. The Great Lego City (1972), the Scalextric World Championship (1979), the plan to become Music Director of the Berlin Philharmonic by the time I was fifty (1989–1994). Projects large and small, all discarded, fecklessness always marginally outpointing enthusiasm.

I know myself well enough to recognise that without a tangible goal my project will fizzle out. I have to set a target. Maybe it's a boy thing.

The statistical side of birdwatching has me torn. On the one hand I'm happy to take the birds at face value, to note their existence, observe their habits, derive pleasure from the way they flit from branch to branch or riffle through their feathers with their beak.

On the other hand I have an irrational feeling that if I can see more birds this will in some subtle way make me better. Better at birdwatching; better at life.

It's pathetic, this need for validation through something so inconsequential. Ludicrous, absurd, laughable.

It's also just a bit addictive.

A part of me dies inside to consider this compartmentalising of nature, this reduction of the glories of the avian world to a series of ticks in spreadsheet cells. But then there's the other part, the kid who pored over the league tables in the *Rothman's Football Yearbook*;* who memorised the first sixty decimal places of pi from a postcard bought at the Paris science museum; who will never forget that Garfield St Aubrun Sobers was the leading run scorer in Test matches, notching up 8,032 runs,† and that Donald Bradman's 6,996 runs were scored at an average of 99.94. The ability to summon such useless factoids at will has deserted me, but interest in them hasn't waned. That's the kind of boy I was, the kind of person I am. Maybe it's time to come to terms with that. And that sad, tragic, spoddy me loves the counting, the ticking off. He is, in fact, secretly thrilled by it.

How many birds could I see in a year? 100? 200? 300? Which would be my 100th, 200th, 300th?

Come to that, how many birds are there in Britain?

I don't know.

I take to the Internet. There has to be a list somewhere.

There's a list. Oh boy, is there a list. Birders love a list. Day lists, week lists, month lists, year lists, life lists, garden lists, county lists, walk-to-work lists, seen-from-the-train lists, glimpsed-out-of-the-bathroom-window-while-doing-a-poo lists.

So inevitably there's an official list, compiled by the British Ornithologists' Union, of all the birds seen in Britain since records began in 1879. At the time of my looking it up, it numbers 601.

I go through it, tallying. Lacking a napkin or the back of an

---

* Oxford United, 20th in League Division Two in 1976 with 33 points and a goal difference of -20 – relegated, along with York City and Portsmouth. You're welcome.

† Dammit, now I need to change my PIN.

envelope on which I can do the calculation in time-honoured fashion, I resort to a Moleskine notebook. It'll have to do.

About half the 601 are classified as 'rare'. In some cases (booted eagle, eastern towhee, Scopoli's shearwater), they've been seen in this country just once. Even when sightings have been reasonably regular (Bonaparte's gull, Blyth's reed warbler, semipalmated sandpiper), they're sporadic enough for an amateur like me not to bother with them. So, much as I'd love to see a dark-eyed junco, Moussier's redstart or yellow-bellied sapsucker, I'm not going to hold my breath.

One bird, the great auk, is an even less likely prospect. It was hunted to extinction in the nineteenth century.

Well done us.

I divide the birds into four categories: Already Seen, Will Probably See, Might See and No Chance. The Already Seen column, after some hawk-eyed feeder-watching and a couple of trips to the park, numbers nineteen. The No Chance column kicks on towards fifty and beyond.

As the columns fill I find myself mentally reorganising my year. Maybe I can wangle a gig in west Wales, nip out in the break, lean over a cliff and tick off a chough.

Quite a number of birds go into the Might See column simply because I've no idea where or how they're to be found. Is a long-tailed duck commonplace in the right part of the world or a notable rarity? What is the right part of the world? What the hell am I doing?

There are birds of whose appearance I have only the vaguest impression. If a garganey sat on the table in front of me, could I identify it? Beyond knowing that it's a kind of duck, I'd be stumped. The same with waders. What's the difference between a dunlin and a knot? Hold on, I know this. Umm, no I don't. And just reading the list of warblers, all of them small, greeny-brown and – to my inexperienced eye – identical, is enough to put me off the whole idea.

But I persevere, and in the end, through a combination of 15 per cent rigorous scientific research and 85 per cent what-the-hell guesswork, I land on a possible total somewhere between 180 and 210. Let's say 200, a pleasingly round number. Achievable but not ridiculously easy.

As I delve deeper into where and when these birds might be found, I discover that while 200 seems a lot, for some people it's merely a launch pad for their annual birding activities. There seem to be plenty of birders who regularly see 300 or more in a year. Should I be setting my sights higher?

Not if I want to retain my sanity, dignity and family.

My provisional schedule is already full of controversial jaunts, diversions and enforced family days out. I envisage Tessa and Oliver trailing twenty yards behind me in the hail on a December day in the Cairngorms, muttering to each other as I reassert my conviction that we're bound to see the ptarmigan just after this next peak. Devoted wife and son they may be, but I fear that extending the target would stretch the limits of my expertise and our family unit to, and possibly beyond, breaking point. It would mean crossing the line from nascent birder to apprentice twitcher.

There's that word. Twitcher. Commonly misused to denote anyone with a passing interest in matters avian. I've done it myself.

But twitchers are a breed apart. Where a birder* goes out prepared to enjoy any bird that might cross their path, the twitcher's agenda is more specific. Rarities.

Distance and inconvenience are no object. If a Hudsonian whimbrel is reported in Penzance, off to Penzance they rush,

---

* They were called 'birdwatchers' when I was young. If the current mania for abbreviation runs to its logical conclusion, it's only a matter of time before they're known as 'brdrs'.

even though they live in Swaffham and have a meeting with Derek from HR at half two. If, on the way, news comes in of a gull-billed tern at Grangemouth, well that's Sunday morning sorted, and never mind the trip to Alton Towers with the kids.

The twitcher exhibits little interest in commonplace birds. Show them a blue tit and a faint sneer will cross their face, as if to say, 'Really, though? A blue tit?' But tell them a semipalmated plover has been seen in Cley and they'll pause only to grab their spotting scope before setting the satnav and disappearing in a cloud of exhaust.

Like any obsessive, the twitcher is easy to mock. But their affliction is no different from the one that drives Andy Murray or Jonas Kaufmann to be as good at tennis or singing as they possibly can.* There's the thrill of the chase too, the sublimation of the primitive hunting urge. Until really quite recently the standard way to identify a bird was to blast it out of the sky and then have a look. Only with the development of sophisticated optics and a more benevolent approach to the environment has the modern way of 'look but don't touch' become prevalent. The twitcher is part hunter, part collector. Find the bird, log it, on to the next. This isn't to say that the twitcher is without sentiment. For most of them the driving force, albeit sometimes masked by a frenzied desire to see more birds than his† competitors, is a genuine love of birds. And this is matched by identification skills of which I can only dream. So if I mock, it's from a place of affection and admiration, even jealousy. But, fascinating though twitching is from an anthropological point of view, it's not how I want to spend my year. So there's my first rule: no twitching. I'll travel – a year watching the birds in the back garden would

---

*   Other tennis players and singers are available, but you're not going to do much better than those two.

†   And yes, they are, as far as I can tell, mostly men.

see me fall short by a distance – but there will be no careering across the country because someone in Liskeard thought they saw a wryneck.

Another factor restricting my final total is my second, unbreakable rule: no cheating. I intend to be firm with myself on this, almost requiring that any bird wear a lapel badge and greet me with a warm, 'Hello, Lev. I'll be your gadwall for today. Do tell me if I can be of any assistance,' before I admit it to the list. Not only is it a moral imperative, I'm keen to avoid a repeat of the Swimming Test Incident.

I have my rules: no twitching, no cheating. Let the game begin.

January ticks (19)

West Norwood & Dulwich

Blue Tit *Cyanistes caeruleus*, Woodpigeon *Columba palumbus*, Great Tit *Parus major*, Blackbird *Turdus merula*, Robin *Erithacus rubecula*, Rock Dove/Feral Pigeon *Columba livia*, Magpie *Pica pica*, Carrion Crow *Corvus corone*, Goldfinch *Carduelis carduelis*, Starling *Sturnus vulgaris*, House Sparrow *Passer domesticus*, Wren *Troglodytes troglodytes*, Dunnock *Prunella modularis*, Mute Swan *Cygnus olor*, Canada Goose *Branta canadensis*, Mallard *Anas platyrhynchos*, Tufted Duck *Aythya fuligula*, Moorhen *Gallinula chloropus*, Coot *Fulica atra*

FEBRUARY 2016

Richard Strauss was not a man plagued by self-doubt. As he lay on his deathbed at the end of a long and fruitful life, he said to his daughter-in-law, 'You know, Anna, it is just as I wrote it in *Death and Transfiguration*.'

The work he's referring to was written sixty-five years earlier. It has a notably transcendent ending, the foreboding and turmoil of the opening twenty minutes resolving into peaceful acceptance. So if he's to be believed, your passage to the hereafter will involve little more than lying on a gilded Hungarian goose-down duvet while winged cherubs spoon Alphonso mango juice into your mouth and unicorns bear you heavenwards on gossamer wings.

He knew a thing or two, did Strauss. He knew the full extent of an orchestra's capabilities. He knew how to write music that transports you to another realm.

And he knew how to make violinists suffer.

I stand in front of twenty of them on a Monday evening in February. They look dispirited, as well they might. Not their fault, not my fault. Strauss's fault. It's only five seconds of music, but to them it lasts an age. Strauss has a way of driving his music forward with turbulent rhythmic figures, repeated and varied, striving ever upward. It's only when the ratchet is fully cranked that he strips away the complex web of orchestral texture and abandons the violins to their fate.

Into those five seconds Strauss has packed a wealth of technical difficulty, but that's not the problem. The problem is that just as they have to contend with these notes, everyone else stops playing, leaving them as vulnerable as a chaffinch in the path of a sparrowhawk.

The violins, committed to a high register, cascade downwards, as if thrown over the edge of a cliff. Somehow, grabbing at tufts of grass and protruding branches to slow themselves, they make it to the bottom, where their fall is cushioned by the reassuring weight of orchestral sound rejoining the fray, and we're off again, tossing and turning to yet another climax.

In performance, it's a precarious moment, even with seasoned professionals. With non-professionals, it's a reason to give up the violin. But I've decided to programme the piece anyway, because it's a cracker, and I'm not one to spoil the ship for five seconds of particularly glutinous tar.

It seemed like a good idea at the time.

They're good people, these violinists. They play in an orchestra for enjoyment, to slough off the cares of their jobs, to take part in a cultural endeavour that can be larger than the sum of its parts. This isn't what they signed up for.

But I've committed them to it, and now, standing in front of them armed only with a white stick and limited powers of persuasion, I look for words of reassurance. 'Try not to panic,' I offer. 'Try to play at the same speed as everyone else. Remember: whatever happens, nobody died.'

I'm rewarded with a small chuckle. They've heard that one before. They've heard them all before. I need new material.

'OK, one more go. From letter L.'

A voice from the back of the orchestra.

'Excuse me, Maestro.'

The capital 'M' is clearly audible.

'Steve.'

I've known Steve for twenty years, our friendship surviving the potentially fractious relationship between trumpeter and conductor. When he uses the audible capital 'M', it's because he knows I hate it.

'Can you clarify when you're going into two between L and M?'

It's a reasonable request. Players like clarity from conductors. Grappling with an unruly instrument is hard enough without the incoherent gestures of the person at the front.

I know the passage in question. At the beginning, the music is firmly in four beats per bar, march-style. But by the end the feel has changed and the pulse is felt with only two beats per bar. Steve wants to know where I'm going to make the change so he can mark it in his part. It will facilitate his next entry, leading to greater security and confidence. As I say, it's a reasonable request.

But I have other ideas.

The trouble is, you pigeonhole the arcane gestures of a conductor at your peril. The transition between the two characters of the music isn't clearly defined. It's like asking when blue becomes green or when your depression first came on. A definite answer isn't always possible. If they have it marked in their parts the players will subconsciously pay less attention to the conductor, and we wouldn't want that.

It's not that conductors crave attention for reasons of deep-seated insecurity.

OK, it is that. But not completely. The more the players pay attention to the nuances of a conductor's gestures, the more likely they are to react as one with their colleagues.

In theory.

So after due consultation with the text, I say, with a quiet smile, 'I don't know.'

A nervous chuckle eddies round the room. Steve, a wise old hand, accepts the answer with a rueful shake of the head. I'll explain my thinking to him later over a pint. He'll understand.

I can understand their nervousness. Conductors aren't supposed to say 'I don't know'. We're leaders, knowers, certainty brokers. Orchestras are like horses. They sense fear. They also suffer in silence when people in strange clothes climb aboard them and make them do things they don't want to. And they like sugar lumps.

And like horses, to stretch the analogy to breaking point, they can get lazy unless kept up to the mark. Not because of any inherent character flaw, more because the natural instinct of any group of humans is to get away with as much as possible. They want to play the music to the best of their collective ability, but unless someone is there to nudge them, it's easy to follow the path of least resistance. And on the wayside of that well-worn path is a cosy pub called Ignoring the Conductor.

A simple tactic is to ask people to watch, but everyone, conductor included, gets bored of that. By saying 'I don't know' I'm hoping the players might be curious enough about the exact point of transition to cast the odd glance in my direction.

So it's a tactic, underpinned by the confidence of two decades of experience, and a fundamental feeling that I basically, more or less, some of the time, with a clear road ahead and a light prevailing wind, know what I'm doing.

As for that tricky violin passage, I'm sure it'll be fine in the concert.

The rehearsal continues, and into my head, from nowhere, pops the arcane knowledge that 'Strauss' is the German word for 'ostrich'.

The 'I don't know' that echoes in my head repeatedly on my birding trips in early February is a beast of a different hue.

What's that bird?

I don't know.

Not that one. The other one, flitting into that bush.

I don't know.

Ooh, that's a lovely song. There, in that tree. Oh, it's gone. What was it?

I don't know.

Was that a goldfinch that just flew over?

I don't know I don't know I don't know shutupshutupshutup.

I'd forgotten just how much of birdwatching is uncertainty and guesswork. It's one thing sitting in your favourite armchair, musing on the plumage differences between first- and second-winter black-headed gulls, but that doesn't help identify the scrubby little blighter that's just jigged into that bush, never to be seen again. And it's no use asking them politely to damn well sit still blast you while I jot down the distinguishing features of your plumage in this notebook dammit which pocket is it in now where did I put the pencil ah here it is oh bugger it's gone. They just won't. Most disobliging.

I'm on relatively secure ground, as you'd hope and expect, in the back garden. South London isn't a hotbed of exotica, and as I charge the feeders with the RSPB's finest suet balls, buggy nibbles and no-mess sunflower mix, I'm fairly confident of the birds it will attract. It's not as if I've been completely blind to the charms of the avian universe all these years. They've just been in the deep background, like extras in a crowd scene.

The birds that have been coming to the feeder all these years, the ones that come now in some abundance, these are the birds of my childhood.

With one exception.

Among the tits, scattering scraps of fat onto the rosemary bush below like dandruff onto a dinner-jacket collar, the blackbirds hopping around the lawn, and the robin without which no British garden would be complete, is a bird whose abundance today was undreamt of when I was growing up.

Psittacula krameri.

In the late 1980s I started playing for a friendly cricket team called the Fulham Taverners. Starting life as the radical cricketing wing of the Fulham Young Conservatives, the team evolved, eventually welcoming players of all political persuasions and cricketing abilities. In that time – taking as our ethos the theory that sometimes it's better to be truly atrocious at something than merely mediocre – we've experienced the highs, lows and middles familiar to any amateur sportsperson, while providing regular entertainment for literally tens of people.

One Sunday, during a game in Teddington, I was distracted by a flash of green. This would have mattered less had the object it distracted me from not been the ball, which, in accordance with the conventions of the game, I was expected to catch, but which whooshed past me like one of Douglas Adams's notorious deadlines. Above the stifled groans of my teammates I heard a mocking squawk, as if my humiliation was the result of a carefully hatched plan. I retrieved the ball, restricting the batsmen to a paltry five runs,* and turned to see the colourful bird circling me, still squawking and giving me its finest beady look from a livid crimson eye. Notwithstanding this rocky start to our relationship, I started to look forward to my encounters with these exotic birds, their rarity adding to the frisson caused by their appearance. Lovely birds, I would think as I patrolled the boundary. Beautiful. Look at the contrast between the lush green of their plumage and the raw red of their hooked beak. I could almost imagine myself in Delhi, if I hadn't been wearing three jumpers and clamping my hands between my thighs to stop them from dropping off.

---

* My throw made up in enthusiasm for what it lacked in accuracy.

Affection can be eroded by familiarity, and when familiarity becomes intrusion, affection is no longer the word that springs to mind.

One parakeet in the garden? An exotic visitor. Two? Aw look, he's found a mate. Three? OK guys, you can stop now. Four? Fetch the air rifle.

Because, you see, parakeets are bastards. Oiks, louts, hooligans. If they were human they would have angry old men chasing them, shaking their fists and shouting 'I'll get you, you 'orrible kids!'

They encircle the garden, screeching. At first it's hard to discern them from the surrounding foliage, but they're visible enough when they descend on the feeder, stripping it bare like vultures with a fresh carcass. Then with a grawk and a squeal, they're off.

But they'll be back. Oh, I know they'll be back.

Bastards.

Lest you think me unduly harsh, I'd say the same about any bird in similar circumstances. The golden eagle, for example. One of them soaring over a Highland valley is majestic, stunning, primeval. Sixteen in your garden, ripping the hydrangeas to shreds and crapping on the patio? Not so much.

The origins of the ring-necked parakeet in this country are subject to various explanations. One version has a pair escaping the set of *The African Queen* at Shepperton Studios; another holds that Jimi Hendrix released them in Carnaby Street in a drug-crazed stupor. The mundane likelihood is they escaped from an aviary and found the comfortable habitat of suburban Surrey to their liking. With two broods a year, high survival rates and few predators to disturb their spread, they've thrived, and their population has grown to the extent that they're now considered, like many non-native species across different branches of wildlife, a pest. Grey squirrels, Spanish bluebells, rhododendrons, Canada

33

geese and now the ring-necked parakeet – strange how the mere mention of an invasive species can make a mild, left-leaning nature enthusiast foam at the mouth like a UKIP supporter.

The parakeet that clings to the feeder and destroys the suet ball with a maniacal glint in its eye one rainy morning in February goes on my list. It's a naturalised bird, and therefore a permitted species for those who care about such things. The bird was admitted to the British list in 1984, so it counts, and while part of me resents it for its parakeet-ness, I am, on the whole, glad to have seen it. My list is in danger of stalling. I've enjoyed getting to know the garden birds. Each appearance of a goldfinch or great tit delivers a little jolt of pleasure, lifts my day a fraction. But while this celebration of the familiar adds a dimension to daily life, it merely whets my appetite. If I'm to make significant inroads into my target, I need to spread my wings and venture to pastures new.

I need to visit a bird reserve.

It's chilly in the hide. Comfort and warmth aren't what it's designed for. The thinking seems to be, 'Look pal, the birds out there, wading up to their wingpits in cold sludge, they're not comfortable, are they? So why should you be?'

Yeah, but they have feathers to keep them warm. And they're birds. They're used to it.

I adjust my binoculars and scan the scrape again.

Gull. Gull. Gull. Duck. Duck. Gull. Duck. Cormorant. Duck. Gull.

Loads of gulls and loads of ducks and not much else.

I'm aware that my descriptions of 'gull' and 'duck' are woefully inadequate. I would love to be more specific, but am hindered by two things.

Firstly, my binoculars.

That's right. Blame the binoculars.

The trouble with the binoculars is that they're of the pocket variety. They've been knocking about the house for years, nobody really sure whose they are or where they came from. Looking through them is frustrating, because they improve your view of anything by a degree that can be described as 'not quite enough'. But really the problem isn't so much with them but with the birds. They're too far away. There's a lovely stretch of water just in front of me. Why can't they float there?

But all this kvetching is by way of diverting attention from the real problem. Me.

I'm assailed by voices from the past.

Have you done your homework, Parikian?

Yes, sir.

Really?

Well, I've done some, sir, but...

Well?

There are so many birds, sir, and they never look like the birds in the books, and they all have different plumages at different times of year, and... sorry, sir.

I recognise the mallard. We all recognise the mallard. It's the park duck. Dark head, ring neck, purple feather on the wing. Waddle waddle. Quack quack.

And I know the tufted duck. That's the other park duck, the blackish and white one with the tuft on its head and a disconcerting yellow eye.

Ooh, and I know the shoveler, because of its outsized bill. It's not grotesquely big, like the spoonbill's or the toucan's or the pelican's. It's just big enough that if you were talking to a shoveler you'd go to great lengths not to look at it or refer to it, but would inevitably blow it all with a stray comment about the size of this month's gas bill, er, I mean invoice.

35

So I'm fine with those. But then there are the others, all sounding like firms of solicitors. Pochard and pintail. Gadwall and garganey. Goldeneye, scaup and smew.

There's ducks out there, Jim, but not as I know them.

Luckily, the good folk of the Wildfowl & Wetlands Trust have thought ahead, providing for the hapless apprentice a bird guide, firmly attached to the wall with theft-proof wire. I never knew birders were so untrustworthy.

I riffle through it, finding the wildfowl pages. There are illustrations of birds in various plumages: male, female, winter, summer, juvenile. The plumages I know, the ones I wish the bally birds had the decency to wear at all times, are the adult males. These are generally the most striking, females being largely brown, and juveniles not yet fully developed and therefore not needing colourful plumage with which to attract a mate. The awkward fact is, however, that not all birds are adult males, which is good news for the survival of the species, but bad news for me. Not only do we have to learn the difference between all the species, we have to learn the variations too.

In the case of the duck-like object floating nearest to me, I'm in luck.

The bird's body is predominantly silver, with black-and-white hindquarters. Its head is a warm chestnut, with a light pink below. There's nothing overstated or gaudy about this bird. It seems to have been designed by someone with expensive taste. I look back at the book. The vagueness of 'some kind of duck' quickly coalesces into certainty.

'Wigeon. You're a wigeon.'

I murmur the words under my breath. They're not loud enough for the wigeon to hear – I'm not mad – but just loud enough for them to be real, for it to be real, for my tiny moment of triumph to live for a second on the air.

I've taken to doing this. Hearing a bird singing in a tree, I'll stop and scan the branches. When I've found it I allow myself a quiet, 'Ah, there you are,' as if it's just arrived ten minutes late for a meeting. Then I move on, my day fractionally enriched.

They say birders are eccentric. I'm going to fit right in.

The lagoon where these birds are floating is part of the larger entity that is the London Wetland Centre, miraculously created on the site of old reservoirs in Barnes, in West London, in 2000.

In my research I've ascertained that the answer to the question, 'Where should a Londoner go to see 200 species of bird?' is basically, 'Don't live in London.' I concede this is an unfair assessment, giving the impression that London is a concrete jungle devoid of wildlife, except for swarms of rats, mangy foxes and one-footed pigeons.

While it's true those creatures are present in some abundance, it's not beyond the wit of man to scrape the surface and find the delights hidden within, not least because London has a lot of green common land, by some estimates more than any city of a comparable size in the world. While these havens are welcome, the presence of a full-on nature reserve just a couple of delayed train journeys from my doorstep is a boon, so I've come to Barnes to see what's about.

As an introduction to wildfowl, the wetland centres administered by the WWT around the country could hardly be bettered. This one, nestled in a curve of the Thames, has a welcoming visitor centre, with a family-friendly cafe and a shop selling gifty knick-knacks, cuddly ducks and general birding paraphernalia. On leaving the visitor centre through an attractive brick courtyard, you're immediately beset by ducks and geese. These, I quickly realise, are part of their captive collection, terribly tame, and prolific excreters. They – and the captive otters whose feeding time twice a day coincides with an opportunity to see flocks of west London yummy mummies in their natural habitat – lend the immediate environs a zoo-like atmosphere. Everything's well cared for, but nothing's going anywhere soon.

Venture further out, however, and you quickly find yourself on a nature reserve, with paths leading through wooded areas and reed beds, and hides overlooking lagoons and grazing marshes. These carefully managed habitats are attractive to all sorts of waterbirds, including the wigeon I've just masterfully identified.

The addition of just two species to my list is a result of my general ignorance more than anything else. The other birds that were no doubt there remained unidentified by my overwhelmed brain. Nonetheless, there's a spring in my step as I walk back to the station for another round of 'Train Cancellation Bingo'. *Rus in urbe* can do that to you.

With one visit to a bird reserve under my belt in a relatively busy period, I prepare to draw a line under the list for this month.

But we all like a bonus, the little treat that appears when you least expect it.

It's not a long drive to the hotel near Windsor for a family wedding on the last weekend in February, but fear of forgetting vital items (clothes, wallet, child) on any trip away, no matter how short, blanks my mind to anything else. Only when we've checked in and are exploring the hotel's television options does the possibility of an unexpected addition to my tally become apparent.

I get a text from my sister-in-law, two rooms away.

'Kites!'

At first I'm confused. Is it Chinese New Year again already? Have I neglected a vital aspect of the celebrations? What a fool I will look in the photos, the only guest not clutching a kite.

Then the penny drops and I go to the window.

To see a red kite hanging in the air, manoeuvring its lithe body with agile movements of its wings and controlling the airflow with precise and fluid wriggles of its forked tail, is to witness an aeronautical miracle.

To see six outside your window is to risk missing a wedding and causing irreparable family ructions.

When I was a child, the red kite had near legendary status, its numbers having dwindled from pest-like abundance in earlier centuries to a handful of breeding pairs in South Wales. It was firmly on my list of romantic must-sees, as forlorn a hope back then as my desire to see a golden eagle. The reintroduction programme initiated in the Chilterns in 1992 came too late for me to realise my childhood dreams, but even in the midst of my thirty-five-year ornithological lull I was aware of their resurgence, and any car journey on the motorways to the west of London was lent an added frisson by the possibility of a sighting.

I summon Oliver. He's the same age as I was at the height of my birding passion. His enthusiasms lie elsewhere, but he's always had a fascination with birds of prey, and here is a free display just for us. We stand at the window until we absolutely have to get changed, then, just before we go down, I sneak another look. They're gone, no doubt seeking a less fickle audience. This is how it should be, a natural puncture to the birder's rampant egotism. I'll see another kite the next day, nearly crashing my bike into the Cumberland Gate in Windsor Great Park as I crane my neck trying to prolong my view of it. But the bike ride will yield a tick yet more outlandish.

Give a five-year-old a box of crayons and ask them to draw the brightest bird they can imagine. When they've finished, ask them to add a few more colours.

You now have a picture of a male mandarin duck. This striking bird's scientific name, *Aix galericulata*, means 'bewigged waterbird', but that's just the start of it. It's a cartoon bird, the extravagant decoration of its exotic plumage immediately catching the eye, and the sail-like feathers on its back offset by

39

a boa round its neck. Not for the mandarin the subdued pastels of the wigeon or subtle grey specklings of the gadwall. The male mandarin is gagging for attention, not just from females of its species, but from everyone.

Like the red kite, this bird's population has increased since I last looked. But where the kite has benefited from conservationists' desire to reintroduce a declining bird, the mandarin's spread is the result of birds escaping from wildfowl collections and going feral. Birders sniff at escapes, or 'plastics', but when those birds gain a toehold as a breeding population, they reluctantly add them to their lists while reserving the right to carry on sniffing.

I don't sniff at the mandarin duck I see on Virginia Water the day after the wedding. It sits on the water, oblivious to my approval, bobbing gently among a group of altogether less showy wildfowl. There's no identification difficulty here, no comparison of primary projections or problematic bill shapes required. It's a male mandarin duck in breeding plumage. There's no bird quite like it.

Tick.

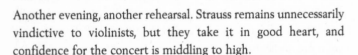

Another evening, another rehearsal. Strauss remains unnecessarily vindictive to violinists, but they take it in good heart, and confidence for the concert is middling to high.

Afterwards I walk to Victoria rather than take the single-stop tube journey. Whichever way I go I'll end up standing on the station concourse while a Southern employee sees how many times they can cram the word 'cancelled' onto the departures board, so I take the healthier option.

It's a crispish and still evening, and as I walk I review the rehearsal in my head, mostly oblivious to the few cars crawling along the back streets around Eaton Square.

My thoughts are interrupted by a totally unexpected sound. High up in a tree, piercing in the prevailing tranquillity, a bird sings. It stops me in my tracks. A soft 'Oh!' escapes my lips as I scan the tree.

It's a mellow song, by turns fluting and warbling, short phrases tailing off, a gap, then another phrase, related but not the same. I stand underneath the tree, searching. What can it be?

I think of the newly purchased CD box set sitting on my desk. *British Bird Sounds* – its authority confirmed by the reassuring words 'British Library' on the front. Useful as this might prove in the coming weeks, it's not much help right now.

Without the aid of the permanent ambient light of London's streets, I would never find it. It also helps that the bird stands still throughout the recital. Colours are difficult to discern, and as I'm standing directly beneath it all I can see are the underparts. They are, as far as I can tell, uniformly beige.

I have a small songbird, perching in a tree, drab in colour and singing a song I don't recognise. I wonder if, unlikely though it is, I've stumbled on some sort of rarity. Maybe one of those exotic warblers I've glossed over in the field guides. I begin to get a little excited. Eager to record the moment for posterity, and hoping I'll be able to shed more light on the mystery when I get home, I take out my phone and record a snippet of song. I'll send it to Andrew. He'll know.

Andrew is my birding mentor. Not that he knows it yet. It's just a decision I've made, like Benjamin Braddock deciding to marry Elaine Robinson in *The Graduate*. Andrew works in IT, but we know each other through music. Formerly a violinist in the very orchestra I've just come from rehearsing, he clearly divined the direction things were taking and jumped ship, choosing to pursue his musical activities in a choir, where the technical challenges are presumably less terrifying. But we've kept in touch, according to modern custom, via Facebook, and it's there

41

that I've seen the occasional post that reveals him to be a keen and accomplished birder. He's just the person I need to guide me through my year, and I've been gearing up to email him about it. This is the perfect opportunity. I send him the recording.

Andrew,

Hope you're well. Just wondering if you can help identify this bird. Something exotic?

All the best,

Lev

Within a few hours I get my answer.

Hi Lev,

Depends what you mean by exotic. It's a robin.

Best,

Andrew

This is going to be harder than I thought.

February ticks (8)

London, West Norwood, WWT Barnes, Burnham, Windsor Great Park

Cormorant *Phalacrocorax carbo*, Black-headed Gull *Chroicocephalus ridibundus*, Ring-necked Parakeet *Psittacula krameri*, Rook *Corvus frugilegus*, Wigeon *Anas penelope*, Lapwing *Vanellus vanellus*, Red Kite *Milvus milvus*, Mandarin Duck *Aix galericulata*

Year total: 27

MARCH 2016

It's the strangest thing I've seen on a football pitch. Play begins in the usual way, both sides easing themselves into the game without attacking intent. After a few passes, the ball comes to a midfielder, who – unprovoked and under no pressure – blasts it deliberately out of play. The ball soars over our heads into the trees lining the cycle path. There's disbelief among the players, but the most offended party is a tall, angular bird, whose nest, perched on top of a telegraph pole, the ball has narrowly missed. It flies up in a flurry, its wingbeats deep and powerful, circles for a few seconds and returns, quickly settling into a dignified pose, like an elderly classics professor.

I'm amused by the footballer's overenthusiastic amateurism, but transfixed by the bird. It's glorious, not dissimilar in shape and size to the grey heron which landed on our shed roof a couple of weeks earlier, causing me to splutter toothpaste over the floor. Tall and upright, it tucks its long carrot bill into its chest, giving it a bashful appearance. But what it does next is anything but introverted. Leaning forward, it bangs the upper and lower parts of its bill together in quick staccato bursts. It takes me a few seconds to connect the loud clattering sound with the bird in front of me. It sounds more like a piece of machinery than a sound of nature – an industrial-sized sewing machine or those deafening pavement-pounding whacker plates. I watch, engrossed, until I feel Tessa and Oliver's impatience wafting across the path towards me. Reluctantly I tear my eyes from the bird. It's a white stork, my first ever. A lifer, as birders have it. As we trundle onwards, I take a backward glance, keeping it in view for as long as I can.

Marvellous bird, the stork. The only thing is, it doesn't count. We are in Germany, so this bird has no place on my list. To avoid miring myself in murky political waters, I should stress that this distinction is purely geographical. I've sworn to maintain a British list, so a British list it must be. Birds seen on foreign soil, however beguiling, cannot be part of this challenge. I'll remember the stork, and have already added it to the 'Cycling' and 'Rainy Tuesday in Germany' lists, but as a contribution to the grand project it's worthless.

The merits of a cycling holiday up the Rhine in late March are many. The terrain is flat, a boon for cyclists whose thighs seize up on the smallest incline; there's interesting scenery; and the mild discomfort caused by the cold and rain is offset by the smugness induced by strenuous exercise and the heartiness of the meals we allow ourselves each evening.

But from the project's point of view, the holiday disrupts a month of solid progress, new knowledge and burgeoning obsession. A month that starts with me standing in the middle of the road, staring at a bush.

It's an unremarkable road, likewise the bush. Suburban south London at its blandest.

A first-floor window opens. A lady, courteous but puzzled, asks if I need help. She's in her sixties, well-spoken, enquiring. I can feel her worry from fifteen paces. Normal people don't stand in the middle of the road staring at bushes.

I have options. I could scuttle away with a muttered apology, but that might disturb her even more. Or I could explain the circumstances, my journey back into birdwatching, the significance of this bird.

Instead I steer the middle path.

'Oh... thank you. I'm just... looking for a bird.'

She makes a little exclamation of understanding and closes the window in an exaggeratedly unobtrusive way. But I'm grateful to her for not calling the police, and revert to staring at the bush.

In keeping with its surroundings, the bird is the embodiment of anonymity. But it represents a breakthrough, a moment of triumph. A minute ago I was a man walking down a road. Then I heard an agglomeration of scrabbling birdsong, the word 'dunnock' popped into my head, and now I'm nothing less than a mighty birdsong god.

I didn't even have to think. The connection between song and name was instinctive. My hard work is paying off. The dunnock's song has filtered into my synapses and is making a little home there. It won't be the first I've seen – there's one in the garden, the first sign of its presence often a jelly-like trembling in the lavender – but it is the first I've identified from song alone. Now I just need it to show its face so I can confirm its identity.

Bang on cue a small brown bird appears, perched on the perimeter of the bush. I drink in the distinctive streakings on its back, the grey around its head, the slender, pointed bill. I nod and smile, as if granting it permission to leave, and off it flies to destination unknown. I watch as it bounces away. There have been many pleasing moments in my return to the avian world, but this is the most satisfying. There's an absurd sense of achievement about it, like the moment in learning a piece of music when things slot into place after weeks of struggle, or when you finally work out what that button on the dishwasher does. This is the nature of all learning: you think you're treading water, but your brain is sorting things out in the background without telling you.

In the wake of the Great Robin Identification Debacle, I've prioritised the learning of birdsong, an area of birding I mostly ignored in my youth. I remember a desultory attempt to record a blackbird using a portable cassette recorder, a cheap microphone, and a dustbin lid, but otherwise the sounds birds produced went unexplored. I was aware of the obvious ones – the grawings of crows, squawkings of gulls, the cuckooing of our annual cuckoo – but the mysterious world of songbirds passed me by.

Buying the *British Bird Sounds* CDs was one thing. Now it's time to listen to them, from avocet to yellowhammer. It's a bewildering array of scrawks, grunts and chirrups, and I've honed my playlist to the birds I'm expecting to encounter locally. It's a good time to be doing it. The explosion of spring is imminent, and male birds are clearing their syrinxes in preparation for the mating season. The air is already beginning to fill with confusing noises, and I'd like to be ahead of the game by the time they hit mid-season form. I've read that a lot of birding is done with the ears. If you can recognise a bird's song, there's no need to dive into the undergrowth in search of it. You can merely cock an ear, mutter, 'Ah yes, icterine warbler,' and continue with your day.

You would have thought a conductor, trained to perceive faulty intonation, poor tone, wrong notes in the back desk of the violas and myriad other discrepancies in a complex web of orchestral sound, would be able to learn the songs of a few common birds.

You would have thought.

I've listened to recordings of the dunnock. I've also listened to blackbirds, robins, great tits, blue tits, coal tits, wrens, goldfinches, chaffinches, bullfinches, greenfinches, blackcaps, willow warblers, garden warblers, whitethroats, goldcrests, starlings, mistle thrushes, song thrushes and nuthatches, and I'm buggered if I can remember which is which.

My inability to learn birdsong is partly down to my conviction

46

that I can do it all at once, a disastrous policy whose futility I explored as a panicked teenager, wondering whether if I stayed up all night I could memorise all the German words starting with M.

But it's also down to the very nature of birdsong. For every cuckoo, with its 'specially for foreigners' two-note song, there's a capercaillie, which sounds like a mixture of a ball going down a plughole and someone sanding a grasshopper.

With the songbirds I might encounter locally, there are several confounding factors. Speed of song is one, predictability of trajectory another. If a dunnock were to sing 'Danny Boy' or the main theme from Mussorgsky's *Pictures at an Exhibition*, I'd be fine. But it doesn't. The dunnock's song is a scrabbly, indeterminate bunch of nearly-notes which lasts a couple of seconds and then stops. After a short pause it starts again, similar but not identical.

It's not the only bird whose song can be described as scrabbly and indeterminate, and my apprentice ears aren't able to sort them all out.

Take the wren, the very-nearly-smallest British bird, which hammers out its explosive song at twelve notes a second. If it were playing a pattern with predictable contours, like a G major scale, this would be less problematic, but to my ears the wren's song skitters around randomly, the only constant a machine-gun trill near the end – except when the cheeky devil chooses to omit it. As I get to grips with it, I begin to recognise an easy distinguishing feature: the volume of its song is out of all proportion to the bird's size. Tiny bird, the wren, weighing no more than a pound coin, but when it sings the air around is electrified.

Compare this with Britain's actual smallest bird, the goldcrest. Its thin, piping song is recognisable partly because of its stratospheric pitch – it clocks in at 7 kHz, 2.5 kHz higher than the highest note of the piccolo.* It also restricts itself, more or less, to three notes, with a squiggly flourish to round it off. The most heavily thumbed page in my copy of *The Reader's Digest Book of Birds* was the goldcrest's. I loved it hard. Perhaps it was because (and here I encourage you, in sympathy with Britain's smallest bird and 1970s Oxfordshire's smallest child, to play the world's smallest violin) I was what my mother called a 'late developer'. While my contemporaries rocketed skywards, I needed a ladder just to sit on a chair. At one point I thought I was shrinking. I was so desperate to grow that I indulged in what might generously be called 'wishful thinking', but more accurately 'measurement fraud'. The pencil marks on the kitchen doorframe indicated a miraculous spurt of three inches in one twenty-four-hour period in 1975, the result of judicious standing on tiptoes and dirty work at the pencil. I yearned to grow, but remained minuscule until well into my teens, by which time I had other problems.

So it was solidarity with a fellow titch, as well as the bird's undeniable charms, that kick-started my unrequited love affair with the goldcrest.

Yes, unrequited, for of all the common birds I might have expected to see in the normal course of events, this one eluded me.

And then, one bright spring day in 1977, there it was. My goldcrest. Not, as I'd been led to expect, flitting around in the upper tiers of a conifer, but perched on an apple tree, head cocked and staring directly at me with an appealing look. Its crown was

---

* Human hearing is at its most sensitive between 0.4 and 3 kHz, approximately equivalent to the top half of the piano. A cuckoo's 'cuck' usually comes in at about 0.57 kHz, with the 'oo' at around 0.52 kHz, well within our hearing and singing range. By contrast, the bittern's 'blowing across the top of a milk bottle' boom comes in at around 0.17 kHz. While one of the lowest sounds made by any bird, it's comfortably within the range of a cello and slightly higher than the lowest note on a viola.

alive with the yellowy-orange stripe that gives it its name, and its tiny body quivered with energy. This adorable bundle of fluff, the same weight as a 20p piece* but much cuddlier, constituted an overwhelming onslaught of cuteness. It felt like 'my' bird. The bond between us was a momentary thread of eye contact, but no less strong for that. To me, at any rate. History doesn't record the goldcrest's feelings. And now, thirty-nine years on, as I wrap my ears around the squeaky 'tsee-ba-da-tsee-ba-da-tsee-ba-da-scabba-diddle-oo' on the recording, I make a special effort to add it to my repertoire of recognised songs. I'm buoyed by my success with the dunnock, and have started listening with renewed application, determined to nail more of them down.

The difficulties, I realise, aren't just to do with speed and unpredictability. We find it difficult to differentiate and transliterate the specific tone and timbre of much birdsong because we're not equipped to do so. There are birdsongs you can slow down and notate in conventional musical language, but how do you transcribe the screechy part of a blue tit's call? And how does it make it anyway?

Step forward the syrinx, avian equivalent of our larynx. Birds' control of this flexible voice box, the tubes that run through it, the lips that can either partially or completely close either of those tubes, and the windpipe through which the sound travels after leaving the syrinx, make them capable of astonishing vocal control. And because there are two tubes and two pairs of lips within the syrinx, those vocalisations make up a range of sounds not available to any other animal.

My research into the sound world of birds leads me to sonograms. These graphic representations of birdsong (frequency on the y axis, time on the x) mean we can examine differences

---

* All birds are measured in terms of their weight compared to coins.

our ears might struggle to recognise. Unfortunately I'm as easily befuddled by sonograms as by birdsong, so after a contented but confused few hours exploring their fuzzy and mysterious world, I admit this might be a project for future years.

I realise the truth, obvious to anyone who knows anything about anything: expertise takes time, practice and patience. What made me think bird identification would be different?

I think of my conducting teacher, the incomparable Ilya Alexandrovich Musin. He was ninety-two and still going strong when I went to St Petersburg to glean what I could from him. An interviewer once asked how he knew so much about conducting. His reply was simple: 'I've thought about little else for seventy years.'

I can't imagine devoting seventy years to the song of the dunnock. And perhaps there's my problem. It's why the Great Lego City never got past the planning stage.

I think too of my father, dedicated to the art of playing the violin from the age of five, when his uncle – leading light for a generation of Armenian musicians in Cyprus – gave him his first lessons. The lifelong pursuit of musical excellence brought him to England as a teenager, and, apart from the intervention of the war, he stayed here for the rest of his life. As a very young child I sat cross-legged on his music-room floor listening to him practise. In my memory these sessions lasted for hours, but more likely I got bored after ten minutes and pootled off to play with my toy cars. But the image remains. The worn red rug on a wooden floor, music stand in the middle of the room, grand piano filling the bay window, which looked out onto the garden. It was a room of warm wood, light and space, an old partners' desk and a glass-fronted cabinet containing rare Armenian books and miniature scores adding to the studious atmosphere. And at the centre of it all my father, seemingly oblivious to my presence, to everything but the music.

His stature in my eyes as a musician of exemplary rigour and taste was established early on. Everyone told me, and I heard it for myself. But growing up with the sound of excellent violin playing in my ears was a mixed blessing. It instilled an understanding of the single-mindedness required to excel at a discipline, but also set a benchmark I could never hope to reach. So in my mind, whatever I did, I was always failing. It wasn't his fault. He was merely doing what he did, and there never was a less pushy parent. But when you grow up in the foothills of Everest, there's a danger you never learn to appreciate the myriad qualities of the Cotswolds.

My own violinistic career was brief and disastrous, the impossibility of the task obvious to me even at six. The piano seemed a more realistic undertaking. The notes were already there, the only challenge being to press the keys in the right order, like a typist. That there was much more to it than that gradually dawned on me as I progressed through the grades, and I hit the wall in my early teens, my indolence by then so overwhelming I could barely hold myself upright at the keyboard.

This wasn't a problem when I was sitting behind drums. The appeal of percussion instruments, when I had my first lessons at thirteen, was instant, and I found whether it was the timpani in the orchestra or the drum kit in a jazz band, the rhythmic hitting of pleasingly resonant instruments energised me. And boy, did I need energising. That orchestral life as a percussionist consisted of so little actual playing seemed a bonus, this leaving plenty of time for mucking around at the back. But even then the seeds of my future career were being sown. You can learn a lot about conducting from the back of an orchestra, even if subconsciously, and I found the long rests were enlivened if I knew the context of my next biff. Knowing the cymbal crash or snare drum roll came at the end of the oboe solo or just after the trombone chord soon became second nature, and so an interest in the whole score, rather than just my own part, was born.

51

As my school career progressed, it became clear that the only things I was prepared to devote time to were percussion, cricket and fecklessness. My piano-playing deteriorated to such an extent that I was reduced to repeating the first twenty bars of the same Beethoven sonata, this being all I could manage. I decided to give it up. I steeled myself to tell my parents. The announcement came in an incoherent welter of tears. My mother, phlegmatic and nobody's fool, received the unsurprising news in silence, then allowed herself one comment:

'Well, it's a shame, because I think you're going to be a conductor, and it might come in handy.'

It's the kind of moment that sticks in the memory. I was fifteen and showing no signs of interest in any kind of career, which is only right and natural at that age. Was she being amazingly prescient? Or was it blindingly obvious that somewhere in the disaster area of my early teenage years, with all my uncertainty, foot-shuffling, 'dunno-sir-sorry-sir' mumbling and shyness, there lurked a monstrous egomaniac waiting to be unleashed? Or did I take her words, lodge them in the depths of my brain, and run with them, tentatively at first, but with gathering speed and confidence as I realised, many years down the line, that I wanted to be a conductor?

I didn't realise that my flusterment was misguided. I was in a pother because I thought my parents wanted me to play the piano. I was wrong. All they wanted was for me to be happy. The tricks the mind plays.

This lack of dedication to the piano came back to haunt me, and in my weaker moments haunts me still. The nagging voice of paranoia reminding you of your own failings can be difficult to silence, no matter how many other skills you amass to counteract them. So for all that I'm comfortable standing in front of an orchestra, for all that I've developed the myriad skills required for the job, for all that I've found a niche in a notoriously difficult field, there will always be a small part of me insisting it's not enough.

For two weeks I give bird identification the devotion I should have given my piano practice all those years ago. I immerse myself in bird guides, absorbing indigestible volumes of information, hoping some of it will stick. I memorise the names of all the warblers likely to appear in Britain in spring, much as I memorised the batting averages of all the Kent batsmen in 1976. Gulls and waders receive the same treatment. I note aberrations of plumage, leg colour and bill size, distinguishing features which will help me identify birds in the field. This barrage of information bounces around in my head like socks in a tumble dryer.

The similarities between this study and my regular homework, absorbing the details of an orchestral score through familiarity and repeated revision, are striking. But while my brain is used to the language of music, it finds this new vocabulary overwhelming and confusing. Nonetheless I persevere. The more firmly entrenched this information is, the easier it will be to summon in the heat of battle.

But even as I'm immersed in this improving activity, I'm troubled by a small but disproportionately noisy question.

Why?

Why bother learning the difference between a snipe and a woodcock? Or a goldcrest and a firecrest? Or any of the myriad confusion species you might encounter while out birding?

Come to that, why go birding anyway? What kind of sad loser am I?

These questions lead down a dangerous path, encouraging an Eeyorish outlook on life, introspective ponderings spiralling gradually downwards into a grisly vortex of existential anguish.

What, when you come down to it, is the point of anything?

Not to be a downer, but there is none. All human activity serves merely to fill the time between birth and death. In any case, if you're after a bit of perspective, our planet will be consumed by our dying sun in a few billion years. So why bother?

Well, while we're here, why not pass the time before our inevitable decrepitude by learning the difference between a shag and a cormorant? It's the equivalent of the courtesy we extend people when we take the trouble to call them by their names instead of addressing them with a vague description of their physical attributes and personality. 'Henry' instead of 'tall, slightly weird dark-haired guy', 'Diane' instead of 'nice but dull bespectacled lady'.

By referring to shags and cormorants as shags and cormorants, and not 'blackish beaky waterbirds', I do them, and nature in general, a service. A barely measurable service, but a service nonetheless. And nature, as we hardly need reminding, needs our services more than ever.

This period of intense absorption brings on a familiar feeling. I realise I'm falling back into the pattern of my youth. My strength as an ornithologically obsessed child was as a theorist. I was able to reel off names of birds I was never likely to see, and would have identified them without a tremor if they'd been obliging enough to stand on the kitchen table in the exact pose they assumed in the guides. Where I fell down was in my ability to apply this knowledge in practice.

The thirty-five-year layoff hasn't made me any better equipped, and my excursions so far amount to little more than dabbling. I need to get out regularly, and where better than my local patch? I plan, in time, to cast the net wider, but I'm keen not to run before I can walk, so I set aside the books and head to Streatham Common.

In choosing my patch, I've been ruled by laziness. London

is blessed with many open green spaces, several of them within walking distance of my house. I plump for the nearest one.

Streatham Common and its neighbour Norwood Grove form a good solid patch of green with a mixture of open ground and woods, with the added bonus of a semiformal garden called The Rookery dividing them. It's a modest patch, but while expectations of special sightings are low, that's not why I'm there. Regular patchwatching, as advocated by all the bird books, will give me practice 'in the field'. I'm confident that after a few weeks of keen study and observation I'll begin to master the dark art of identifying a small brown bird from a brief glimpse of its disappearing hindquarters.

The books are also unanimous in their advice to go birdwatching early in the morning, when activity is at its peak. There is a word in Swedish, *gökotta*, for the act of getting up early to listen to birdsong, but the knowledge that this word exists, while heartwarming, doesn't make it any easier. It's a bitter pill, this early rising, but my enthusiasm propels me to acts of previously unimagined heroism, and I set the alarm for an optimistic 5 a.m., before reality prompts me to change it to 5.15, no 5.30, OK then 5.45.

In the event, and in strict accordance with Finnemore's Law, which states that the likelihood of waking on time is in inverse proportion to the importance of the thing you have to be up for, I'm lying awake at 4.26, eyes wide open and my brain performing mental gymnastics worthy of Olga Korbut.

What the hell. It'll be light soon. *Gökotta* ahoy.

It's a strange and unfamiliar feeling, being up before everyone else. The musician's life is geared towards late nights. I almost expect to be arrested. As I walk past a fellow early riser at the bus stop I'm assailed by a frisson of self-consciousness. I feel him glance at me, and am suddenly aware that to appear in public with a pair of binoculars round my neck is to invite the judgement of strangers. Birdwatcher, confused operagoer, or incompetent spy? But the zeal of the recent convert overcomes this shyness. Let people think what they like, I nearly convince myself.

Once on the common, my hope that I'll be alone with the birds is confounded immediately. I was forgetting about dog walkers. There's a clutch of them as I arrive, owners and dogs of different shapes and sizes, not resembling each other nearly as much as we've been led to believe. I greet them with a hearty, 'Morning!' They look at me as if I've farted poison gas. I can almost see them clocking my binoculars and thinking, 'Incompetent spy.' But worst of all, I've broken the first rule of the Living in London Club.

Never say hello. Ever.

They hurry past. If they had children they'd be herding them away from me. A Labrador shoots me a look of hatred as it scurries off.

It's not the ideal start. I hear mocking laughter from the copse down the hill. It takes a few seconds for the sound to register in my befuddled early morning head. I've heard it before. Recently, in fact. I've heard it on the CDs. But I can't put my brain on it.

It bothers me as I walk down the hill, following the path around Norwood Grove. It takes me down to the bottom corner, then back up towards the copse, skirting the edge of the grove. I hear the sound again, back up the hill from where I've just come. I lift my binoculars, but it's a token gesture. Whatever the bird is, it's taunting me from afar.

As I explore this unfamiliar territory I feel like a stranger in a foreign land, overwhelmed by the new, everything tantalisingly beyond my grasp. When I do see a bird I recognise, I dismiss it as easy. 'Oh, it's just a robin. Everyone knows a robin.' And when a bird flies off without giving me enough clues to its identity, I berate myself for not instantly recognising it from its flight pattern, or rump colour, or jizz.

Now there's a word.

It's common in birding circles, conceived in a more innocent age. For those unaware of the word's secondary, earthier, meaning, I offer one simple exhortation.

Do not google it.

The word 'jizz' is commonly thought to come from the World War II RAF abbreviation of 'General Impression of Shape and Size'.* GISS becomes gizz becomes jizz. Whatever the explanation, birders continue to use it, either ignorant of or impervious to its darker connotations. Jizz is an important concept in bird recognition. Birds often disappear before you've had a chance to note the colour of their primary coverts or supercilia or whatnot, so a working knowledge of the 'feel' of a bird is indispensable. We use it to recognise people from their gait or body shape. Sports commentators know about jizz. Paula Radcliffe's bobbing head became instantly recognisable to athletics watchers in the 2000s. Likewise the run-up of Asif Masood, the Pakistani fast-medium bowler – memorably described by John Arlott as 'like Groucho Marx chasing a pretty waitress' – or Ian Botham, 'like a shire horse cresting the breeze'.

Although I reckon I could recognise Ian Botham a mile away from his jizz alone, my skills are less reliable with birds, especially when they're in flight. The little beggar that just bounced over my head often goes unidentified.

But the pastel-shaded beggar I glimpse through foliage one morning in the small copse in The Rookery rings instant bells. It's attached to the tree as if with Velcro, has a jaunty set to its body, and, crucially, is facing downwards. It descends a couple of feet, pecks at the bark for a second, then flits into the undergrowth, where I can't follow.

---

* A theory tragically undermined by the fact that the term first appeared in 1922, but never mind.

But I've seen enough. The soft pinks and blues, combined with the acrobatics, give me the information I need to murmur 'nuthatch' under my breath. Because, as I learned many years ago and have somehow retained for just such a moment, the nuthatch is the only British bird that climbs trees downwards.

I have a similar experience with the stock dove by the pond, its 'kind' eye and lack of white on its body distinguishing it from the much commoner feral pigeon, with its variations of plumage and 'lunatic staring' eye. With both these birds there's a feeling of intimacy, a sense that there's a thread of communication between the bird and me, something to which nobody else is privy. I see them both in a little nook away from other people, and the proximity of the encounters renders them memorable, the exact moment of contact imprinted on my mind.

Over the next fortnight I visit my patch several times. I become familiar with its birds and where they hang out. A pair of jays occupy the top of the wood, clacking noisily as they fly away from me. A song thrush – living by the adage 'If it's worth singing, it's worth singing twice' – serenades me down the east side of Norwood Grove. Greenfinches, with their zuzzing snore of a call, herald spring from the copse in the middle. There's always a blackbird on the path as I arrive. More often than not, as I walk that path, a wren buzzes across in front of me, wriggles through the railings, and loses itself in the bushes.

There's something irresistible about the wren, its tail cocked at a ludicrously perky angle, its entire demeanour redolent of bundled energy and small-birdy flittiness. It's a low-level bird, say the books. Look down, not up. And they're right. I'm getting better at spotting it, its direct flight fizzing the air. And when it perches on the railings and treats me to a five-second recital, complete with machine-gun trill, I smile for the rest of the morning. Admittedly it's 11.53 at the time, but a seven-minute smile isn't to be sneezed at, and to be world-weary about a wren is to declare yourself a curmudgeon of the first order.

I spend most of those seven minutes walking through the wooded area to the north of the patch. The walk takes me to my habitual resting point before the stroll home, one of a long line of benches in The Rookery. It's a pleasant place to spend a few minutes, looking down the hill over twin lawns which lead to the formal gardens. The lawns are dominated by two conifers just in front of the benches. Furthest away is a large cedar, an arresting and noble tree, elegant branches sweeping down close to the ground. I sit and enjoy the early spring sun on my face while updating my notebook, my clumsy scrawls mostly indecipherable. My memory tells me I saw a mute swan and a parakeet the day before. The notebook insists they were a mule swat and a parapet.

I've walked a fair distance, and I'm trying to summon the energy to go home. The air is thick with birdsong. To my left, my new friend the dunnock, scrabbling indeterminately. From the thickets to my right, a great tit. In the distance, the mocking laughter, remembered now, and never to be forgotten, as a green woodpecker.

And now, from the depths of the tree in front of me, a new sound.

'Tsee-ba-da-tsee-ba-da-tsee-ba-da-scabba-diddle-oo.'

It clocks in, I'm guessing, at roughly 7 kHz.

Just as my mind plods to the conclusion that this is the song of the goldcrest, Britain's smallest bird, a goldcrest, Britain's smallest bird, hops to the edge of the tree and cocks its head in my direction. As slowly as possible I reach for my binoculars and lift them to my eyes. They're not that good, but they help bring the bird closer. It stares with its tiny button eyes into the blank infinity sign of the binoculars, and with a quizzical look that seems to say, 'Don't I remember you from somewhere?' hops into the heart of the tree and out of my life.

It's the first goldcrest I've seen for thirty-nine years. I walk home with the carefree energy of a twelve-year-old.

We leave the stork* behind and continue towards Karlsruhe. Our daily schedule of thirty-five miles isn't overambitious, but the short stops add up, and I've already caused too many delays with a series of 'ooh look' moments. The route takes us through mixed landscapes, some beautiful, all in some way interesting, and birds are never far away. Birdwatching isn't entirely compatible with smooth and continuous progress on a bicycle, and I'm aware these interruptions are eroding my family's patience. Oliver, eleven and cycling-mad, whizzes up and down the towpath as I scour the evergreens for a woodpecker, but his appetite for this form of cycling is limited. Tessa, not eleven and cycling-sane, takes the reasonable view that to stop too often is to risk not only seizing up with cold, but also arriving at our destination under the cover of darkness. So when I see a flash of activity as we skirt an industrial plant with ten miles still to go and time getting on, I hesitate. Family peace is more important than this, surely?

Maybe.

For this, if I'm right, is an historic bird, at the heart of my mendacious past and directly responsible for my current obsession. I need to see it if I possibly can.

But the rusty flash that caught my eye might have been its only appearance, and a return to the spot might mean a fruitless few minutes scanning the aggregate heaps in the face of increasing familial impatience.

It won't take long.

---

* Approximate weight: 474 pound coins or 4,639 £10 notes.

'Carry on!' I call. 'I'll catch you up.'

There's a slight rolling of eyes. I wheel round and head back to the spot, trying to remember exactly which bit of the chain-link fence it was behind, which gravel heap to scour. Gloriously, it's still there, perched on the fence in the lee of a scrubby bush, not much bigger than a robin, its rusty tail doing fifty to the dozen and the rest of its body looking as if it's been dipped into a coal scuttle.

Black redstart.

It's a restless soul. As I slide the pocket binoculars out of the saddlebag, its head darts to left and right and it's off, disappearing into the bleak industrial landscape it likes to call home.

This is the bird that made me pause in my reading of *The Reader's Digest Book of British Birds*, the one with a shaky tick next to it. I make a mental note to reinforce that tick when I get home, and cycle like the wind to rejoin my long-suffering family.

We have three more uneventful days of cycling, then three days in Mainz with friends. Old friends, good friends, friends who know how to make you welcome. For a while I forget about birds. Almost.

But by the time we say our goodbyes, load up the car, and set off down the wrong side of their quiet suburban street, I'm itching to rejoin the fray. My enthusiasm is at a peak, stoked to boiling point by the stork and the black redstart, all the more so because neither of them counted. I have plans to exploit a quiet period at the beginning of April. There's work to be done, for sure – preparation for an intense period of rehearsals and concerts in the next couple of months – but there are gaps in the diary for forays further afield.

My list stands at a derisory forty species. Pathetic. I need to kick on. Those scaup, whimbrel and guillemot aren't going to come looking for me. I have to go looking for them.

March ticks (13)

West Norwood & Streatham Common

Green Woodpecker *Picus viridis*, Chaffinch *Fringilla coelebs*, Fieldfare *Turdus pilaris*, Redwing *Turdus iliacus*, Great Spotted Woodpecker *Dendrocopos major*, Jay *Garrulus glandarius*, Long-tailed Tit *Aegithalos caudatus*, Nuthatch *Sitta europaea*, Mistle Thrush *Turdus viscivorus*, Song Thrush *Turdus philomelos*, Stock Dove *Columba oenas*, Goldcrest *Regulus regulus*, Grey Heron *Ardea cinerea*

    Year total: 40

APRIL 2016

We have the Nazis to thank for the return of the avocet.

In 1940, with invasion imminent, preparations were made to defend East Anglia from German forces. Anti-tank blocks and scaffolding were constructed and areas behind coastal dunes flooded.

Some of the concrete blocks at Minsmere, just north of Aldeburgh, are still there, close enough together to tempt you into jumping from one to another. But it was the flooding that had lasting significance for wildlife. By the end of the war extensive reed beds were established, and grazing marshes, coastal lagoons, heath and woodland contributed to the burgeoning biodiversity on the site.

In 1947 avocets – piebald waders with delicately upturned bills – bred at Minsmere, after an absence from the UK of over a century. Also in that year the Royal Society for the Protection of Birds took over management of the site, and visitors and birds alike have been constants there ever since.

In 1977 I wanted to go there so much it ached. The summer holidays dragged by with nothing to do except mooch, fester and pester. My father was away on tour, my brother staying with friends. It fell to my mother, as well as running her own antiquarian book business, to bear the brunt of this torture. She reached the pragmatic conclusion that a trip to Suffolk for two days of birdwatching, tedious for her, would at least shut me up.

Suffolk friends were called, the trip arranged, and, doubtless, no gratitude from me either expected or received.

My memories of the visit are mixed. Some are razor sharp, as if newly minted. Sand martins – brown and white darts – flitting in and out of their nest burrows in the sandbank near the car park; the hushed atmosphere of my first bird hide, dark wood rough and raw; adults, taller than tall, letting me perch on bare Dickensian benches to train my childish binoculars on the marshy lagoons; my first sight of an avocet – smaller than I'd imagined, the black patches on its wings, neck and head sparse enough on a predominantly white body to lend it an air of daintiness, and its retroussé bill, perfectly adapted for sifting the silt for prey, making it, to my eyes, the embodiment of cuteness.

But at the same time I felt an undertow of uncertainty, a feeling of 'is that it?' Having scanned the scrape for birds, failed to identify most of them, and watched them pongling around for a while, I wanted to move on. They were lovely, but now what? The bench was uncomfortable, sharp edges digging into the backs of my legs, and I was aware that my mother was tolerating rather than enjoying the experience.

I'm still unsure what I expected. The birds could do no more than exist, and the enterprise would have been pointless without them. But part of me wanted more, without knowing what that meant. So this formative experience was confusing: part exhilaration, part anticlimax.

And after that? Did we drive across the country just for me to spend ten minutes in a hide before declaring, 'I'm bored, I want to go home'? I don't remember. I'd like to think I had the grace to spin it out for the sake of decorum. But I'm not betting on it.

These memories flood my mind as I approach Minsmere one sunny morning in early April. I have two days blocked off in the diary, family permission for the selfish excursion, and a new pair of binoculars on the passenger seat.

I've decided I can't arrive at the flagship reserve of the RSPB ill-equipped. It would be like making my Test debut at Lord's armed with the Slazenger bat of my childhood. Not knowing the first thing about binoculars, I've thrown myself on the mercy of the salesman, who is so relieved to have human company he treats me to a lengthy and informative dissertation on the merits of half a dozen models. I'm tempted by the top-of-the-range Swarovskis, which are so magnificent they almost deliver the bird, with identification, to your visual cortex in surround-sound 3D, but for my level of expertise and commitment £2,000 seems excessive, so I buy the first pair I saw. Mid-range, mid-price, mid-aspiration.

The roads narrow, but Minsmere remains tantalisingly out of reach. Woodbridge, Ufford, Saxmundham, Yoxford. Fields, trees, hedgerows, lanes narrowing and winding.

A movement to the right.

The most fundamental principles of common sense and road safety say you shouldn't birdwatch while driving. But it's too tempting. I know what it is, nailed it from its jizz within a nanosecond, but I just need a sight of it. I slow to what I consider an uncontroversial speed. The bird is still there, its miraculous understanding of airflow allowing it to hang motionless in the air like… well, like a kestrel, because that's what it is.

The sight is like a time machine, dumping me back in 1976 as surely as the smell of linseed oil, the straw colour of parched lawns or the word 'standpipe'.

We'd see them above the verge of the A40. 'Sparrowhawk?' someone would ask. And I'd reply, after a calculatedly casual glance, 'Kestrel.' It was the shape of the wings, I'd explain with irritating world-weariness. The kestrel's are narrower, more pointed. And the hovering. If it's hovering, it's a kestrel.

Instinctive recognition of a kestrel is one of the few birdwatching skills I retain. It's not much, but I'm grateful for it as I add the tick.

Lost in thought, I nearly run over a pheasant and two red-legged partridges. Their efforts to escape an untimely death under the wheels of a Škoda Octavia are comical. They have wings. Why don't they fly? At the last second one of the partridges does indeed take off in a frenetic burst of flapping. This has no discernible effect on its speed, and barely any on its altitude. Maybe that's why.

The game birds are my second and third ticks for the visit and I haven't even arrived yet. This is going to be a doddle. The birds are actually throwing themselves at me.

I park and enter the visitor centre, a new addition since I was last here thirty-eight years ago.

'You don't need a map, do you?'

Something about me gives the volunteer the false impression I know my way around. I finger my binoculars nervously, fearing their obvious newness will betray me as a beginner. He hands me a sheet of paper.

What's about at Minsmere? it reads.

Quite a lot, apparently.

Shelduck on The Scrape. Stone-curlew near the North Wall. Black-tailed godwit on The Levels.

The word 'godwit' triggers a memory. Me and Michael, fellow Young Ornithologists and relentlessly competitive in every sphere. I've invited him on holiday in Scotland, and we've spent three days outdoing each other in ornithological smart-arsery.

Michael is better than me at everything. Birdwatching is the one area where I have a chance. It's a miracle my mother hasn't killed us both.

We're on a beach, looking at a flock of waders.

'Dunlin, look. Knot on the right.'

'Oystercatchers over there.'

'Common sandpiper to the left. Greenshank.'

Competitive birding for kids.

Michael gets excited. 'Ooh look! Godwits!'

I train my binoculars on a group of brown birds with long bills. His identification is plausible. But there are two kinds of godwit: black-tailed and bar-tailed. To tell the difference we need to see their tails, tantalisingly hidden by folded wings. We're going to have to flush 'em.

That's what we tell ourselves, anyway.

A proper birder wouldn't do that. A proper birder would work it out from other indications. Bill or leg length, subtle plumage variations.

And a proper birder wouldn't run screaming at a group of harmless waders just for a tick.

In my defence, I'm not the first to run, nor the first to scream. But I am the first to see the identifying bars on the terrified birds' tails as they scatter to the four winds.

If my mother is unimpressed by our behaviour, she doesn't show it. Much.

And now I'm fifty, not twelve, and sitting in a hide overlooking The Scrape at Minsmere. There's a godwit in front of me and I know it's a black-tailed, partly because of its bill shape and leg length, but also because it was on the list at the visitor centre, and I thank the birding gods for the expertise of others as I jot 'Blank-taped golmit' in my notebook.

The hide is populated by four men, two women and a telescope. The women ask questions, the men answer them, and the telescope points at a reed bed. The tallest man, a study in lugubriousness, looks at me gravely and asks if I want a look. I accept, hoping it will become clear what I'm supposed to be looking at.

Reeds, apparently.

I'm torn. Admit I can't see anything, or make appreciative cooing noises?

'I'm sorry... I can't... there doesn't seem to be...'

I relinquish the telescope and he takes my place. I hold my breath, expecting to be exposed as an idiot to six strangers and an expensive piece of optical equipment.

'Oh. It's moved.' He adjusts the scope. 'There. Jack snipe.'

Flushed with relief, I look again. Even now it's difficult to see, its camouflage highly effective. It's a dumpy-looking thing, yet the fine streaking of its variegated brown plumage, highlighted in the dappled sunshine, somehow lends it a quiet elegance. It skulks in the reeds, safe in the knowledge it can't be seen.

Little does it know.

I murmur thanks, vacate the scope, and revert to surveying The Scrape through my own, newly acquired optics.

Before long, in an orgy of ornithological discovery, I've seen a dozen new birds. A shelduck – half duck, half goose – is easily identifiable by the large orange knob on its head. A dozen oystercatchers, black-and-white bodies finished with a snowman's carrot nose, patrol the far side. With a fishwife squawk, an avocet, protecting its territory with the tenacity of vintage-era Rafael Nadal, chases a dunlin until the smaller bird is forced to take wing and forage elsewhere. So much for the daintiness of the avocet. But the disruption is temporary and soon both birds are back to normal, the dunlin scurrying around the foreshore pecking at the mud for morsels of food as if nothing had happened.

I make jottings in my notebook, occasionally checking my identifications with the Collins app on my phone. The list spills over to a second page. Herring gull, shoveler, lapwing. Knot, dunlin, redshank. Little grebe, teal, gadwall. A great big pile of birds right in front of me and I don't know where to look next. Here's the world-famous birder, mopping them up like there's no tomorrow.

I take a moment to admire the understated plumage of a gadwall, the vermiculated greys of its chest and subtle brown streakings on its back a pleasing contrast to the block colours of the shelduck and stark monochrome of the avocet. It's a fine duck, easily overlooked. I overhear the tall gentleman talking to his lady friend.

'Gadwall there. Underrated bird.'

There's reverence in his voice. He could be talking about a cricketer or an author, a Rikki Clarke or J. L. Carr, but I know what he means. He's a connoisseur, rejecting the accepted hierarchy that places the gadwall below flashier birds. We exchange glances, a slow smile and a nod, and this simple shared moment buoys my perception of human nature. People are good, on the whole; bird people especially so. It's such a simple thing, to share pleasure in a slice of nature, yet so enriching, so life-affirming.

Leaving the hide before I'm overwhelmed by my own cloying sentimentality, I crack on. There's a lot to cover. Minsmere has seven hides, as well as extensive heath and woodland. The reserve, with spring blossoming, is buzzing with activity. Some wintering birds are still around, promising themselves they'll leave soon, but just one more dabble in this nice warm mud; early spring arrivals are trickling in, possibly disappointed it's not warmer.

I reach another hide, overlooking the main scrape from the other side. The view is dominated by a flock of about forty gulls, ranged along a narrow spit of land. I'd tentatively identified them as black-headed gulls from a distance, while secretly hoping they might be something more exotic. Now I'm close enough to check.

They're black-headed gulls.

The name is misleading, their heads a warm shade of chocolate. They're attractive enough, delicate compared to the brutish great black-backed gull or everyone's favourite chip-stealer, the herring gull. But they're not noted for their taciturnity, and their rabid squawking has me considering an early departure to pastures more peaceful.

Two men enter. They exude expertise, scanning the lagoon with occasional mutters which are neither designed for public consumption nor particularly secretive.

'Med gull there.'

A small nod from his companion, a mild yelp from me.

The 'what's about' list noted the presence of seven Mediterranean gulls on The Scrape, but I'd assumed the arcane knowledge required to identify one would be beyond me. There are about a dozen gull varieties to be seen in Britain, each with several age groups, and to my untutored eyes they're a confusing mess of interminable variations of black, white and grey, with some brown thrown in for good measure, depending on the age of the bird. The guides cite arcanities like scapulars, primary projections and gonys angles as ways of telling them apart. I've tried, I really have, but it's too much for my tiny brain. I'm drowning in a frothing cauldron of gulls.

But now, with a possible tick before me, and experts at hand, I'm incentivised. I check the Mediterranean gull on my phone. The adult bird is described as 'unmistakable', a sure sign I have no chance of identifying it. I pluck up courage.

'Excuse me... so sorry... which is the Mediterranean gull?'

Sometimes all you have to do is ask.

'You see the left edge of the island? Count... hold on... one, two, three... sixteen birds in.'

I count sixteen birds in.

'That's your Med gull.'

'I see. Thanks.'

I don't see, but keep looking, searching for clues. I suppose the bill is a shade heavier, and there's a deeper red to it. And maybe its nascent balaclava is black rather than chocolate brown. I flick between it and the neighbouring bird, comparing and contrasting.

Yes, I've got it now. I think.

I take my notebook out and note 'Med gull'. Then a small tick and, as an afterthought, a question mark.

Honesty in all things. Well, most of them.

As I drive to Minsmere the next morning, rosy-fingered dawn doing its thing on the horizon, I cram the hotel's complimentary shortbread into my mouth and call it breakfast. I've lived in Britain for fifty years, but it seems I still haven't twigged that April is fundamentally a cold month, and my thin jumper offers inadequate protection. I'll just have to think warming thoughts.

From the car park I hear a sound like someone blowing across the top of a milk bottle. It's instantly recognisable, and adds purpose to my stride as I make for the Bittern Hide.

The bittern is a secretive bird, fond of hiding in reed beds, a habitat with which Minsmere is amply equipped. The expanse of reeds is so vast it's difficult to know where to start, but I assume if someone's gone to the trouble of naming a hide after a bird, that's as good a place as any.

All is calm. A little egret sloshes around in the swamp to my right, the pure white of its plumage reminiscent of 1970s detergent adverts. A little grebe dives, leaving concentric ripples in its stead. The bittern is notable for its absence, but there's no hurry, and it's hard to imagine a more tranquil environment.

CHACK!

I jump two feet in the air. My skin stays on the bench, while my binoculars opt for the floor.

CHACK-A-DACK!

A big noise. Explosive, harsh and close to my left ear.

CHACK-A-DACK-ADACKADOCKADIGGADOGGA-DACK!

I recover my composure. I heard this sound yesterday, but

from much further away. This bird seems to be in the hide with me.

The Cetti's warbler didn't exist in my day. Not in Britain, anyway. It was filed under 'rarities', with just a handful of sightings ever recorded. But it started breeding here in 1973, no doubt drawn by the variety of Britain's cuisine and the open and welcoming character of its people, and has made inroads since then. This novelty factor makes it particularly alluring, and I'm keen to see one in the flesh.

The song strikes up again, strident, insistent. I leave the hide on a whim, tiptoe and tenterhooks. Finding its exact source is surprisingly hard. Just as I think I've narrowed it down to a single bush, it stops. I have the bush in my sights, poised to pounce. I'm relying on the naked eye to spot the first movement, but have the binoculars ready so I can pinpoint the bird when it shows its face.

It's lying low, waiting for me to make the first move. But I can outwait it.

A minute passes. No dice. A chill wind slices through me. This is silly. I should give up.

One more minute.

CHACK!

I wheel round. The crafty blighter's behind me. I get it now. It sings to make you look, and immediately flies somewhere else and watches you looking in the wrong place, a maniacal grin plastered over its scheming face. But I'm wise to it, and after a mere six repetitions of the game, I nail it. It's sitting lower than I thought, hidden in the shade, but there's no doubting its identity. Just as I catch sight of it, it gives another peremptory 'CHACK!' as if admitting defeat, and whirrs off to torment someone else.

I am birder. Hear my mighty roar.

Buoyed by my victory over the hapless Cetti's warbler, I almost forget I was after a bittern. I return to the hide, but twenty minutes yield nothing but a philosophical shoveler and an ominous numbness in my toes, so I move on, disappointed. Bittern Hide? Yes it does.

As I follow the path out of the woods, I realise I'm yet to see a human being. This solitude, the slow pace of the day allowing thoughts to percolate and coalesce without the distraction of conversation, is one of the joys of birding. Nothing against my fellow humans. Well, most of them.

A ramp leads up to the Island Mere, the newest hide on the reserve. I scan the reed beds below, hoping for a water rail, another secretive bird. A lady walks towards me, bright and breezy. Her smile is one of sympathy and understanding.

'I always hope to see a water rail down there, but I never have.'

It's so similar to what would have been my own opening gambit that I'm thrown off guard. I feel my friendly smile turn into a self-conscious rictus. I try to formulate a response, fail, feel obliged to make some sort of noise so as not to be thought a lunatic, mumble something that sounds to my appalled ears like 'meffroonle', trip over my feet, and escape into the safety and solitude of the hide.

If I'd hoped for a few moments of peace and quiet to lick my wounds, I'm disappointed. Eyes swivel towards me, swing doors flap, the pianist in the corner stops playing.

My new companions are four men, two women and industrial quantities of Tupperware. They're set in for the day. They seem unmoved by the glory of the scene before them, but I've already learned that birders are undemonstrative souls. They keep their enthusiasm under a veil.

The frisson occasioned by my arrival abates, and peace descends. A fierce wind whips through the half-open windows and cuts my neck in two as I look across the broad lagoon with its loose girdle of reed beds. A pair of teal nuzzle around in the silt; sand martins swoop, up, down, diagonally, aerobatic miracle made flesh; a marsh harrier, a shallow V in the distance, floats over the straw-coloured beds; greylag geese veer across my view like honking fighter planes on a recce mission; two great crested grebes in the middle distance choose that moment to instigate their famous courtship display. The words 'get a room' spring to mind, but for them a cold lagoon on the East Anglian coast is a room – we humans, with our insistence on snuggly duvets, forty TV channels, a minibar and a loo roll with the end folded into a V, we're the weird ones.

I let the scene nourish my soul. I'm freezing, but at least my heart's cockles are warm.

The lady behind me, eating granola from a Tupperware tub, shifts slightly, issues a clarion call.

'Bittern up!'

She moves across behind me. She doesn't need to point. Above the hide a brown bird, larger than I expected, lumbers across the blue sky on rounded wings. I crouch forward and crane my neck to keep it in view. As it circles over the reed bed I know this pleasure will be all too fleeting – ten seconds at most. As if sensing my thoughts, it banks, flops into the bed with a palpable sense of relief, and disappears from view.

Cross it off the bucket list. No longer will my mental picture of a bittern be composed from photographs and illustrations. I have my own image now; ill-lit, distant and fleeting, but mine.

The ping of a coiled spring being flicked with a triangle beater. A flash of movement. A glimpse of a small, warm-brown shape flitting across my view. A reed sways under its paltry weight.

Bearded tit.

The name is sadly inaccurate. The beard is a droopy, Mexican-in-a-1970s-cartoon moustache, and the bird isn't a tit. True, it's small and flits around very much like its great, blue, coal, long-tailed, marsh, willow and crested nearly-cousins. But its habitual milieu is a clue to its proper name. Officially, it's a bearded reedling.

I realise, in a rare moment of ornithological self-congratulation, that I'm the only one to have seen it. Everyone else is looking at the bittern, or at least the place where it was last seen. I should say something. That's what people do, isn't it? That's what jack snipe guy did. He shared his knowledge.

I hesitate. What if these people aren't interested in bearded tits? They didn't show any enthusiasm for the grebes or the teal or the geese. And I've already experienced the humiliation of a dozen eyes boring into me, not to mention the engulfing embarrassment of the 'meffroonle' moment. But still. It's a bearded tit. Gorgeous little bird, sitting there with its droopy moustache, guitar and sombrero. I should definitely say something.

I clear my throat. The sound echoes around the hide like the voice of God. Six heads swivel in my direction. Before I speak, something makes me glance across to the swaying reeds.

It's gone. The bearded tit has gone. Disappeared into the reeds, never to be seen again. I sidle to the door and make my escape.

There are four of us, peering earnestly into the depths of a tree about a mile off the North Circular. Yes, we're all male, and yes, we're all middle-aged. Stereotypes are generally built on fact.

The bird's in there somewhere. It's been around for a week, showing no inclination to leave, and occasionally disporting itself in full view of the few people interested enough to visit it.

I'm not twitching, I tell myself. I was coming here anyway. It's mere coincidence that I stumbled on the 'recent sightings' section of the London Birders website. If it's a twitch, it's an accidental one. I'm not breaking any of my self-imposed rules.

No matter how much I rehearse this argument, it rings false.

If there's such a thing as a birding hangover, I'm suffering from it. The Minsmere trip yielded thirty-four ticks, but in the aftermath I'm overcome by anticlimax, a feeling that I'll never again have it so good. I've seen those birds now, and despite my good intentions there's a tiny and hateful part of me that regards a ticked bird, seen again, as a disappointment.

There's only one antidote to this lassitude. More birding. Rack them up while spring is young. At some times of year birds are difficult to find, but right now you can't avoid them. I'm keen to exploit opportunities closer to home, so I've come to Brent Reservoir, supposedly one of the best birding locations in central London. It turns out to be quite a trek, but, while not dripping with the natural atmosphere of Minsmere, has a charm all its own. You have to warm to a place where the location of a bird is described with reference to a submerged supermarket trolley or wheelie bin.

But before I reach the hides, I've found myself caught up in this accidental twitch.

It breeds in the Siberian taiga, this bird. If it's to be found in this country, it's usually in autumn, either blown off course by easterly winds or as an extension of normal migration patterns. Quite how it's arrived in this tree in NW9 in the middle of April, and what it thinks of its new surroundings, will remain a mystery. Its presence here is unusual. If it were a restaurant in provincial France, the Michelin guide would describe it as 'worth a detour'.

I feel sorry for it. Illogical, I know. Did I feel sorry for the chicken that died so I could slather its flesh in mustard mayonnaise and eat it in a granary roll for lunch? I did not. This bird, unlike the chicken, has its life and liberty; and no doubt it was in pursuit of happiness that it got diverted. But I can't help wondering what it makes of the attention bestowed on it by this group of skulkers whose number I have briefly joined. Does it know where it wants to go? Is it hunkering down in the safest spot it can find while it summons the energy to continue its journey?

Does it, I wonder, anthropomorphising wildly, miss its mum?

After a while I ask myself how long I'm prepared to stay. I've come on a recce, not a twitch. I'm keen to visit the hides overlooking the reservoir, just twenty yards away. But the lure of the twitch is strong.

A shower sweeps over us. I juggle with binoculars, notebook and rain jacket, and by the time I'm organised, the rain has passed and there's still no sign of the bird.

When it does appear, fifteen minutes later, our initial view is fleeting, no more than a flicker of activity from the back of the tree. It pops up, disappears, pops up again, plunges back into the depths. Then, like a diva toying with her admirers, it emerges and bathes in its reception.

Even more interesting than the behaviour of the bird is the behaviour of its stalkers. There's a sharpening of focus, an intake of breath from the man standing next to me. He's muttering to himself, shifting his head to left and right to stay with the bird as it hops from branch to branch. Its camouflage serves it well, and we have to be on our mettle to keep track of it.

'There it is. Midway back, to the left.'

I shift my binoculars as deftly as I can, but it's too quick for me.

'Behind the bough now. Out again. To the right.'

He's pointing. I can see it, and bring my binoculars up again. It's gone. No it hasn't. Wrong branch. I lower them again, locate the bird, readjust the binoculars.

Got it.

My companion is all of a twitter. His breathing is shallow, the tension in his face palpable. This might be the highlight of his year.

'Got the dark eye-stripe. Pale supercilium. Yes. Wing-bars. Yes. There it is. Yes.'

He lowers his binoculars. His hands are shaking. I'm happy for him. He's been genial enough company, but for the last five minutes the only way to divert his attention would have been to do a convincing impression of an ortolan bunting, or some other rarity that might outrank the yellow-browed warbler we've just seen.

I try to put myself in his shoes. I'm glad to have seen it, grateful for the tick. But what am I missing? It hasn't made my pulse race, put a tremor in my hands, made me shaky with relief once the sighting's been snared. It seems that at least part of the attraction was not just to see the bird, but to have seen it, to have ticked it off the list. My birdwatching adventures have been therapeutic and energising. For him this seems to have been an almost religious experience. This bird is fine enough, but I would have derived as much satisfaction from watching the miracle of a blue tit hanging upside down on the feeder at home.

Maybe we're not cut from the same cloth. There's room for different kinds of enthusiasm within the sphere, after all. And yet here I am devoting my year to the collection of ticks. Hypocrisy, anyone? Perhaps. Or perhaps I'll just call it ambivalence and confusion.

How far would I have gone to see this bird if I hadn't already been coming here? Not that far. Certainly not the trek across London I now know this trip to be.

Still, a tick's a tick.

We're joined by a silver-haired gentleman. He, it transpires, was the first person to see it.

'Is it your first?' silver-hair asks me.

I mumble my usual disclaimer.

'I'm a beginner, really.'

He perks up a bit, addresses me like an uncle dispensing life advice.

'Coal tit. That's how to recognise it. The beginning of the call is just like the coal tit. OK?'

I nod earnestly. I daren't admit it, but as I still have difficulty discerning the call of a coal tit, his tip is little help to me. But it's the thought that counts. I log the information for future use, and we go our separate ways, he to I know not where, me to the hide to search for green sandpipers amongst the upturned bins.

You should always treat yourself on your birthday, so I go to RSPB Rainham Marshes.

It's been a good day, Minsmere's abundance replicated closer to home, the arrival of summer visitors guaranteeing a continued supply of new sightings.

A clutch of itinerant yellow wagtails, flitting around on a patch of mud *this* close to the hide; linnets, bouncy and excitable, spring in their bones and bursting out of their mouths; a reed warbler, singing its scratchy song from deep cover, but flitting up to adorn the top of a reed like a figurehead on a ship's prow; a whitethroat, rewarding my homework with a song I knew from the moment it started, before popping up onto a protruding branch to congratulate me, as if it knows it's my hundredth bird. I'm halfway there. I raise my bat towards the pavilion and take guard for the second hundred.

I'm delighted and amused to see a skylark, its silver chain of music soaring upwards, higher and higher and higher, into the boundless sky, just as Ralph Vaughan Williams wrote it.

Definitely a skylark, not a nightingale.

The only downside has been the absence of the short-eared owl. I've come here three times this month, and each time it's eluded me, but that's a disappointment I can live with. Owls, it seems, aren't my thing. There are five varieties in the UK, and I've had neither hoot nor feather of any of them.

Not so with the lapwings. They're abundant at Rainham. The visitor centre is in sight, and I can hear a plate of beans on toast calling me from the cafe, but the lure of the lapwings is greater. Just one more minute.

A man approaches. Like me, he's about fifty. Like me, he's wearing binoculars round his neck. There the similarities end.

My demeanour is exaggeratedly buoyant, enhanced by exercise and the richness of avian life. His is downbeat, possibly exacerbated by the massive telescope/tripod apparatus that sits on his back and threatens to devour him like some monstrous sci-fi alien. As I hear the crisp tread of his feet on the gravel I tear my gaze from the glorious spectacle before me and acknowledge his existence with a brisk nod, a tight smile and what I hope is a birder's 'morning'.

We stand in silence for a few seconds.

One of the attractions of birds, I've realised, is all too easily overlooked.

They can fly.

Honestly, think about it for a second. They can actually bloody fly. It's a miraculous thing.

They may not be able to invent the wheel, design cathedrals, make lavender bags, temper chocolate, merge mailing lists, bake an olive and rosemary focaccia, write haiku, work out when it's bin day, dance a cha-cha-cha, remember all the words to Tom Lehrer's 'Elements Song', do a passable impersonation of Michael Caine or open a bottle of wine using the heel of their shoe, but they can fly – so, frankly, they win.

We can fly, but we need a lot of help, and the experience is undermined by the whole AAGGHHH WE'RE IN THE AIR IN A METAL TUBE WE'RE NOT SUPPOSED TO BE IN THE AIR IN A METAL TUBE GET ME OFF BEFORE IT GOES SPLAT thing.

But maybe that's just me.* Although we don't know exactly

---

* And yes, I *know* it's much safer than clipping your toenails or buying a Toffee Crisp from a vending machine. Just allow me this one irrational phobia, OK? Oh, and spiders.

how flight evolved, there are two main theories. The arboreal theory contends that flight is basically Gliding+, a fully integrated gliding experience enhanced by FLAP technology. It's an enticing thought, undermined by the fact that none of the current non-avian gliding vertebrates uses flapping to help them – they're gliding purists, if you like. So there's no connection between this and the flapping method, and no evidence that the development of flight was a result of adaptations using it.

Pitched against this is the cursorial theory, which has it from the ground up, as it were. The idea here is that a running dinosaur would leap in the air to evade predators, and the development of small proto-wings to help that process led to ever-increasing hops and leaps, and then to, 'Woo hoo, I'm flying, look at me, Mum!' (WHIFLAMM). This theory is undermined by the objection that strong-legged dinosaurs wouldn't need help from wings, so why did even a partial one evolve? This objection is in turn undermined by the example of the chukar partridge, which indulges in wing-assisted incline running, or WAIR,* using a mixture of flapping and running. This means that partridge chicks can whizz up steep hills with the greatest of ease. From there it's easy to imagine an adaptation which takes this process a few flaps further to WHIFLAMM. When I nearly ran over those partridges at Minsmere, it might not have looked as if their wings were helping them, but they probably made the difference between safety and partridge pâté.

Whatever the truth, it crosses my mind that there must have been a moment when some creature nailed it, realised this was the way forward, and embraced the future with the fervour of Frasier Crane assessing a 1988 Château Lafite.

After that there was no looking back, the combined

---

* This, unlike WHIFLAMM, is an actual thing, corroborated by scientists and everything.

intelligence of evolving life forms exploiting the myriad possibilities afforded by a life in the air.

Flight in all its forms, from the whir of a hummingbird to the soaring of an albatross, never fails to boggle the mind. And when there's an exhibition of virtuosity right in front of you, it would be rude not to give it a minute or two. So I'm watching a group of lapwings give their courting display. In this case, it's not their mum they're showing off to, but the 'woo hoo, I'm flying, look at me' bit holds.

The lapwing's decline since my childhood has been marked, but it's still the most widespread British wader. I have memories of flocks of them billowing up in the wake of tractors ploughing the fields around our village. As those fields are now a golf course, I suppose the lapwings are no longer there. But visit an estuary or mudflat and you're likely to see some.

If the gadwall is underrated, then spare a thought for the lapwing. Superficially black and white, it's easy to take for granted. But the green and purple iridescence on its back and neck show beautifully in sunlight and at close quarters, and its crest, no more than a flick of the pen, lends it a quizzical air.

Attractive enough when standing on the tidal flats, in display the male lapwing is mesmerising. It's an aerobatic trick show of effortless virtuosity, combining tumbles and swoops and sudden upward dashes with a song that brings to mind the soundtrack to the 1980s video game *Galaxian*.

For many years I assumed the bird's name came from the lapping of its wings. The discovery that it is in fact a corruption of the old English for 'crested bird' was a kind of betrayal, and made me question all the easy assumptions I've made over the years. Be that as it may, the lapping of the lapwing's wings lends plausibility to my supposition, the limbs in question broad and rounded at the ends, like wide-handled table-tennis bats. Yet from this apparent languor it produces astonishing control, improvising airborne flourishes and curlicues before gliding in to land with casual understatement, a Clooney-esque, 'Hello ladies,' to cap the display.

If I were a female lapwing, I totally would.

I've been watching four of them, rivals in love, each determined to advertise its suitability as a mate to its adoring lady-lapwing public. It's a captivating sight.

My new companion seems immune to the joys of lapwings. His voice is flat.

'Anything about?'

It's the conventional birder's opening gambit, and already I'm on the back foot. What is 'anything'? I can't list everything I've seen. What he means is 'anything unusual'. Because I've stopped on the path, he assumes I've found 'something'. But all I'm doing is watching lapwings. So what do I say?

I shrug, vaguely apologetic.

'Oh, no... I was just... watching the lapwings. Amazing display.'

I might as well have given him a pair of grey socks for Christmas. After a short and unimpressed silence, he tries again.

'No sign of the water pipit? Or the gropper?'

A month ago I would have been flummoxed by 'gropper', but I've learned a bit about birding nicknames, so I'm on sound footing. It's short for 'grasshopper warbler'. Advocates of the use of such abbreviations ('sprawk' for 'sparrowhawk', 'mipit' for 'meadow pipit', 'PG Tips' for 'Pallas's grasshopper warbler' etc.) claim it saves time, and there's truth in that – but there's also an element of the unnecessary shibboleth in there too. 'We belong,' users of these nicknames are saying, 'to a club. Learn the lingo or don't join.' As an apprentice, I don't feel either that I've earned the right to use the lingo, nor that I particularly want to.

The grasshopper warbler is shy, but advertises its presence with a high reeling sound that indeed recalls the chirp of a grasshopper. This one's been around for a few days, but is elusive.

I shrug. 'Afraid not.'

Disappointed beyond endurance, he moves on. The lapwings send him off with an intensification of their display. I wonder if he and I inhabit the same planet. It's the flip side to the feeling I had at Brent with yellow-browed warbler guy.

Perhaps I'm being unfair. Perhaps he was pecked to death by a mob of lapwings as a child and has been traumatised ever since. Or perhaps he's secretly enraptured by them but doesn't want to show it.

Nonetheless, I make a silent vow never to submit to complacency, never to lose the sense of wonder at the glories of the everyday, that childish feeling of awe and discovery that fuelled my heinous sprint at the bar-tailed godwits all those years ago.

Hunger soon gets the better of me and I head for the cafe. As I pass a patch of reeds, I hear a high-pitched reeling from its depths. There's a grasshopper warbler in there, but it's too well hidden, and I'm too hungry. As I continue, I wrestle with two questions. Should I retrace my steps and find my lugubrious companion to tell him about it? And does it, heard but not seen, count towards my target?

I've just reached the answers 'no' and 'yes' when a distinctive shape flies over my left shoulder and perches on a bush twenty yards ahead of me. Neither pigeon nor hawk, crow nor kestrel, it stops me in my tracks. A cuckoo, many times heard but never seen, the sound of my childhood made flesh, breaking cover for just a few seconds before fleeing to the woods.

That one definitely counts. Happy birthday to me.

April ticks (68)

WWT Barnes, RSPB Minsmere, RSPB Rainham Marshes, RSPB Dungeness, Brent Reservoir

Jackdaw *Corvus monedula*, Greylag Goose *Anser anser*, Shelduck *Tadorna tadorna*, Gadwall *Anas strepera*, Teal *Anas crecca*,

Shoveler *Anas clypeata*, Red-legged Partridge *Alectoris rufa*, Pheasant *Phasianus colchicus*, Little Egret *Egretta garzetta*, Little Grebe *Tachybaptus ruficollis*, Great Crested Grebe *Podiceps cristatus*, Marsh Harrier *Circus aeruginosus*, Sparrowhawk *Accipiter nisus*, Avocet *Recurvirostra avosetta*, Oystercatcher *Haematopus ostralegus*, Black-tailed Godwit *Limosa limosa*, Dunlin *Calidris alpina*, Redshank *Tringa totanus*, Jack Snipe *Lymnocryptes minimus*, Mediterranean Gull *Larus melanocephalus*, Lesser Black-backed Gull *Larus fuscus*, Herring Gull *Larus argentatus*, Great Black-backed Gull *Larus marinus*, Coal Tit *Periparus ater*, Sand Martin *Riparia riparia*, Swallow *Hirundo rustica*, Chiffchaff *Phylloscopus collybita*, Kestrel *Falco tinnunculus*, Bittern *Botaurus stellaris*, Ringed Plover *Charadrius hiaticula*, Turnstone *Arenaria interpres*, Knot *Calidris canutus*, Bearded Tit *Panurus biarmicus*, Stonechat *Saxicola rubicola*, Greenfinch *Chloris chloris*, Buzzard *Buteo buteo*, Egyptian Goose *Alopochen aegyptiaca*, Pintail *Anas acuta*, Pochard *Aythya ferina*, Little Ringed Plover *Charadrius dubius*, Kingfisher *Alcedo atthis*, Firecrest *Regulus ignicapilla*, Cetti's Warbler *Cettia cetti*, Willow Warbler *Phylloscopus trochilus*, Blackcap *Sylvia atricapilla*, Pied Wagtail *Motacilla alba*, Sedge Warbler *Acrocephalus schoenobaenus*, Wheatear *Oenanthe oenanthe*, Reed Bunting *Emberiza schoeniclus*, Common Gull *Larus canus*, Collared Dove *Streptopelia decaocto*, Skylark *Alauda arvensis*, Meadow Pipit *Anthus pratensis*, Little Gull *Hydrocoloeus minutus*, Green Sandpiper *Tringa ochropus*, Snipe *Gallinago gallinago*, Yellow-browed warbler *Phylloscopus inornatus*, Hobby *Falco subbuteo*, Whimbrel *Numenius phaeopus*, Whitethroat *Sylvia communis*, House Martin *Delichon urbicum*, Whinchat *Saxicola rubetra*, Cuckoo *Cuculus canorus*, Swift *Apus apus*, Reed Warbler *Acrocephalus scirpaceus*, Yellow Wagtail *Motacilla flava*, Linnet *Linaria cannabina*, Grasshopper Warbler *Locustella naevia* (heard)

Year total: 108

MAY 2016

The swifts are back.

Two of them scream over the terrace as I'm hanging out the laundry, Maverick and Iceman, writhing in and out of each other's slipstream, slicing through the atmosphere so close to my head I can hear, for a split second, the miniature whoosh of their displaced air.

Summer isn't summer without swifts. I saw one at Rainham, a lone harbinger, on my birthday, but in my head it didn't quite count, the excitement reserved for the moment we hear the screech of our own birds circling overhead then swooping into the eaves and out again in a flurry, never stopping, evolved for nothing but flight.

Their season is short. If you see one in Britain in April, you're lucky. Throughout May they arrive with a flourish, their excitable screaming and extravagant aerial displays enlivening the skies for the next three months. And then, one day in August, they're gone, leaving a sickle-shaped hole in our lives. In those short months I will drink them in as deeply as I can, standing on the terrace with a gormless look on my face as they swoop and sweep and glide and flutter, a top-class aerial ballet company performing at no cost to the taxpayer.

We had swifts when I was a child, but mostly we had swallows, which arrived a few weeks earlier and more surreptitiously. It was their departure, advertised for days beforehand by the gradual build-up of chattering birds on telephone wires, that sticks in the mind, a memory as much a part of my childhood as blue tits pecking through the foil to get to the top of the milk.

But while the swallows were abundant in 1970s Oxfordshire, they're not really city birds. So for us now it's swifts all the way.

I count twenty of them circling high over Streatham Common one Saturday morning early in May. As I stand, head tilted back, revelling in their display, I become aware of a bundle of energy approaching on the path.

He's eight or so, wildly overexcited, carrying a pair of purple binoculars and a colourful bird guide. Five paces behind, his mother, weary, amused, has the air of someone who's wondering where the cafe is. I know how they both feel. I've spent a contented hour roaming the common. Sun and birds are out, the air full of the sights, sounds and smells of spring. All is well with the world. But now I need coffee.

I've just spent ten minutes watching a nuthatch feed its young. They've nested in one of the boxes in the little wood, and as I stand underneath I can hear wheedling cheeps as the parent whirrs back and forth acceding to the chicks' demands. Occasionally, if it's away for too long, a chick pops its nose out, wondering where the food is. Even from a distance the adult bird looks haggard, flown off its wings by the demands of parenthood. How it must long for the day they fledge and it can kick back with a vat of pistachios and a cold beer.

The mother of the young boy has a similarly careworn air, but she's indulgent, obviously pleased by her son's mania, and presumably relieved he's chosen to spend the morning outdoors rather than staring at a screen.

'Look, Mum! Great tit!'

He shows her the bird with an extravagant wave of his binoculars. A great tit does indeed flit past us into a bush. The boy whirls round again, pointing.

'Robin!'

His overt enthusiasm is a pleasing contrast to the demeanour of most birders I've encountered, a valuable reminder of why we do it. He's clearly unaware that his shouting and flailing are more likely to drive the birds away than attract them, but his excitement is infectious. Just once I'd like to see an adult birder let out an involuntary, 'SHIT! DID YOU SEE THAT?' And I like to think, underneath their impassive exteriors, that's exactly what they're doing.

He sees my binoculars.

'Are you birdwatching?' Flattering awe. I smile at them both.

'I am. Beautiful bird, the great tit, isn't it?'

He scowls.

'It's the bully of the feeder.' He's admonishing both me and the bird.

Duly chastened, I change the subject.

'Hey, you know what I've just seen?'

'What?'

'A nuthatch.'

He's wide-eyed, looking through his book. But it only lists the commonest birds, and the nuthatch, abundant enough but not everyday, isn't there. I bring out my phone, show him a picture. He's beside himself.

'Look, Mum! A nuthatch!' he screams, as a blue tit zips past. A mistle thrush emerges from the undergrowth, its alarm call reminiscent of the teleprinter from *Grandstand* in 1976, and I fear the lad might explode. He's unstoppable now, naming all the birds in the vicinity with equal fervour and inaccuracy.

'Lovely to see such enthusiasm,' I say to his mother.

'He's obsessed. I can't keep up.'

I point up the path.

'If you go up there you'll reach a fenced area. Just past that on the right there's a tall tree with a nest box halfway up. That's where the nuthatches are.' To the boy I say, 'Have fun.'

'Yeah,' he replies. And he's off, bouncing up the path. Despite his inadvisable waving and shouting, there are birds aplenty knocking about the place, more than I've seen at any time that morning.

I go home for my coffee. The future of birding is in safe hands.

I'm buoyed by my role, however brief, as mentor to the next generation, but I'm under no illusions. I need mentoring myself.

Tempting though it is, with my total topping 100, to think the battle is half won, I'm not kidding myself. Most of those birds were easy fodder. All I had to do was turn up and point my binoculars out of a hide. The months ahead present a tantalisingly short window to see our summer visitors, and while some will be commonplace, plenty are more elusive, and their identification will require skills I don't yet possess. Despite my deep-seated vein of independence, I realise I must swallow my pride and enlist help from older and wiser heads.

Andrew isn't older, but he is by some distance wiser. He took my woeful ignorance of the robin's song with laconic good humour, and now he's agreed to show me a couple of favourite haunts. I present myself outside a PC World in Walthamstow one Sunday morning, and we drive to the Norfolk/Suffolk border, in search of cranes, stone-curlews and, in my case, enlightenment.

RSPB Lakenheath Fen was converted in 1995 from arable farmland back to the kind of wetland habitat that used to be dominant in this part of the world. It's been a spectacular success, wetland birds falling over themselves to breed here. They include cranes, graceful and elegant birds, as tall as an eight-year-old but with a bigger wingspan. The crane disappeared as a breeding bird in this country 400 years ago, victim of hunting and diminishing habitat. But recently it's established toeholds, in Somerset thanks to a reintroduction programme, and in East Anglia of its own accord. Lakenheath has other attractions, but secretly I'm holding out for cranes.

My hopes are immediately dealt a blow.

'If you see them, they'll probably be very distant.'

I take the RSPB lady's use of the word 'distant' to mean 'far away', rather than 'stand-offish'. Having lowered our expectations, she gives us a map of the reserve and a list of recent sightings, many of them familiar from Minsmere. My eye alights on the word 'garganey'. Like the gadwall, this is an unflashy duck, its plumage a subtle mix of grey, black, brown and white, the distinguishing feature of the male a white crescent which runs down the nape from above the eye. Underrated bird. Scarce. Worth seeking out.

The difference between Andrew's and my levels of expertise is highlighted within a minute. As we crunch our way along the gravel path, Andrew, while apparently concentrating on my thrilling tales of ornithological derring-do, interrupts to point out the song of a blackcap.

I stop, concentrating. Sure enough, in the distance there's a jumbled song I hadn't even heard, let alone identified. We were walking. Talking. The scrunch of the gravel obscured all other sounds, and conversation left no room for background listening. But Andrew seems always tuned in to both landscape and soundscape. It's a matter of awareness. Useful though my recordings have been, they're like practising conducting in front of a mirror. There's no substitute for hands-on experience.

We come to a separation of the paths with a view across a broad stretch of water interspersed with the inevitable reed beds. The sky, Tupperware-grey now the early sun has yielded to unthreatening high cloud, remains large, the flatness of the landscape inviting the eye across it. Some of the commoner birds float across the water. Coots, Canada geese, mallards. Amongst them is an unflashy bird, white crescent stripe running from its eye and tapering as it slides into the browns and greys of the bird's plumage.

Bonus garganey.

An early tick is like an early goal in a football match – it injects energy and purpose, the anticipation of a good day. How misguided. The cranes fail to appear, and no matter how pleasant the walk and abundant the birdlife on offer, there remains the tiniest needy tug at the back of my mind as we drive the short distance to Weeting Heath.

News of the stone-curlews sounds hauntingly familiar.

'I'm afraid they're quite distant today.'

I've never been more grateful to have an expert with me. An expert with a telescope.

The stone-curlew viewing hide is a short walk from the visitor centre, overlooking an expanse of rough grass with gentle hills in the distance. I scan the horizon through my binoculars, knowing they're not strong enough but doing it anyway. Rook, stone, rook, rook, rook, stone, grass, more rooks, nothing but bloody rooks, their stout black shapes stubbornly not morphing into anything resembling a stone-curlew.

'They've just gone over the brow,' a gentleman offers.

About a hundred yards from the hide the ground slopes gently away. The stone-curlews are nesting just beyond that ridge, laying their eggs in a bare scrape on the ground among the occasional stones that give them their name. Camouflage is all-important for both bird and egg, vital protection against predators. This leads me to wonder why they choose to nest out in the open. Doubtless there are sound evolutionary reasons, but it does seem mildly perverse.

These birds are picky. They like chalky, stony ground with short-clipped grass to ensure an abundance of their favoured diet of little scrabbly things like woodlice and millipedes. It's a habitat

91

nurtured by the Norfolk Wildlife Trust, with the help of a willing army of sheep and rabbits. With the changes in farming practice and gradual loss of natural habitats, the stone-curlew, along with dozens of other birds, has declined in this country. Depressing though this is, it's heartening there are people who care enough to try to halt the decline.

Andrew touches my shoulder.

'Got one in the scope.'

I want to find them myself. It's like struggling with a crossword clue that someone else has already got – I'm torn between desperation to know the answer and an almost equal urge to prove myself. But my binoculars aren't up to the task. I look. Even through the scope the birds are indistinct, this very lack of clarity somehow making the sight more moving, like footage of the moon landing. Barely visible just above the ridge, a brown blob, its eye and bill a yellow dot and dash, moves slightly towards us. It stops, turns, is met by a twin blob. Their paths intersect briefly, then move apart. If I concentrate really hard I can make out more detail, and then, just as I think I have the bird in my sights, it moves. I step away from the scope.

I don't quite know why I'm so moved by them. Maybe it's their appearance, slender legs and startled look coupling with a notably yellow eye to lend them a certain vulnerability. Maybe it's the thought of the work that's gone into preserving their status as a British breeding bird. Or perhaps it's because we've had to work a little to see them. There are dozens of rooks between us and the stone-curlews. They're interesting, intelligent, attractive birds in their own right, the blackness of their plumage showing a purple gloss when caught in a certain light. But their abundance renders them, today at least, comparatively insignificant. I can see a rook any time. The stone-curlew is different. I doubt I'll see another this year.

I spend a couple of minutes admiring a rook to redress the balance.

The stone-curlews trundle over the brow of the hill. We've had a good sight of them, but it's time to go home. We pick up our stuff and leave.

It's an ambitious schedule, dependent on train connections. A day trip from London to a bird reserve is rarely straightforward by public transport. But I have the day off, Tessa needs the car for work, and faint heart never made birder. And so I find myself sailing through the north Kent countryside on my Brompton one sunny morning. I wish I could say that I do so without a care in the world, a warm spring wind whistling through my hair and a song on my lips. But my ill-fitting helmet itches, third gear gets stuck, and the Tesco vans of the Hoo Peninsula seem hell-bent on nudging me into every ditch in the area. It's a relief to arrive at the reserve, padlock the bike to a post, and start my circuit.

The RSPB reserve at Cliffe Pools, a mix of saline and freshwater lagoons, grassland, salt marsh and scrub, isn't one of those with a tea room and gift shop. There's a car park, but otherwise it's just you and the great outdoors. I like this. It makes me feel like a member of the hard core, eschewing the namby-pamby creature comforts of life.

But twenty minutes in I could murder a flat white.

The path is long, with no visible end. To the right, fields, greylag geese grazing in the distance. To the left, an expanse of water, the occasional coot floating aimlessly on its surface. A kestrel glides over, hovers for a few seconds, decides against it and veers off in search of richer pickings. The song of warblers from the bushes competes unavailingly with the exuberant croakings of marsh frogs from the ditches lining the path. A stoat emerges, glances disdainfully in my direction, then trots calmly ahead of me, rightly confident it could take me down mano-a-mano should the need arise. It ducks under a fence and loses itself in a field.

If I've learned anything about this game, it's a modicum of patience. My first glance at the large area of bushes to my left yields no more than an unending vista of hawthorn and bramble, but rather than assuming there's nothing there, I stop, consider my options, and head up the narrow path into denser undergrowth. I force myself to walk slowly, senses on full alert. I'm alive to every twitch and rustle. A scurrying at knee level. My head jerks round, but it's gone. A flurry to my right, flickering leaves, a trembling of branches. A shadow dives into the impenetrable depths. A cheep from... where exactly? No idea. Another cheep, an answering chirp, activity everywhere, but none of it doing what I want it to, which is to sit down in front of me in order of height, and bloody well shut up while I work out what they are.

Seriously, how do people do it? It's next to impossible. I read reports of a day's birding, all certainty and no question marks. 'Whinchat: 4, wheatear: 6, linnet: 35.346, goldfinch: 1,398.' No mention of 'unidentified little brown jobs overhead: 76', or 'nearly identical cheeps from the middle of a bush – your guess is as good as mine: 137'.

I stop and take a few seconds to drink it all in. One obliging bird seems to sense my frustration and pops up onto the bush in front of me, showing its bloodied nose and holding still. It has earned my gratitude.

'You, my friend, may be just a goldfinch, but you are most welcome, and I thank you for your generosity.'

It returns to its bush without reply, my soul brother for a second.

I stay for a bit, willing the birds to come out and play. But it's as if they've sensed my volatility and are keeping clear. I can't blame them.

I'm about to move on when it begins. One sound at first,

a preparatory cluck. Once heard, never forgotten, so they say. They're right, and now I'm treated to an outpouring of fluid, liquid music of astonishing richness and depth, as if the shrubbery has been turned into a Marshall stack and turned up to eleven.

It's no more than five yards away, somewhere in the bush in front of me. It's one of those low scrubby bushes, variety unknown. But the bird is well hidden. I inch forward, desperate to lay eyes on it, but equally desperate not to interrupt the music that seems to suspend me a foot above the ground, worldly burdens momentarily shed.

I'm two feet from the bush. The song is all around, the bird still nowhere. I lift my eyes, and there, in the bush behind the one I was looking in, five yards away and with a glint in its eye that says 'What took you so long?', is my bird. We make eye contact. It knows I'm there, seems to be singing solely for me. It isn't, of course. It's singing to find a mate. My wishful thinking can't change the laws of nature. But at that moment, in that maelstrom of miraculous sound swirling around me, there's no way on earth you can tell me that this nightingale, this anonymous-looking bundle of life, isn't directing its love directly towards me, through my ears and into my heart.

And then, too soon, with a flick of its rufous tail, it's gone. But it carries me away, out of the reserve and all the way back to the station and home.

Recommended. Would encounter again.

The year's nearly half over and I haven't seen an owl, a failure denoting a heinous lack of dedication. While London isn't the first place you'd think of as natural habitat for these alluring birds, there are plenty of places where they can be found. A short-eared owl has been seen regularly at Rainham Marshes, just not when

I've been there. And Richmond Park, Wimbledon Common and Kensington Gardens all have tawny owls, so I've read. I've even made a couple of early morning forays to Streatham Common, where they've been reported in the past. Zilch. But I'm confident a week of glamping in Dorset over half-term will supply at least one.

Despite my professed aversion to canvas, I've allowed myself to be persuaded by majority vote to submit to a week under it. I protest too much. My memories of camping holidays of my youth mostly involve rain, beans on toast, and campfires brought to flickering life by my father's typically fastidious attentions. These rustic outings gave way to foreign trips involving hotels and fine dining as we got older, but some tiny part of me must remember that true happiness lies not in luxury and warmth, but in endless games of Owzthat and rummy played in a leaking caravan while waiting for the drizzle to relent. Nowadays, give me a well-appointed shower block and the opportunity to do dad stuff involving charcoal and tongs and bacon, and I'm in.

The glampsite is idyllic – a large field given over to a well-spaced clutch of yurts, with clear skies, empty roads and a stream running down one side, it's a welcome release from the grind of urban life. Rosie, the farm's border collie, greets us at the car and accompanies us loyally to our yurt. Our fellow glampers say hello and nothing else. Everything is as it should be.

I don't want my birding to disrupt the family dynamic, so I get up half an hour before going to bed and drive to Portland.

Birds like an extremity. Those places that stick out of the coast are often the first land they see after a long journey, so it's natural they should gravitate towards them. Dungeness, Spurn, the Isles Scilly and Fair – all heavily populated by birds and birders. And so it is with Portland Bill, that little skin tag hanging off the base of Dorset. There's a bird observatory by the lighthouse, one of nineteen dotted around the coasts of

Britain and Ireland, each doing valuable work monitoring the movements of migrating birds. It's from there that I start my first morning's reconnaissance.

I'm not alone. It turns out that unimaginably early for me is the middle of the afternoon for a dedicated birder. The two I speak to, both younger men, have been out for an hour already, and even this is regarded by one as 'lightweight'. Blanching slightly, I ask them where I should head for, thank them, and take my leave.

The early-morning fog is localised and beginning to clear in patches, but lends a mystical air to the place, shrouding the base of the old lighthouse so the top half seems to hang magically in the air above it. The sea isn't yet visible, although its presence is unmistakable in the taste of the air and the background shushing of waves on the rocks below.

The feeling that I'm on the set of a Hammer horror film is enhanced by a deep *graw* to my left. There are two of them, perched on adjacent fence posts, noticeably huge for corvids, their heavy bills dimly silhouetted in the mist. Dark birds, associated in many cultures with death. Ravens. Huginn and Muninn, Odin's eyes and ears, come to freak me out.

My inner birder does brief battle with my inner superstitious idiot and wins a narrow but painful victory. Rather than flee for my life, I watch the birds for a while, struck again by their size and the deep, other-worldly quality of their gronking and crawing.

A nice early morning tick to start me off.

As I explore, it becomes clear why Portland is a haven for birds. As well as its unique situation, the Bill has a wide variety of habitats in a relatively small area. From the fields to the cliffs is a short enough walk, and by the time I reach my vantage point over the sea, I've clocked up two more ticks: a fulmar, floating above me on stiff wings like a mini-albatross, and a rock pipit, small and perky, its boldness allowing me ample time to confirm the identification.

Whenever I'm within a mile of a cliff edge my mother's voice rings loud and clear in my head. 'Don't go near the edge!' It became a running joke, repeated when any of us went near the shallowest of inclines, even occasionally when we approached the kerb to cross the road. I'm disinclined to go near edges at the best of times, but here there are ways to do so without risk, and I'm afforded a decent view of the sea from a safe vantage point. From here, after a bleary start when it seems there are no birds on the sea at all, I realise I can see little black dots whizzing out from the cliffs, describing a parabola over the sea and back again. These must be guillemots. Or razorbills. Or are they little auks? I watch as their whirring wings propel them through the air. Definitely some kind of auk, the family of marine birds known as 'the penguins of the northern hemisphere'. A dim memory wafts into my head. They use those stubby wings to propel themselves underwater, and this stubbiness isn't conducive to easy flight through the much thinner air. No wonder they look so panicky.

Auks aren't comfortable on land, using it only to breed. All they need is a tiny bit of rock to perch on. There they lay their single, noticeably pointy-ended egg. Just looking at the birds huddled together on minuscule ledges on the cliff face makes my head spin. Guillemot eggs used to be much sought-after, both for eating and collecting, and the people who gathered them would risk their lives climbing down the slippery rock face, bringing back bags full of eggs and bartering with waiting collectors at the top of the cliff. Unthinkable, in more ways than one.

As I train my binoculars on these almost comical birds, I can discern differences between them. I'm looking at two species here. And now I can see a couple of them silhouetted against the dawn sky, I see that their profiles are markedly different. Slim pointy bills: guillemots; short, blunt ones: razorbills. Tick and tick.

I could watch their frenetic forays all morning, and am also hoping for an appearance from other seabirds, a shearwater maybe, or a skua. But seawatching is a specialist's game, the distances involved usually too much for binoculars in the hands of a beginner. As well as a telescope, you need the patience of a saint, and the ability to see a blob a mile away in a sea fret and accurately identify it as a Manx shearwater or a juvenile gannet.

Besides, there's plenty else to see here, both late migrants and resident breeders. And although I've stuck religiously to my 'no twitching' rule, I can't help thinking about a rare and unusual bird that's been in the area for a few days now, showing itself happily at times but lying determinedly low at others. Wouldn't it be a happy coincidence if my path were to accidentally cross with that of a great spotted cuckoo?

I head north from the cliffs, aiming to do a large loop which will return me to the car with a clutch of exciting ticks in the bag.

Three hours later I collapse behind the steering wheel, undone by the early start, miles of trudging, and the stubborn determination of Portland's bird life to avoid me.

Tiredness and hunger impel me to curse all birds, and especially great spotted cuckoos. It's almost as if the guillemots, razorbills, rock pipits and ravens had never existed.

It's our last day at the glampsite. All is idyllic. We play football with Rosie, the border collie. She trounces us. Barbecuing takes place. A robin, whose song has accompanied me to the car every morning at 4 a.m., is still giving it large as daylight morphs to gloaming. A yellowhammer joins it in duet from a telephone wire behind the yurt. The song, according to every single bird book, is supposed to sound as if the yellowhammer is singing 'A little bit of bread and no cheese'. Handy mnemonic it might be, but this particular bird clearly hasn't heard of it. It sounds to me as if it's trying to emulate the French horns at figure 15 of Gershwin's *An American in Paris*.

Each to their own, I suppose.

Accompanied by these calming sounds, I light the fire and, cradling a glass of red wine, and then another, ponder the week, the month, the year. What started as rekindled interest has blossomed into obsession. I carry my list in my head wherever I go. Where ten years ago I might have assessed a new place on the quality of its architecture, bookshops or restaurants, now this valuation is based on its proximity to birding havens. I've walked more in these five months than I did all last year, and have got used to lunching on a small sandwich and a packet of crisps, or even, when I misjudge the availability of such things, nothing at all. I've lost weight, gained energy, and rediscovered a world hidden in plain sight for three decades.

The disruption to family life I nervously anticipated hasn't materialised. Tessa and Oliver allow me my strange ways, smiling indulgently as I return from a birding trip and recount the day's events, and dutifully admiring the photo I show them of yet another distant bird that must seem to them no different from all the others. In a strange way my new-found interest complements theirs. Tessa, embarking on a garden design course, is always on the lookout for new gardens to visit. If I can wangle it so there's a bird reserve nearby, so much the better. And if we can cycle there, so Oliver can have his training session at the same time, he's more than happy to be dragged round one or other of his parents' favoured habitats as a quid pro quo. He's also proved a dab hand with the camera, getting to grips with its many features far more quickly than me. Any middle-aged person wanting to learn about technology only has to hand their apparatus to an eleven-year-old boy and wait for ten minutes.

While May has yielded a comparatively small number of ticks, that's not my only yardstick of success. It's about seeing the world through new eyes, reassessing values, making use of one's time. The list is the driving force, but the new birds are valuable because of their intrinsic beauty and fascination, not just because they've swelled my total to 124.

But still. 124. Yay.

I saw my cranes after all. Missing them at Lakenheath gave me an itch I needed to scratch, so I granted myself a day and a half at Slimbridge in Gloucestershire, home of the Wildfowl & Wetlands Trust, and drop-in centre for some of the birds from the Great Crane Project – a reintroduction scheme on the Somerset Levels. It was the wrong time of year to go there. I knew that. For the full panoply I needed to be there in winter, when the reserve throngs with thousands of wildfowl. But the sight of two cranes taking off, circling, then coming in to land again, counts among the more moving spectacles of my birding year. They're at the same time gawky and delicate, long necks straining forwards as they heave themselves off the ground with an elegance that belies the hard work and sheer power required for the task. And at rest, standing tall, they have a majesty enhanced by their rear feathers, which stick out like a bustle, lending them an air of Victoriana.

Also at Slimbridge were common terns, refined cousins to gulls, elegant, delicate and deliciously skittish. A pair appeared over my shoulder as I cycled along the canal on the second morning. I engaged in an exhilarating but inadvisable race, me and my folding bicycle against their deceptively languid wingstrokes. I held them until they decided to fire up the afterburners and I pulled out of the competition rather than condemn myself to a watery demise.

This week in Dorset has been terny too. First, Sandwich terns, seen up close on their nests next to the hide at Brownsea Island in Poole Harbour, shaggy crests on the backs of their heads lending them a punky look, and matched by a decibel level which would put a crooked smile on John Lydon's face. But their elegance in the air, suspended above the water as if held on a thread from above before plunging to spear an unsuspecting fish, brought to mind the hover of a kestrel.

And then the little terns, their fragile breeding colony protected by a roped-off area on the shingle beach at Ferrybridge near Weymouth. Tiny for a seabird, their delicate appearance is deceptive. They're robust enough to fly to Africa and back every year.

How easily we say that. 'They fly here from Africa,' as if it were a routine trip to Waitrose. To give myself some sense of the enormity of the feat, I try to visualise it from the bird's point of view. Guided by forces beyond our comprehension, and endowed with astonishing stamina and doggedness in the face of constant sapping of energy by the elements, these birds make the journey because it is, believe it or not, the most efficient thing for them to do, their chances of survival enhanced by chasing perpetual summer across the globe.

As dusk beckons, and to the accompaniment of a steady trickle of gulls heading south to their nightly roost, we go for a stroll round the site. A family of 'mule swats' drifts towards us on the stream, parents keeping their two cygnets firmly in view and offering an admonitory hiss if we stray too close. A third cygnet takes the easy option, nestled on the mother's back between her large angel wings. I wonder if the cygnets take it in turns to go for a ride, or whether this favour is the result of special pleading.

It's approaching prime owl time, and I leave Oliver with the swans as I take a brief and aimless saunter, hoping to catch a glimpse of a barn or tawny owl against the darkening sky. But no. Not tonight.

I head back to the yurt, aware of my dereliction of duty in the barbecuing department. Oliver stays, pongling around with a stick. Dusk is slow, and the light has that crepuscular quality that makes shapes indistinct.

I'm putting sausages on plates when Oliver returns. His is the saunter of one who knows they're about to go one up. He's casualness personified as he delivers the killer news.

'Just seen a barn owl, Dad. It flew over my head and went into the next field.'

I'm delighted for him. Just.

May ticks (16)

Isle of Wight, RSPB Cliffe Pools, Beddington Farmlands, RSPB Lakenheath Fen, Weeting Heath, WWT Slimbridge, Frampton-on-Severn, Portland, Brownsea Island, Chesil Beach

Yellowhammer *Emberiza citrinella*, Gannet *Morus bassanus*, Nightingale *Luscinia megarhynchos*, Garden Warbler *Sylvia borin*, Common Tern *Sterna hirundo*, Garganey *Anas querquedula*, Stone-curlew *Burhinus oedicnemus*, Crane *Grus grus*, Bullfinch *Pyrrhula pyrrhula*, Fulmar *Fulmarus glacialis*, Raven *Corvus corax*, Rock Pipit *Anthus petrosus*, Guillemot *Uria aalge*, Razorbill *Alca torda*, Sandwich Tern *Sterna sandvicensis*, Little Tern *Sternula albifrons*

Year total: 124

JUNE 2016

It starts with the lightest smattering, a few unthreatening drops no bigger than commas, and then a mist so fine as to be almost unnoticeable. Refreshing enough on a warm summer's day, especially halfway round a long walk on undulating terrain, but also a portent of things to come. From our vantage point over Ashdown Forest we can see the future, the heavy mass of clouds still distant but moving in our direction. About five miles away a village is shrouded in grey, as if shaded by 4B pencil. I suggest to Andrew that we consider returning to the car. He agrees. Oliver's relief is palpable.

I place myself in Oliver's shoes. He's not here under duress, but nor was the trip his idea. I sold it to him on the possibility of raptors, the certainty of photo ops, and the Winnie-the-Pooh connection. Cynical move, that last one. Eleven is a bit old for that finest of bears,* but the familial devotion is deep, and mere mention of him is enough to bait the hook. Sure enough, Oliver gave the resigned assent of a boy who knows he has no choice. He's played cricket in the morning while Andrew and I birded, and Tessa has dropped him off and gone to visit

---

* This is not strictly true. You're never too old for Winnie-the-Pooh, but you can be too eleven. When it comes to beautiful things of childhood, there is an age of least appreciation, and eleven is on its cusp. It could be argued, in fact, that eleven is both too old and too young for W-t-P.

a garden. Everyone's happy, more or less. We've visited the Enchanted Place, narrowly evaded a heffalump trap, and are now on an expotition to the North Pole while scanning Eeyore's Sad and Gloomy Place for Dartford warblers. Oliver has found a stonechat to photograph. Stonechats are great for that, perching considerately on a gorse bush with the patience of a film star on the red carpet.

A bird sings in the distance. I ask Andrew what it is. He looks at me slightly askance.

'Song thrush.'

Ah yes. Silly me. I've heard loads of song thrushes this spring. I'm nearly on first-name terms with the one in Norwood Grove. So why didn't I recognise this one?

There's a phenomenon, familiar to conductors, called podium deafness. It works like this. When sitting in an auditorium observing someone else's rehearsal you're an aural genius.

'Second flute's flat. Bass trombone's late. Inside fourth desk second violins just played C sharp instead of C natural.'

But standing on the podium, baton in hand and the weight of responsibility on your shoulders, confidence evaporates and all you hear is a raging white noise occasionally punctuated by something that might or might not be an oboe. If mistakes are made, all your brain can formulate is the vaguest thought that something, somewhere, has gone wrong. Beyond that all is mush. So you intensify your expression of passionate immersion, make a sweeping gesture with your left hand, and shout at the third horn for a non-existent missed entry. That's conducting.

If I've got used to podium deafness over the years, I still suffer from its birding equivalent. Andrew has pointed out redstarts, tree pipits and a marsh tit, all familiar to me from pictures and recordings. I've seen the birds, heard them, observed and enjoyed them, and nodded sagely while noting them in my book. But I am nothing in this unfamiliar environment without the expertise of others. In truth, I've flailed in Andrew's wake, adrift on a sea of novelty. They're all ticks, but I can't help feeling they're plastic ticks, as cheap, shoddy and fake as a Bolex watch.

For all my undoubted effort, it's clear I'm entirely dependent on my mentor. But isn't that what mentors are for? He's showing me a way of doing things, of being alert but relaxed, that only comes with experience. I've never seen any of these birds before. Why on earth do I expect to recognise them straight off the bat?

It's all part of a familiar pattern. Wanting to be the expert, dazzling others with my knowledge, and plunged into paroxysms of gloom when I fail. Better, surely, to be the one who wants to learn?

I shake these negative thoughts from my head and concentrate on the acres of gorse all around, hoping to discern the flutterings of a Dartford warbler in the shaggy depths.

'There's your redpoll, Lev.'

I wheel round. He's pointing upwards. I scan the skies, trying to locate the source of the staccato chattering that alerted him to the passing presence of these little finches, and eventually find three dots bouncing out of sight over the brow of the hill.

Trying to retain a snapshot of the sight and sound of the birds as they passed overhead, I add common redpoll to the list.

As we make towards the car with one eye on the clouds and the other on warbler-watch, it becomes clear we're not going to avoid the tender ministrations of the English summer. The smattering has turned into a dogged mizzle which looks like being just the support act. After a while, acutely aware of the increasing dampness of my son and heir, I call a halt. If we kick on we should make it back before the rain really takes hold.

There's only one thing wrong with this plan. I'm in charge of the map.

The confidence with which I lead us to the path on the right is matched only by the inaccuracy of my navigation. We tramp off, unaware we're heading in completely the wrong direction. Andrew and Oliver trust me. Why shouldn't they? I'm a conductor.

There comes a moment during a rainy day in England when the rain shelves any pretence that it's a passing shower and sets in for the long haul. 'Think you're wet?' it seems to say. 'Think again.' And then it rolls up its sleeves and gives of its best, applying itself to the task of delivering a countywide drenching with the attention to detail of a true professional. The idea that it doesn't bear you a personal grudge is a pathetic fallacy.

We reach the drenching stage a mile from the car, and it's quickly replaced by a veritable Crocodile Dundee of rain production.

'That's not rain,' it declares. 'THIS is rain.'

The intensification of the soaking means I consult the map less often than I should, and this leads to an inevitable straying from the righteous path. Only when we hit a road do I decide to look again, and realisation dawns.

They take it well, all things considered.

Fans of Winnie-the-Pooh will know that the best way to get somewhere when confronted with a flood is to turn your umbrella upside down, climb inside it, and paddle your way across the forest to wherever it is you want to go, whether it's to rescue a Piglet or to return your long-suffering child to an environment where he can breathe without the risk of drowning.

We have no umbrella. Shanks's pony it is.

I try to imagine how I would have reacted to the afternoon's events at the age of eleven, and come to the swift conclusion that the young man walking with resigned good humour by my side deserves a treat when we get home. I put a consoling arm round his shoulder.

'Nearly there.'

'Thanks, Dad. You just squeezed a river down my back.'

The perils of compassionate parenting.

We reach the car, nostalgic for a time when every movement didn't induce a torrent of splashing. There we assess the wisdom of continuing our day as planned.

Ashdown Forest, good for bears of little brain and terminally depressed donkeys, is also one of the key spots in the south of England for a particular crepuscular summertime bird, and it's pivotal to my plans for the day.

The composition of my 200 birds has been fluid. If I fail to see any of those seafaring bullies, the skuas, for example, it won't be a disaster, because I should be able to make up the numbers elsewhere. But there are some whose presence on the final list I'm regarding as non-negotiable, and not just because of the numbers. Some birds have an aura about them, something that sets them apart from the run of ordinary things. The golden eagle is one; the bittern another. I would argue, too, for the inclusion of the relatively common kingfisher – any sighting of this bullet of iridescence is imprinted on the synapses for later recall.

Firmly on my Aura of Greatness list is a bird that used to be known, for all the wrong reasons, as the goatsucker.* Its scientific name, *Caprimulgus europaeus*, retains the link.† Nocturnal, mysterious, its appearance more giant moth than bird, the nightjar is in a category of its own, neither owl nor raptor. Perhaps that weirdness is part of the attraction. Being nocturnal, it holds a natural fascination for the diurnal human brain. Creatures of the night are almost by definition sinister, lurking in the shadows of our darkest fears. And the nightjar's song only adds to the mystique. Where other birds have song or calls that are recognisable as such, the nightjar has its own sound, a rattling

---

* You hang around goats long enough, you get a bad name, even if all you're doing is hunting moths.

† *Capra* = nanny goat; *mulgere* = to milk. Pay attention at the back, will you?

and continuous reeling known as 'churring'. I've been brooding about the nightjar for weeks, my desperation to see one having to be kept in continual check. It needs to be a warm midsummer evening, and you need to go to a specific spot where they're known to be found, usually on the edge of a forest clearing. They generally appear shortly before night descends and makes further sighting impossible, so there's a window of about an hour. Right time, right place, right conditions. My opportunities will be few, and even then there's no guarantee I'll see one.

Rain, for nightjar sightings, is bad news.

We sit in the car and consider our options. The forecast says the rain will clear. But the forecast said light showers earlier, so my faith in it is shaky.

After twenty minutes of gentle steaming, I heed the prevailing mood and, like an umpire calling off play for the day an hour after everyone else knew it was inevitable, announce that we're going home.

Birds vs family. Family wins. There will be other nightjars. There had better be.

Mao Zedong was a delusional old cove, as illustrated by his bizarre vendetta against a humble bird which had been part of China's culture for centuries.

Passer montanus, the tree sparrow. One of the ultimate 'little brown jobs'.

In 1958 the Great Leader decreed that all the tree sparrows in the country be killed. This wasn't just a whim. He'd thought it through. Sparrows, he reasoned, ate too much grain. Get rid of them, and the people would be able to realise the fruits of their labour.

To be fair, it wasn't just sparrows. Also targeted in the Four Pests Campaign were rats, mosquitoes and flies. If only he'd restricted it to just the three pests, nobody would have batted an eyelid. But sparrows?

When you have a population of 600 million people on hand to obey your every wish, the extermination of a whole species moves from the realm of 'lunatic' to 'lunatic, but it might just work'. Birds were shot, nests destroyed, eggs broken and nestlings killed. People went out every evening, banging pots and pans to stop the birds from roosting, with the result that the exhausted birds dropped out of the skies like dead sparrows. The Chinese sparrow population plummeted.

The fatal flaw in this Baldrickian plan soon became apparent. Sparrows don't just eat grain. They also eat insects. Locusts, for example. The catastrophic effect of removing an entire link from the food chain would have been obvious to any remotely attentive eight-year-old, but that wasn't Mao's style. Locusts swarmed, crops failed, and the Great Leap Forward became the Great Chinese Famine, which accounted for the small matter of between 20 and 45 million deaths from starvation.

Dictators, eh? Tsk.

It's almost the definition of irony that the tree sparrow was one of two species suggested in the early 2000s as China's national bird.*

For anyone over fifty and even vaguely interested, the tree sparrow and its cousin, house, will be familiar birds. The reason you have to be over fifty is that they've declined by over 90 per cent since the late 1960s. It's widely thought that this decline is the result of agricultural policy – hedgerows were cleared, scrubby bits beside fields spruced up, old trees removed, farming techniques became more efficient. By the time the adverse effects of these policies became apparent, the damage was done, and the

---

* It lost out to the red-crowned crane, whose scientific name, *Grus japonensis*, proved equally controversial.

tree sparrow is now on the Birds of Conservation Concern red list.*

From the top of the hill on Beddington Farmlands in south London, you feel as if you can reach out and touch the famous IKEA chimneys of the Purley Way. It's not St Paul's or the Angel of the North, but it'll do. By contrast, the large refuse incinerator being built on the edge of the site won't do at all, and the sludge beds next to the sewage farm on the other side, while good for birds, are best viewed from a distance.

This 400-acre mixed habitat site also includes lakes, reed beds, scrubland, meadows and shallow pools. Its attraction to me is partly that it's near where I live, but also that it's home to a tenacious breeding population of tree sparrows. It's a permit-only site, so I've signed up to a guided walk in the hope that some of them will present themselves to my eager scrutiny.

We're a small but select group, of mixed ages and genders. Peter, our guide – younger and more dashing than I'd expected – leads us to a vantage point above two lagoons, one of which is home to the largest daytime roost of herons in the London area. The sight of thirty or more of these prehistoric-looking birds lends the lagoon a hint of the primordial swamp.

It's sunny, breezy, June-y. An agitated gull flies over, followed by a bird of prey. I'm still sketchy on birds of prey,† so defer an attempt at identification. They disappear over the brow of the hill, combat still ongoing, the gull easily repelling the shambolic efforts of the raptor. Peter laughs.

'That'll be one of the Sutton peregrines. Juvenile. Not quite got the hang of it yet.'

I've never seen a bungling raptor. The possibility hadn't occurred to me. The ones I've seen have been full of quiet

---

* There has recently been a tiny revival in the population and range, thanks in great part to cooperation between conservation groups and farmers.

† Yes, OK, and on all other kinds of bird too. Thank you for your input.

menace: marsh harriers coasting low and slow over reed beds, kestrels balanced on the air above an unsuspecting vole, buzzards soaring on thermals, scanning the landscape for movement. The peregrine is sold to us as a killing machine, the emphasis on speed and ruthless efficiency. But this one's like a gawky teenager. It can fly all right, but it's being outwitted and outsped by a black-headed gull. Fine bird, the black-headed gull, but you wouldn't normally back it against a peregrine. But it stands to reason that the ability to stoop at 200 miles an hour and pluck a pigeon out of mid-air, while partly intuitive, might require some honing.

No sooner has the peregrine disappeared than Peter draws our attention to something fast-moving and distant behind us. Two bird-like birds, flying like birds, with the distinctive shape of birds. While I'm upgrading my identification from 'some kind of bird' to 'some kind of small or medium-sized bird', Peter has identified them as ruffs, fired off a burst of photographs, and is examining the results on the camera's screen.

'There you go. See the distinctive flight shape? And the wing-bars.'

Just as I thought. Definitely some kind of bird.

We continue towards tree sparrow central, and I take stock. I have two bonus ticks, taking my total for the year to 134. It'll be a rum do if I don't see another ruff or peregrine before the year's up, but it's nice to have them under the belt. Now, if I can see these tree sparrows it'll leave me on 135, which as everyone knows is a number inextricably associated with Alex 'Hurricane' Higgins and his historic last-frame break in the 1982 World Snooker Championships final.*

If you ever find yourself looking for a tree sparrow on a 400-acre site, the thing to remember is that one of them is

---

* It's also my childhood hero and great England wicketkeeper Alan Knott's highest Test score. I do have a life. Honest I do.

very big and the other is very small. This realisation hits me as we trudge around the area where the birds are supposed to be. A whitethroat pops up and serenades us. Lovely bird, the whitethroat. Enchanting song, fascinating behaviour. Now piss off and don't come back unless it's with a tree sparrow.

Despite the growing body of evidence to the contrary, I still have a fond fantasy of arriving at a site and being greeted by a line of birds, perched out in the open, in good light, their features exactly resembling the ones so painstakingly represented in the field guides. In these fantasies the birds serve at my pleasure, tailoring the activities of their day according to my whim. So the possibility of not seeing any tree sparrows today simply hasn't occurred to me. But as time passes without a whiff of a sighting, I have to accept it as not just a possibility but a likelihood. Accordingly I seize on any small bird as a possible tree sparrow. The merest hint of a flitting shadow in the corner of my eye has me wheeling round and scanning the rank vegetation that surrounds us, even though I know the bird was a blue tit. I try my best to hide this desperate behaviour from the others, who are showing signs of wanting to move on. For them, the stakes are low. Tree sparrows or no, they've had an enjoyable and informative morning. Peter is vastly knowledgeable about things besides birds: trees, grasses, wild flowers, butterflies, moths, everything. It's knowledge worn lightly, shared as a matter of course, but what I really want him to do right now is conjure up a tree sparrow.

One of my companions, an older lady, is making 'shall we leave?' noises, the occasional 'Well...' and 'So...' accompanied by a vague drifting down the hill towards the exit and home and tea. She's had enough, hoping we'll all take the hint and drift away with her.

This won't do.

'Are you mad? Nobody leaves until we've seen these tree sparrows, you imbecilic poltroon.'

The words form in my head, but I'm saved from myself by an 'Ah!' from Peter to my left. I follow the direction of his pointed finger with my binoculars until they alight on a small, dumpy, stout-billed silhouette. The light is good enough to discern the diagnostic black cheek patch and red-brown crown which separate it from the commoner* house sparrow. As we watch, it's joined by two more. They jazz around for a few seconds, almost as if they know they have an audience, then disappear into the depths of the bush.

We're done. We can go.

The sight of the tree sparrows brings home just how vulnerable these birds are. If I wanted to see one as a child I went into the garden, and now here I am, on a fenced site in south London, so desperate for a sighting I'm on the verge of abusing a stranger. That such a common bird should decline so sharply in a lifetime should be unthinkable. It makes me wonder what a 1950s birder would say if they were around now.

'What have you done with the sparrows? And the yellowhammers? And the corn buntings? And the grey partridges? And the turtle doves? And the pretty much everything? Where are all our birds?'

'Ah, yes. We wondered if you'd notice. Well, we've sort of, you know, killed them off. Sorry about that.'

It's almost impossible to address this subject without coming across as a gloomy and earnest eco-warrior thumping a well-worn tub. But it's also essential to do so. The birds, the bees, the insects, the flowers, the trees, the absolutely bloody everything, they all need our help. We are, after all, the cause of their problems. And

---

* But still declining, by the way. Don't think you're getting off that easily.

it's no longer acceptable to sit around doing nothing. Joining one of the conservation organisations listed at the end of this book would be a start. The bare minimum, some would say.

There's no doubt wildlife is in trouble, most of it man-made, but, misty-eyed optimist that I am, I like to find the good news amidst the torrent of bad. There are birds, more than you might imagine, whose populations have increased and spread in the same time. I've seen more marsh harriers in the last month than were alive in Britain in the 1970s. Little egrets and Cetti's warblers are now regular sightings where before they were scarce or non-existent. And nowadays if I go out birding and don't see a buzzard – a prospect back then as remote and unattainable as Grace Kelly – I write a letter of complaint to my MP.

I remember my first buzzard sighting as if it was this morning. It's hard-wired into my memory, not just for the bird's proximity, but also because it triggered another, different kind of first.

We are on a family holiday in the Jura mountains on the France/Switzerland border. My father drives happily round hairpin turns that remind him of his Cyprus childhood, seemingly oblivious to the steep ravines beside the road. My mother prays silently in the passenger seat. My brother and I sit in the back seat, me naming every bird I see, him responding with a sullen 'shoot it'. I'm twelve, so a natural irritant to an older brother. He's sixteen, and therefore unimpressed by most things, especially annoying younger brothers with a bird fixation.

Our one piece of common ground is Monty Python, which we quote incessantly, flitting from one sketch to another randomly and without preamble, neither of us needing any explanation of context.

'I'd like to have an argument please. Jackdaw.'

'Shoot it. Certainly, sir. Do you want the full argument, or were you thinking of taking a course?'

'Don't give me that, you snotty-faced heap of parrot droppings! Song thrush.'

'Shoot it. I think it's slightly more runny than you'll like it, sir.'

'Woodpigeon. It's a stiff! It's shuffled off this mortal coil and joined the bleedin' choir invisibule!'

'Shoot it. I don't care how bleep runny it is.'

Our lucky, lucky parents.

The 'bleep' is a matter of necessity, neither of us quite having the confidence to swear in front of our parents, despite overwhelming evidence that my mother, at least, is no stranger to the joys of verbal profanity. It was from her lips that I first heard what I still consider the rudest word in the English language.

Christmas Eve, 1972. The milkman, instead of delivering the specified sixteen pints of gold top, twelve cartons of double cream and enough butter to sink the navy of a small seafaring nation, has deliberately fobbed us off with a pint of semi-skimmed and two tubs of strawberry-flavoured Ski. As I sit at the kitchen table I become vaguely aware of some sort of whirlwind streaking through the room and out of the back door. It's an image I recall many years later when John Simpson reports seeing a cruise missile 'fly down the street and turn left at the traffic lights' on BBC news.

But this isn't a cruise missile. It's far more dangerous than that.

My mum, on the warpath.

It's a few seconds later that I hear the very bad word.

Poor milkman. We never saw him again.

Despite this, Step and I are still shy of the bad words.

Until the buzzard.

It curtails our Pythoning activities. It curtails everything. It does this by flying up from the sheer cliff to the left of the car, veering across in front of us and keeping pace with us at a distance of no more than five yards. It's a majestic and unforgettable sight. It even manages to halt the relentless flow of Python.

'Fuck me sideways.'

The words, not entirely appropriate for one of such tender years, slip unbidden from my innocent twelve-year-old lips. My parents, I think, are so shocked they forget to tell me off. And so a lifetime of unfettered profanity begins.

The buzzard flies on ahead of us after a few seconds, and then down into the ravine and out of sight. And today, whenever I see one, I silently repeat those three words in homage to my younger, better self.

The lure of the nightjar is strong, and Ashdown Forest on a Saturday evening isn't a long drive from south London. One more try. Oh, go on then.

I go down early. A couple of hours in the late afternoon sun, maybe mopping up a crossbill or even a turtle dove, an hour of nightjar vigil, then home. I might even snaffle a woodcock if I'm lucky.

This time I'm alone, without the responsibility of keeping an eleven-year-old entertained and dry, but also without the guidance of my mentor. What could possibly go wrong?

As if to underline the futility of my endeavour, six birds, little brown dots against an early evening sky, fling their mocking calls at me like bullets before bouncing out of view in the middle distance. Linnets. Or goldfinches. Or greenfinches. Not crossbills. I don't think.

Look, I don't know, OK? They were small and brown and vindictive. That's all I've got.

Before I descend into an impenetrable slough of despond, I'm saved by another bird. I remember it from the previous visit. Andrew and I had almost given up on seeing it when a couple of flurries of activity alerted us first to its presence, and then almost immediately to its absence. It had done what all birds do when they see me: dive under cover and wait until the coast is clear. But Andrew exerted his god-like powers of birdery on it, and it emerged, eventually perching on top of a spruce like a Christmas angel for a few minutes before flying off to taunt someone else.

This one is treating me to a display of vocalisation and acrobatics that catches the attention from a hundred yards away. I inch towards it, hoping it will ignore my presence and continue with the show. As its song sinks in, it triggers long-lost memories in my brain, and before I know it I'm humming the piccolo part from figure four of the third movement of Olivier Messiaen's *Turangalîla-Symphonie*.

My first year as a percussionist at the Royal Academy of Music involved total immersion in an unfamiliar world. Not only was I called upon to do more practice than I'd ever imagined possible, it became painfully clear how narrow my musical education had been so far. It wasn't just that I'd never played any of this music before – I'd never even heard of the composers. It was a strange and disgraceful dereliction of my duty as a wannabe professional musician. So when I was told that we would be participating in a festival of music by Olivier Messiaen, one of the major musical figures of the twentieth century, my reaction was one of blank incomprehension, followed by a hasty trip to the Academy's record library.

The music I listened to in the following days, and performed a few weeks later, was like nothing I'd ever heard before. Why had nobody told me about this stuff? It mixed dense and complex harmonies with oriental and exotic sounds from outside the canon of Western classical music I'd grown up listening to. There were moments of chaos, savagery, angularity, peaceful beauty and delicious ecstasy, all underpinned with an overt spiritual quality that spoke even to my uncompromisingly heathen soul.

Most important in my appreciation of Messiaen, though, was

his use of shedloads of percussion. Xylophones, gongs, drums, cymbals, wood blocks, bells, shakers, wind machines and much more, even instruments of his own invention, like the geophone.* His philosophy towards percussionists was admirable: 'Keep them busy. At least it'll stop them going to the pub.'

For one used to sitting at the back and occasionally going ting, this opened up a new world of possibility, but there was another aspect of this music I found just as beguiling.

Messiaen had a fascination with birds, and would spend hours roaming the countryside with a notebook, transcribing the songs he heard. He incorporated these sounds into his music, even devoting whole pieces (for example *Catalogue d'Oiseaux* and *Oiseaux Exotiques*) to capturing the sound world and atmosphere evoked by birdsong, sometimes weaving his transcriptions into the fabric of the music, sometimes allowing them to stand alone, shorn of accompaniment.

This bird is a woodlark, and its distinctive fluting song, with a descending pattern that induces a faint melancholy in the listener, makes it a Messiaen bird. In the snippet it reminds me of, Messiaen used it as one of several layers of sound, each pursuing their own course regardless of the others, but somehow intersecting to produce an entrancing soundscape. Those few bars are on a loop in my head as I make the connection between the piccolo in the orchestra and the bird in front of me. An earworm from a woodlark. There's a title of a piece of music in there somewhere.

The one I saw with Andrew seemed content to perch on its tree, but this one is determined to give me a proper display. It sits atop a gorse bush, bounces across to a neighbouring one, then takes off, climbing half-high before sailing down like a paper aeroplane and

---

* Take a large drum. Fill the bottom with lead shot. Swirl it around to invoke the sound of the shifting and cracking earth.

landing on the first bush again, all the while giving out its plaintive song. It's a magical piece of theatre. I near as dammit applaud.

If only I could say the same for the cricket match I stumble upon ten minutes later. It's the kind of thing I've participated in countless times, an admirable display of sporting incompetence in which error is met with blunder, countered by catastrophe, and then topped with laughable ineptitude.

But it's a cricket match, so I stop and watch. After ten minutes I revise my assessment that the game is unworthy of applause. Collective uselessness of this order is a rare thing, and can only be the result of many hours of hard graft. I offer the players a silent 'bravo' and continue on my way.

Forty-five sweaty minutes later, I'm beginning to think I should have stayed for the end of the match. I've walked along a stream in the woods below, hoping to spot a grey wagtail. But there are none. I've tripped over equal numbers of tree roots and protruding rocks, and the detour has yielded nothing more than a talkative wren and a confiding robin. Cherished birds, both of them, but no more exciting than the ones I can watch from the comfort of my own kitchen.

As I emerge from the woods and back towards the car, I have my reward.

It's a willow warbler, the kind of summer bird an experienced birder would barely give a second glance. But I've identified it from its song, and this is still a rare enough occurrence to give my confidence a bit of a boost.

And then there's the song itself.

This willow warbler's song is a thing of great and melancholy beauty. Soft in tone, its shape resembles the song of a chaffinch,*

---

* The song of the chaffinch is often compared to a fast bowler running to the crease and then delivering the ball, but this is useless to me unless I know which bowler. Fred Trueman? Colin Croft? Wasim Akram? I lean towards Jimmy Anderson, but that's just me.

but one crossbred with Marvin the Paranoid Android. After a reasonably lively opening few notes, it takes on a plaintive quality as it descends, conveying indefinable feelings of regret and loneliness. But then at the end there's an ornament, a skip in the step, a moment of uplift, the unexpected Jaffa Cake hiding beneath the Rich Tea in the biscuit tin of life.

This willow warbler seems happy to share its thoughts with me for fifteen minutes, so I head for my appointment with the nightjar in chipper mood.

According to local knowledge, there's a particular bench from which the birds can be observed, and I'm heading for it when I run into a trim and organised-looking man, mild, about my age, and wearing a pair of binoculars slung round his neck. Call it a hunch, but I think he might be a birder.

He seems to know where he's heading, and doesn't object to my tagging along, but neither of us is particularly inclined towards conversation. I maintain my aversion to the 'Anything about?' gambit, and in any case it wouldn't be appropriate. We both know what's about. There's no need to declare an interest. It's implicit from our very presence.

So there's a nod of greeting, no more, and we make our way to the likely spot and wait for the nightjar to show its moth-like face.

We wait. And we wait. And we wait. Vladimir and Estragon, working our way through Act Two.

Dusk descends, taking away the details of the surrounding heath and wood by stealth. Before us is a broad expanse of bracken and gorse. Beyond, the dark woods, vaguely threatening. The air isn't uncomfortably cold, but neither is it balmy, and I'm glad to have kept my coat on. Nightjar prefer to display on warm evenings, and I suspect early on that this endeavour is a busted flush.

I'm diverted by the appearance of a bird just above the treeline. It has a distinctive dumpy shape, a comparatively long bill, and its outline is stark against the dusky sky. It's flying fast and straight, and in a second it's gone.

Woodcock. Tick.

As it disappears, I hear the faintest sound, an impossibly distant high-pitched purr. Estragon hears it at the same time, and we look towards it, cupping our ears.

It's not until you do this that you realise how effective an amplifier a cupped hand can be. What was almost inaudible now becomes merely very faint indeed. And then, just as we get a handle on it, it dims and stops. I'm half inclined to walk towards it, but the chances of tracking it down are slim. With a shrug we settle back down to the wait, hoping the sound will set off another, closer one. Our efforts are hindered by the insistent trillings of at least two song thrushes.*

The minutes pass, as they do. It becomes obvious our wait will be in vain. It's a good time to remind myself that birding is never a waste of time. At the very least I've had a nice walk in attractive surroundings. It feels like scant consolation.

At about twenty to ten we unanimously decide to call it a night, although I do another lap before returning to the car, just in case the nightjar was waiting for Estragon to leave before making its appearance. The moon is up, veiled behind thin cloud. An invisible stonechat flits among the bracken. Tsip-clink, tsip-clink.

I linger for a minute in the car park, hoping against hope for a low-flying nightjar to come and surprise me. But there's nothing except me and the emptiness of the forest, silent in the moonlight.

* Oh sure, *now* I recognise them.

On 24 June I wake with a sore head. The previous evening's concert was a success, but tiring. My efforts to assuage this tiredness with several doses of a magical grape-based elixir appear to have been unsuccessful.

The main news item of the day doesn't help. The Great British Public has, Lord love 'em, voted by a narrow margin to leave the EU.

I've noticed in recent weeks that my instinctive reaction to moments of difficulty has been to grab the binoculars and head for the nearest green space. The therapeutic effects of birding are enhanced by the physical exercise, and my brain, occupied by the effort of finding and identifying birds, is diverted from thoughts of doom and despair.

On this occasion I opt for a rambling walk to Dulwich Park. The birds, oblivious to national events, continue with their lives as if nothing has happened, basking in the warm sunshine. A hybrid mallard jumps up onto the broad wooden railings on the bridge over the pond and stands no more than a foot away from me. The iridescence of its purple-green head is offset by striking marblings and vermiculations on its body. I'm particularly taken by the contrast between its purple speculum* and the subtle sworls of brown and grey around it. Undeterred by my scrutiny, it eyeballs me boldly. Its nostrils, halfway up its mustard-yellow bill, match the staring intensity of its eyes, to disconcerting effect. It has a tiny bit of down stuck in its bill. Its extreme proximity and the relentlessness of its unblinking gaze make it look, frankly, unhinged.

I briefly consider asking if it's interested in running for public office. Then I walk home, spirits very slightly lifted.

---

* This is the coloured patch you can see on a duck's wing. It's a word I've just learned and I'm eager to use it as often as possible.

June ticks (11)

Ashdown Forest, Beddington Farmlands

Marsh Tit *Poecile palustris*, Common Redpoll *Acanthis flammea*, Tree Pipit *Anthus trivialis*, Siskin *Spinus spinus*, Redstart *Phoenicurus phoenicurus*, Woodlark *Lullula arborea*, Treecreeper *Certhia familiaris*, Tree Sparrow *Passer montanus*, Ruff *Calidris pugnax*, Peregrine *Falco peregrinus*, Woodcock *Scolopax rusticola*

Year total: 135

JULY 2016

He means well, I remind myself every five minutes or so. He's evidently detected in me a kindred spirit, some sort of meeting of the souls, and from the moment I enter the hide he settles into a stream of verbalising that is more cosy monologue than cosy chat. But no amount of meaning well can compensate for the torpor induced by his voice. For forty-five lifetimes, or perhaps they were minutes, I've listened to a litany of bird sightings from a visit to Minsmere earlier in the year, delivered in a grinding monotone that had me wanting to claw my eyes out just five lifetimes in.

But if I claw my eyes out I'll miss the kingfisher.

July has been slow. When planning my year, I naively assumed two weeks on the Isle of Wight would rack up big numbers. My disastrous conversation with Chris was fresh in my memory, even at three years' distance.

The Isle of Wight is grand for birding. Loads of different habitats.

While I'm happy with the 135 I've clocked up so far, I'm hopeful I can add a dozen or more while we're here. A birding bonanza – a bird-nanza, if you will.

In my imagination they'll be falling out of the bushes to oblige, and I've emailed Chris to ask if he might take me to some good spots.

His response doesn't inspire confidence.

'Happy to see what we can find, but can't promise anything. July's pretty quiet. We call it the doldrums! Might see a wheatear or two.'

I've arranged to meet him on Sunday morning on the downs above Ventnor. I'm looking forward to it. But for now I'm staving off a tedium-induced coma.

I've met some lovely people while birding. Kind, helpful and generous people, prepared to share their time and knowledge with a perfect stranger. My companion in this hide is among their number, but, ungenerously, I wish that one of us were elsewhere.

'And in the afternoon we had green sandpiper and spotted redshank. And plovers. Golden, grey...'

A pause in the flow, a nanosecond, a golden opportunity to interject, to stem the tide.

'...ringed, little ringed...'

Bugger.

This early-morning trip to a small nature reserve on the east of the island, two days into our holiday, hasn't been a write-off. Far from it. The barnacle goose staring me in the face as I entered the hide was a feral one,* but I've long since squared the counting of feral birds with my conscience. I've counted feral pigeons and greylag geese. What's one more between friends?

The goose was quickly followed by the bobbing backside of a common sandpiper and the slim elegance of a greenshank, close enough for me to see the fractional upturn of its bill as it sifted the water, and to study the fine barrings of its plumage.

But what use are three ticks in half an hour if the ensuing tedium makes my head explode?

I should leave, just get up and go.

But I want to see the kingfisher.

---

* Wild birds descended from domesticated ones. Birders can get a bit sniffy about them.

I know there's a kingfisher around because my companion told me about it. He hasn't seen it himself, but he was informed of its presence by an earlier occupant of the hide. I have no reason to disbelieve him. He might be boring, but he seems honest.

'It's good for wildfowl, too. We had garganey, gadwall, tufties of course, shelduck…'

I've seen several kingfishers this year. I could just leave. But somehow, having stayed this long I can't dip out now. And a kingfisher is always worth it.

My companion's telescope stands neglected while he mans his camera, complete with monstrous lens, ready for the fleeting appearance of the kingfisher. He's made clear his desperation to get a photograph of it, expanding on the subject at length some time in the early millennia of our friendship.

Time is a funny thing. So far it's been stretched to its limits, but now, all at once, everything happens in a flash.

I see the kingfisher, a rainbow dart in the corner of my vision, fly across from the right and land on the reeds in front of me. The click and scrape of the opening door behind us distracts my companion from his recital, and he turns his head as I say the magic word.

'Kingfisher.'

His head whips round, he fumbles with the camera, trains it on the spot.

Too late. The bird has disappeared into the depths of the reeds.

I vacate my space on the bench, leave the hide, and take a deep breath of the warm summer air. It tastes disturbingly like *Schadenfreude*.

If you stand on Ventnor Esplanade on the south coast of the Isle of Wight, facing the sea, do a 180-degree turn and walk upwards until you can walk upwards no more, you will at some point arrive at the top of St Boniface Down with aching calves and a strong feeling you should have brought the car.

A kestrel perches on the chain-link fence protecting the site that used to be Ventnor radar station, a crucial strategic part of the Chain Home network that gave early warning of Luftwaffe attacks in World War II. Decrepit pillboxes provide a link with the past and somewhere to hide from the roaming cattle, should the need arise. But mostly the place is views. From one side you look out to sea, even if it's sometimes engulfed in fog; on the other the vista stretches across the island – even, on a clear day, as far as the Spinnaker Tower at Portsmouth.

There are five of us. Me; Chris, who is tactful enough not to raise the subject of my skylark-related idiocy; Dylan, his younger brother, with the concomitant cheeky smile and healthy disrespect for seniority;* Jonno, tall, loping, with a droopy moustache and a sing-song north-eastern accent I could listen to all day; Neil, taciturn in a camouflage jacket and hat. Four lads, long friends, birding every Sunday morning together, an opportunity for catching up and indulging their shared enthusiasm. To be part of the group, even briefly, feels like a privilege, but also a little like an intrusion, disrupting the established balance of their group dynamic. But they're nothing but welcome and smiles and chat.

We walk in a loose group, held together by the general direction of the walk, someone occasionally breaking off in search of a bird. Chris and Dylan catch up on family news. Jonno tells me about their friend, dead three years now, who was an integral part of the group. Behind us, Neil wordlessly scans the landscape through his binoculars.

As if on cue, a skylark appears on our left and begins its

---

* Why yes, since you ask, I am a younger brother myself. What of it?

ascent. The loop of repetitive song rippling and eddying above us instantly triggers memories of the larks soaring above the field next to the bus stop in the eternal sunshine of my childhood.

I give Chris a sidelong glance. He says nothing.

They've lived here for years, fleeing the unemployment-ridden north-east in the 1970s for occasional summer work, and finding island life to their liking. Employment was the driver, way of life the clincher. Music festivals played their part, too. Now they seem to know every inch of birding territory on the island's 148 square miles. St Boniface Down is their starting point every Sunday, conveniently local and often thronging with birds.

Chris is keen for me not to come away from the trip empty-handed. Every time we see something, he asks if I have it on my list. I've done a bit of research into what's about, and can give him one target bird I reckon we have a chance of seeing.

'If we can get a Dartford warbler today, I'll be happy.'

We set off, heading east along the path, keeping the downs to our left and taking in absurdly picturesque views across Luccombe Chine to the sea and cliffs beyond. We talk intermittently, mostly about birds. Dylan is pragmatic about my chances of hitting 200.

'It depends how much you want to travel, doesn't it? Have you been to Scotland?'

'Next month.'

'Well, that'll help. I tell you, though, when I lived in Bulgaria we'd have had that 200 in a week. Right on a migration point, we were.' He tells me about Bulgarian birds, the relish dripping from his lips. 'Aw, Lev man, those birds. Six kinds of eagle in a day. We had them over our garden.'

The conversation isn't wildly dissimilar from the one attempted by my erstwhile friend in the hide at Hersey. But the difference is the engagement. Dylan comes alive when talking about birds, and listens to what I say; Hersey guy ignored my every word and killed all sentient creatures within a hundred-yard radius stone dead with one blow of his larynx.

I ask Dylan how his interest in birds started. He gives me a sidelong look and a knowing smile, as if deciding whether to tell me.

'We're like poachers turned gamekeepers, I suppose. We used to go egging as lads.'

Egg collecting. Normal in Victorian times, illegal since 1954. Egg collectors are now universally reviled, and the knee-jerk reaction is to disapprove of such cruel and unnecessary activity, until you discover that David Attenborough used to do it. Not only that, he would be in favour of a change in the law to allow responsible egging as a way of sparking young people's interest in nature.

If it's good enough for Attenborough, it's good enough for me.

I picture Chris and Dylan, fifty years ago, cheeky lads sneaking out, up to no good, climbing a tree and taking an egg, just one, from a blackbird's clutch. No harm done to the bird, which will still rear a healthy brood, and a lifetime's interest taking root. Not so bad, on the whole.

We come to a patch of long, reedy grass. Dylan whips out his phone.

'We had a gropper here last week.'

And now there's the sound of a grasshopper warbler coming from his phone. Using playback to lure a bird is another contentious issue, although not in the same league as egging. Traditionalists argue it's not the done thing, unfair to other birders, and especially that it might be harmful to the birds, making them think their territory is under threat from a competitor or distracting them from essential tasks like feeding their young. Proponents of responsible use of the technique argue that using playback at a suitable volume is often less harmful and disruptive to the bird than thrashing around in the undergrowth looking for it.

Dylan is using the playback subtly enough. Too subtly perhaps, because there is no sign of the bird, and after a couple of minutes he admits defeat and we move on, soon coming to an extended patch of gorse, prime Dartford warbler territory.

I feel Chris at my elbow.

'Dartford warbler!'

Well, whaddaya know?

I follow his pointed finger towards the clump of gorse ahead of us. It trembles, and then an indistinct blur whizzes round to the other side, too fast for certain identification, for me at least. We all know what it is, but this fleeting glimpse merely whets our appetite. That's the thing about birding: you always want that little bit more.

We skirt the bush, hoping not to scare the thing off. Chris moves stealthily, me less so. I lose my balance avoiding an exposed root, and stumble on a clump of earth while recovering. I somehow manage not to fall over, but am acutely aware that my movements, more interpretive dance than walking, might disturb the bird.

'There's three of them.' Dylan, off to my right, ten yards up the hill. 'An adult and two young 'uns.'

I hardly dare join him for fear of falling on my backside, but slowly pick my way through the gorse, the spikes tickling my legs through my trousers. Now I'm by Dylan's side, and training my binoculars on the bush. It's quivering with invisible activity, as if populated by the cast of *Dad's Army* on a camouflage training day.

'They're hiding from you, Lev.'

Chris, a wry smile on his face, appears next to me. I return the smile.

'I do have that effect, I've noticed.'

He's alert again, pointing.

'Can you see it?' He wants to be the one to show me. 'There it goes!'

Indeed it does. My eye catches the flitting flight of the bird as it hops up onto the neighbouring bush, still close, and now directly in our sightline. Through the binoculars I'm able to drink it in, this small bird, no bigger than a robin. It's slate-grey on top, vinous red underneath, tail bobbing up and down, standing upright and proud on top of the bush, looking towards us, seemingly unafraid. Fifty-four years ago a harsh winter nearly wiped them out in Britain. Now their status seems assured, but you still have to seek them out, a sighting not to be taken for granted. And they hold a totemic place in my mind, one of *those* birds from my childhood, the ones that burrowed their way into my memory and stayed there. With this sighting, another piece slots into place.

Chris turns to me, eyes bright.

'There you go, Lev. A nice Sunday-morning tick for you.'

I'm touched by his pleasure for me. It occurs to me that maybe he feels some sort of responsibility for the absence of birds and wants to discharge his duties as a good host. But I just feel privileged to be a temporary part of this close-knit and private group. For me, the Dartford warbler is a bonus.

We're back where we started. The four friends leave the path and head for a bench under a tree, lighting cigarettes and sitting in companionable silence.

A kestrel perches on a tree to the left.

'Do you always end up here?' I ask.

Chris doesn't answer directly.

'We've seen some birds from here, haven't we, lads?'

'Our friend's ashes are scattered here,' says Jonno. 'He came with us every Sunday for years. Three years ago now.'

We sit in silence for a few moments.

'Kestrel's on the move.'

It flies unhurriedly across our sight line and then away to the valley below.

I do a scan across the valley. A whitethroat is in a tree near where the kestrel flew, jinking in and around it. Another bird joins it, small, greenish.

Chris has his binoculars up quicker than you can say 'willow warbler'.

'Willow warbler.' He lowers them again. 'Aye, we've seen some birds from this seat.'

It's time for me to go. They'll move on somewhere else, maybe Brading Marshes or Newtown Nature Reserve. Next Sunday they'll meet again, probably relieved to return to their routine, just the four of them, lapsing into familiar rhythms and cadences without the disruption of an outside force. I'm grateful to them for shifting along and allowing me to perch on their bench even for a short while.

I thank them and take my leave. Chris gets to his feet.

'We're here ten o'clock every Sunday if you want to see some birds, Lev.'

I might just take him up on it.

It's dark in the forest. Dark and creepy. It's the kind of place you might find lions and tigers and bears,* were it not for the inconvenient fact that those animals aren't found in the same habitats, let alone in Britain. But the phobia remains. I expect at any moment to be whisked away by flying monkeys, or at least nibbled to death by a red squirrel.

My quest for the nightjar (24–28 cm) has led me to Parkhurst Forest (395 hectares). Despite my best efforts, I've been unable to find reference to a specific spot where they can be found.

* Oh my.

While it can be helpful for birders to put their sightings online, sometimes they're frustratingly vague. 'One female still by the gate.' 'Two males on common.' 'A juvenile in usual place near river.' You either have to know the patch they're talking about so you can go directly to the place in question without passing Go, or be prepared for a bit of detective work and a lot of walking.

In some cases there are good reasons for this. The precise nesting locations of scarce breeding species need to be protected. The nightjar, while not close to British extinction, is uncommon enough for people to be careful about sharing sensitive information. So while I know that Parkhurst Forest is a place where they might be found, I have no alternative but to tramp round it in search of the most likely spot, using my best judgement and expertise. I know to eschew the denser areas in favour of clearings, but that's about it.

There are several paths leading from the car park. I feel as if I'm in one of those 'tangled string' puzzles – can Lev find the right place for the nightjar before dusk falls? To the right, a paved path leads into the forest, a locked single-bar gate barring the way to vehicles. To the left, a selection of small footpaths, marked trails to help people find their way around. I reject the path to the right as too large and obvious, and strike out on one of the winding trails to the left. It's easy terrain, leading through thick forest, trees looming, their shadows exaggerated by the angle of the descending sun.

The plan is to do a brisk walkaround of as much of the forest as possible for an hour or so, then choose the most likely spot and wait. As I cover more and more ground without finding a single clearing, my heart sinks. This was an idiotic idea. If faced with a choice of turnings, I invariably take the one that leads to even thicker forest. More than once I find myself striding out in what is obviously the wrong direction, but unable to turn round and retrace my steps for the usual reasons of stubbornness, blind hope, and a masculine refusal to admit any kind of mistake whatsoever.

As dusk approaches I realise I've strayed quite a way from the car park, and am not certain I could find my way back. There are marked paths through the forest, trails of varying lengths designed for family walks, but I've long since abandoned them in favour of the complex network of smaller byways, a decision I'm beginning to regret.

Luckily I have my phone with me, although I have to be careful how much I use it, because the battery's a bit flaky and currently stands at 45 per cent, no hold on, 33 per cent, ah sod it 22 per cent, shit wait what 5 per cent?

As I try to work out the best way to retrace my steps, I'm assailed by the feeling that things could turn suboptimal at any moment, that it could be a while before I find the car, and that I might have to abandon all hope of seeing a nightjar. I'm not at the 'foraging for survival' stage, but it's only a matter of time.

The sun's gone now, and the forest is beginning to darken ominously. What were trees are now indistinct shadows, each one poised to turn into a monster at any moment.

I never liked monsters. Not for me the argument that inside every monster there's a fluffy bunny waiting to be released. The one lurking in the lavatory, waiting to drag me screaming into the sewers if I didn't sprint out of the bathroom the moment I flushed, wasn't fluffy; nor was the one that impersonated my dressing gown and hung on the back of my bedroom door biding its time until I fell asleep, when it would jump across the room and stick pins into my eyelids. Those childhood demons remain vivid. I can laugh about them now. Sort of. But my adult mind, while fundamentally rational, is still quite capable of conjuring them and their cohorts out of nowhere.

There are noises, too. Animal life is settling down for the night, and I hear rustlings and shufflings from everywhere, each one specifically designed to sound exactly like an escaped prisoner skulking through the undergrowth.

Oh, did I say there's a prison at Parkhurst? There's a prison at Parkhurst.

Things I'm afraid of: the dark, unidentified noises, criminals. I'm lost in a forest at dusk within half a mile of a prison. Which part of this did I think was a good idea?

Under normal circumstances I'd walk faster and make exaggerated noises to buck up my spirits and keep the frights at bay, maybe even singing a jaunty tune to the words:

I'm not scared,

No, I'm not scared,

I certainly don't fear being attacked by a deranged lunatic with an IQ of thirty-six and an irrational hatred of binoculars,

Tumty tumty tum.

This is a common human reaction, simultaneously logical and nonsensical. On the one hand it makes you feel less alone, but on the other, if you're frightened of being attacked by an axe murderer, why draw attention to yourself?

But I keep quiet, for tonight my watchword is stealth. I don't want to disturb the nightjar, if nightjar there be, which I'm beginning to doubt.

In my heightened state of nervousness, any unexpected sound would be enough to turn me into a whimpering husk, so the eerie, high-pitched mewing that rings out ten inches above my head not unnaturally scares the living bejesus out of me. On sober reflection I realise that the sound is coming from a distance of yards rather than inches, and as it filters into my jittery brain I recognise it as the sound of a circling buzzard,* so the danger is less immediate than I first thought. But coming hot on the heels of my thoughts about flying monkeys, it's enough to make me watch the buzzard until it's spiralled out of sight.

---

*   Fuck me sideways.

The path is both familiar and unfamiliar. It feels as if I've been here before. Maybe I have. Not so much déjà vu as nightjar vu. The trees crowd in on either side of the path for a spell, then open out again. There's a small clearing, just the kind of place you might find a nightjar.

Or not.

I wait for half an hour, eyes adjusting to the encroaching darkness, ears attuned to the ambient sound, hoping to catch the faintest hint of nightjarly movement or noise. But if there is one in this forest, it's not here. And because of my hopeless meanderings, it's now too late to find another spot. Dusk has almost shot its bolt. It's time to go home.

I continue on the path. Five minutes later I stumble – more by luck than judgement – upon one of the forest trail signs. Like Theseus, but without the triumphant sense of murderous achievement, I trace my steps carefully back to my starting point. I stand by the car for a moment in a way that I hope conveys to the forest just how disappointed I am with it, then I get in and start the drive home.

I'm not sure why I glance to the left as I leave the car park. It's the merest instinct. There's no danger of oncoming traffic. The place is deserted. The paved path, which I ignored when I first arrived, is wide enough for vehicles, but it leads back into the forest and is blocked by a single-bar gate. There are no cars there, just a lone figure silhouetted in the pale moonlight against the dark trees behind.

Wait a minute.

Why would anyone be standing on a path in the forest just after dusk?

There are two possibilities. The most likely explanation is that this is 'Desperate' Dave Djibrovic, recently escaped from

Parkhurst and lying in wait for a chance to wreak motiveless havoc on disappointed nightjar-hunters. But it's the other possibility that makes me reverse the car, get out and walk towards him. If I'm wrong, I can always defend myself with my binoculars.

The wing clap of a nightjar in a dark forest is a distinctive sound, like a soft whip-crack or a wet towel being flicked against a buttock.* As it echoes round the forest once, twice, three times, I scan the treetops and see a shadowy shape agitating high in the conifers on the edge of the clearing.

Had I not been so determined to take the path less travelled, I would have found this clearing within a minute of arriving. Still, I've had a nice walk, and now here's my nightjar.

It can't seem to settle. No sooner has it disappeared from view in the upper reaches of the trees than it's up again, clapping and flapping and causing a localised kerfuffle, at odds with my impression of the bird as a stealthy hunter. Then it seems to tire of this activity and with easy wingbeats escapes the clutches of the forest and flies across the clearing towards a single tree by the path. On landing, it squats lengthways and immediately becomes just another branch, its silhouette only discernible if I squat down to view it against the darkening sky, and even then only because I already know it's there.

And now it begins, an other-worldly and mesmerising sound, a reeling so fast and compressed it has a rattling quality. It has two gears, one marginally lower than the other, alternating between the two every few seconds without pause. There's no stopping for breath, no rise and fall of natural phrasing, the mechanical nature of the song an inherent part of its appeal and adding to the nightjar's already substantial mystique, enhanced by the eerie atmosphere of the forest.

---

* Just me? OK then.

Gabble ratchet, they used to call the nightjar in Yorkshire. It seems appropriate.[*]

I haven't moved for five minutes. I remember, belatedly, that I'm not alone. My companion, the shadowy figure without whose presence I would now be halfway back to the cottage, is standing ten yards to my right. Like me, he's doing a decent impersonation of a statue. This isn't an occasion for the usual stilted greetings and awkward exchanges that often colour a birdwatching trip. He's given no sign of noticing my presence. Now, as the churring stops and dusk gives way to night, he turns and walks past me. No words are spoken; none are needed. We exchange a glance, a quick nod, the merest acknowledgement of our shared experience, more potent than a thousand words.

A bat flies by on silent wings. I can still just make out the silhouette of the nightjar on the branch, but the show is over. I walk back to the car, pausing to send the forest a grudging retraction of my former disappointment, and drive home.

The hawk waits, poised for action, its beady eye uncompromising, dark brown plumage blending with the tree. It braces, and then with one mighty flap of its wings launches itself into the air, gaining height and speed quickly before turning towards its prey. There's barely a second to react. I watch, powerless to move, as the bird descends, wings controlling its speed, tail flicking from side

---

[*] At first this seems to be a description of the sound the bird makes, but its derivation is rather more sinister. It stems from 'Gabriel's hounds', 'gabble' being a mangling of 'Gabriel', and 'ratchet' a variant of the Middle English 'racche', a dog which hunts by scent. The birds were supposed to embody the souls of unbaptised infants doomed to wander forever in the air. The name was also used to refer to the sound made by a flock of bean geese in flight, which resembles a pack of dogs. Confusing stuff.

139

to side to make the vital adjustments necessary to its goal. It's a killing machine, awe-inspiring unless you're the hapless individual in its sights. And now the talons come out, sharp and deadly, ready to grasp. A final flurry as the bird homes in on its target, and now it's there, perched on Oliver's head and accepting the applause and laughter of the crowd as merely its due. Oliver, his sangfroid barely disturbed when the bird landed on his falconry-gloved hand a few seconds ago, is laughing, the kind of nervous laughter that says, 'This is amazing just as long as it doesn't rip my head off.'

I've seen more new birds during this falconry display on Streatham Common than I have in the rest of July. None of them count, of course. If tame birds counted I could just pop into London Zoo and my list would be full within minutes. But it's mildly disconcerting to see the barn, tawny and little owls, so elusive in the wild, sitting on their perches, taunting me with their calmness. They're professionals, these birds, tame as your cat. But they do go off-piste from time to time, seizing the chance to escape their trainers and terrorising the local pigeon population.

My feelings on falconry are mixed. On the one hand there's the soft-centred, overemotional, well-meaning-but-muddle-headed part of me that goes, 'Oh, but wouldn't the poor ickle barn owl be happier in the wild?' And then there's the hard-nosed, level-headed, now-let's-just-look-at-the-facts-shall-we part that acknowledges that properly treated, captive birds of prey have longer life expectancies than wild ones, and if you tried to release any of these birds they'd do one lap of the common and come straight back to where they know they'll be fed and kept warm.

And if you asked any of them if they'd like to swap with a battery chicken, they'd give you a look and say, 'You know what, old horse? On the whole I'm happy where I am. Now lob me that vole, will you?'

In the grand scheme of Man's inhumanity towards animals, there are far bigger battles to be fought.

On the way home, Oliver cycles ahead of me. I come across him, stopped by the side of the road, staring transfixed into a front garden. I follow his gaze. Hunched under a rhododendron, watching us with a wary eye, is a sparrowhawk. At its feet, a pigeon, unequivocally no longer of this world. There's something brutally magnificent about the scene, nature in the raw, or as raw as you're going to get in SE27 without venturing into the sewers.

I wonder, as we watch the hawk shield its prey, waiting for us to leave so it can tuck in, how I would react if it were a blue tit or a chaffinch lying dead at the hawk's feet. There's no doubt my first reaction would be of pity for the smaller bird. And I acknowledge that this is irrational, based on an anthropomorphising of the cuddlier birds versus the unlovable feral pigeon.

The fact is, the hawk survives in the urban environment because of the abundance of prey. The presence of an apex predator, rather than threatening the local population of small birds, is a sign of its health. If there weren't plentiful food, the hawk would move elsewhere or starve, and the blue tit population is well able to withstand the relatively minor hit caused by predation. But our natural instinct is to take sides, to attribute the human values of good and evil to any meeting of hunter and hunted. This is a mistake. There is no good. There is no evil. There is just nature, red in tooth and claw as ever it was.

I dwell on these issues as we cycle home. Then I feed the cat a double portion in the hope that it won't bring in a blue tit.

July ticks (6)

Isle of Wight

Greenshank *Tringa nebularia*, Common Sandpiper *Actitis hypoleucos*, Barnacle Goose *Branta leucopsis*, Curlew *Numenius arquata*, Dartford Warbler *Sylvia undata*, Nightjar *Caprimulgus europaeus*
Year total: 141

AUGUST 2016

I'm standing by Portree harbour in bright sunshine, phone to my ear, looking at a millpond in disbelief.

'Sorry? Say that again?'

'I'm afraid we're not going out today. It's just too rough out there, and it's only a wee boat.'

I can feel the eagles slipping from my grasp. I express my incredulity as gently as possible, hang up, and call the second number.

'Well, we're going out, but the advice we're giving is only go if you're comfortable in rough seas.'

And now I'm ten, enduring a Sealink crossing from Dover to Calais. I'm sitting on the top deck, clammy and pale. The sea is calm, the only disturbance a light wind blowing through my hair and ruffling the bag held to my lips. My mother sits patiently beside me, long accustomed to my ability to chuck up at the slightest provocation. I am, she later tells me, a fetching shade of pale green.

The queasiness usually sets in on the A418, about a mile from home. By the time we've reached the ferry terminal we might have stopped three or four times, but these are merely the preliminary skirmishes. It's only when we're at sea that the nausea shows me, quite literally, what it's made of. The roughness of the sea is irrelevant. We're travelling, ergo I vomit. Travel-sickness pills are effective only in the sense that they're brilliant at bringing on a bout of travel sickness.

I've eaten two meals today. The evidence is in the bag.

The vice gripping my stomach relents. There's nothing left to give. I feel marginally better. Better than what, I'm not quite sure.

My mother has a consoling hand on my shoulder.

'How's that?'

I feel a wan need to reassure her I'm not about to perish.

'Not out.'

I eventually muster the energy to go below deck, force down a blackcurrant-flavoured boiled sweet with icing-sugar coating, and lose 70p on the fruit machine.

I've got better at travelling in the intervening forty years, but my aversion to rough seas remains. Lurking at the back of my mind is the fear that to reach 200 I'll be forced to go on a pelagic – specialised boat trips that go far out to sea in search of seabirds like petrels and shearwaters. Today's plan, a tour of the waters around Skye in search of white-tailed eagles, seemed more harmless, but apparently I was wrong. How desperate am I to see a white-tailed eagle? Not quite that desperate.

I hang up and relay the news to Oliver. He goes quiet and stares at a herring gull.

They say you should go birding in all weathers. But the memory of our soggy day in Ashdown Forest is strong, and a forecast of relentless and thickening rain on Speyside, where we're staying, has forced us westwards in search of clearer weather. Locals have expressed surprise at this decision. It usually gets worse as you head west, they say. Are we sure it's not chucking it down even harder on Skye? But the forecast is adamant. Sunshine and scattered cloud, light winds.

Define 'light'.

I've forced myself to watch the road and not the scenery as we've travelled west, the views becoming ever more brazenly picturesque the further we go. And the weather has played ball. The mizzle that accompanied us around Loch Ness has abated, and now we're basking in warm sunshine at Portree. Two apprentice pipers, in full garb and with a combined age of about six, work through their repertoire at the top of the path, the sound wafting towards us on the still air. Up close, it's a pungent noise; down here the edge is reduced, and I stick to my belief that it's an instrument best appreciated from a distance.

I look again at the harbour. I drink in the stillness of the day, the calmness of the water. How is it that a mile away it's too rough to sail? This is a major blow. It's a long day out – three hours each way – and we've risen early. Our reward was supposed to be an almost guaranteed sighting of those enormous, majestic raptors. We won't be in Scotland long enough for a return visit. It's today or bust.

Even in my disappointment I notice that one of the birds strutting around the harbour, scavenging chips and crusts of bread, is a tick. Ten yards away, among the thirty or so gulls of different shapes and sizes, is a grey-and-black bird that until fifteen years ago would have been disallowed. It's a hooded crow, close cousin of the carrion crow, their distributions separated by a firm but narrow line of hybridisation cutting across Europe. Go to France, Germany, Belgium, the Netherlands, Portugal and most of Spain and you will see the all-black carrion crow; in Ireland, Scandinavia, Eastern Europe, Italy and north-west Scotland, it'll be its two-tone cousin. Once classified as the same species, they were separated in 2002, so now I can tick it with impunity. This kind of decision leads to what's known as an 'armchair tick'. Scientists discover that a bird formerly considered a subspecies is a species in its own right, and birders worldwide celebrate the increase of their life lists by one without having to move a muscle.

Funny old world.

This hooded crow, casting a beady eye on Oliver's chocolate brownie, is scant consolation for the loss of the eagles. We'll spend the day here anyway, renting bikes and exploring the hills around

Portree. We'll see birds, each of them enhancing the naturally striking landscape. We'll look out for eagles, trying not to fall into the common trap of mistaking a buzzard (large, a.k.a. a 'tourist eagle') for a golden eagle (massive, a.k.a. an actual eagle). At the end of the day we'll embark on a last-ditch drive across the island to a known eagle spot. We won't see any.

I saw an eagle, back in the day.

I'd just bought, with almost my own money, my first pair of binoculars. They were the most exciting and grown-up thing I'd ever owned, better than my Sanyo cassette recorder, more eagerly anticipated than my copy of 'Bohemian Rhapsody', and more alluring and sensuous, if such a thing were possible, than my lovingly oiled Slazenger cricket bat. Armed with these binoculars, I would take my birding to the next level, rooting out hitherto unimagined riches from familiar territory. No more would Oxfordshire's birds evade my gaze. I would be master of them all at last.

The truth was, as I roamed the village's lanes and paths, the new acquisition slung proudly round my neck, that the birds stayed frustratingly out of reach in the depths of bushes and hedgerows. But at least now I could catch a fleeting glimpse of their disappearing backsides in glorious 8x42 binocular magnification. The ability to approach a bird without causing their immediate absence was a skill that eluded me, and no amount of highfalutin optical equipment would make up for that. It had something to do, I think, with impatience, my idea of a slow and cautious approach being not dissimilar to that of a puppy on speed.

But if I happened upon a distant and motionless bird, for example a white-tailed eagle, I knew they would come into their own.

Eagles aren't generally creatures of lowland England, and this white-tailed would have been more at home soaring on the updraughts above the crags of the Norwegian coast. But odd winds and dodgy navigation plonked it temporarily within reach of the twitchers of central southern England, and the network began to buzz. Communication was understandably less sophisticated in the 1970s, and the twitching community's network seems to have revolved around a single telephone in the hallway of a small cafe in north Norfolk, but word still spread remarkably quickly, and the eagle stayed long enough for the news to percolate towards me. The local farmer, alive to my interest, rang with the news, and I stationed myself, binoculars poised, by my mother's desk, ready to nag her until she drove me to see it. It was no more than a few miles away. The journey was brief, the stay briefer. For all my fiddling and adjustments, my magical new equipment couldn't compensate for the eagle's determination to stay perched on a distant fencepost. With the naked eye, it was a barely discernible dot; enhanced by state-of-the-art binocular technology, it graduated to a blob. As the bird was on private ground, we couldn't get closer without breaking the law. Apart from one notable occasion when she stole a plastic fork from a delicatessen, breaking the law wasn't my mum's thing, so I resigned myself to the inadequate view available, and she settled into a solid bout of hinting that we should leave.

A man stood by a telescope, all beard and gloom. He told us with grave pleasure that the bird hadn't moved all morning, nor was it likely to, as the day before it had only moved to fly further away. Cowed by the density and expanse of his facial hair, and the grim relish he seemed to take in giving the bad news, I was too shy to ask if I could look through his telescope. He didn't offer, so after fifteen minutes, and one last unavailing peer through my now discredited binoculars, I reluctantly allowed my mother to take me and my disappointment home.

My strategy has been founded on a successful trip to Scotland, but time is short. Oliver and I have flown up early, while Tessa will drive up to meet us in Edinburgh, visiting friends on the way. But this boys' jolly has to be run to a tight and considerate schedule. Not only must I cram as much birding into our three days as possible, I can't neglect my duties as a parent. Oliver's as game as a capercaillie – especially if raptors are on offer – but this is my obsession, not his, and I worry that a diet of wall-to-wall birding is a tough sentence to inflict on even the most willing of eleven-year-olds. There's a karting track not far from our B&B, and Speyside offers some mouthwatering cycling opportunities, so I'm hoping we can knock off the necessary birds each morning before embarking on more child-friendly activities later on.

It's the hope that kills you.

Scotland is important because it has several birds I'm not going to see anywhere else, and this period before my patch of work in Edinburgh is my only window of opportunity. A successful trip will bring ten ticks. So far I have two.

The first came easy as winking. A short drive from the B&B to RSPB Loch Garten, an even shorter walk to the osprey centre, a squint through a telescope. A few hundred yards away, sitting atop a specially built platform like an ill-fitting turban, is the ospreys' nest, a mass of sticks big enough to accommodate an ostrich. The bird perched in the middle of it is large, but still dwarfed by the nest. It stands tall, alert, a noble sight, unique amongst raptors in surviving almost entirely on fish. We're lucky to catch them at home and not on one of their regular forays to the fly-through at the local salmon farm.

The return of the osprey to Britain is one of the success stories of the conservation movement. Hounded to extinction in the nineteenth century by hunters and egg collectors,* its

---

* Its old Scottish name, bastard eagle, might contain a clue to its status in their eyes.

return in the 1950s was tentative at first, with a single breeding record in 1954. It's the curse of a rare bird that its eggs become more valuable the rarer it gets, and the commitment of illegal collectors has to be anticipated and outstripped by those devoted to conservation rather than destruction. Ranged against the eggers was a small and dedicated team of volunteers from the Scottish Ornithologists' Club, who ran a determined campaign, protecting the site with barbed wire and guarding it round the clock. Despite this, there were many setbacks and progress was slow, not helped by the pesticides that did so much to destroy the British raptor population after the war.* By the time I was of an age to be interested, the Loch Garten ospreys were famous, figureheads of a growing Scottish population, and visited by thousands each year. Since then, the toehold has turned into a firm grip, with over 200 known pairs in Scotland and a small population in England. These aren't the only ospreys I could see this year, but they're the easiest, and this visit to the bird's spiritual home feels like a pilgrimage.

From the visitor centre we walk into the forest in search of smaller and more elusive prey. The early portents are ominous. The Abernethy Forest, this summer morning, is a welcoming place, the trees tall and widely spaced enough to allow the soft dappling of the sun to fall gently on the pine-cone-bespecked ground. Through the trees we can see glimpses of Loch Garten, its presence lending the place the idyllic quality I always associate with a nearby body of water. It's almost soporifically tranquil.

But it's too damn quiet for my liking.

What I'm after is a particular sound, a gentle and cheery trilling from the treetops. It's the advertising call of the crested tit,

---

*   DDT and other pesticides make the shell of birds' eggs thinner, leading to embryo death. Raptors, at the top of the food chain, consumed more pesticides through their prey, so were worse affected.

Scotland's perkiest bird. Cousin of the familiar great and blue, the crested tit is aptly named, the feathery crest on its head lending added appeal. But first you need to see it, and this is problematic, as it prefers to flit around in the upper reaches of the canopy than to mix it with humans and other ne'er-do-wells down below. And this morning even hearing one seems a pipe dream.

I've also got an ear out for the metallic chipping call of the crossbill, another aptly named species, whose eponymous appendage renders it superbly adapted to prising the kernels out of pine cones, presumably so it can rustle up a quick pesto alla Genovese.

But there's no sign of either. No sign of anything much. This is not unusual. For all the times when the air seems thick with birds, and the moments of excitement engendered by a special sighting, it's easy to forget how much time birdwatching is spent not birdwatching. You never know which way it's going to fall. Part of the attraction is the anticipation. What are we going to see today?

In this case, not much.

Oh me of little faith. We complete our tour of the forest and walk back along the road, resigned to failure, and there's the sound, right above us. Several of them, calling to each other excitedly, high in the canopy. Perhaps they're humanwatching.

The details of the ensuing search, the craning of necks, the scanning of a treescape that will have me dreaming of pine needles for nights to come, the false hope, the frustrated cursing and the eventual triumph, these details need not detain us. We find the crested tits, we enjoy the fleeting views we have of them, and then we leave them to their business and go about ours.

I could insist. I could wield the might of executive parental power and just tell him we're going hiking up a mountain in search of a bird that looks like a rock, is hard to see, and might not be there anyway.

Or I could agree to the bike ride.

The guy at the bike-rental place gives us a hand-drawn map, on which he has marked his recommended route along the trails of Glenmore Forest. I surprise him by saying we're happy to take the longer and more difficult route. He makes a mark on the map, a little blob of green highlighter.

'That's a pretty special place. You might want to go there.'

A London cyclist associates any ride with verbal abuse and a heightened risk of death, so to go on a mountain trail, where the air is clear and the biggest threat to your life is from an allergic reaction to stunning landscapes, constitutes a delicious form of freedom.

We sail up hills, skid round corners, splash through streams. Oliver leaves me floundering on the climbs, his power-to-weight ratio making a mockery of mine. I wreak my revenge on the descents, powered by bulk and gravity.

We stop at the special place. It's as memorable as he indicated, a small loch hidden halfway up a hill, backed by a steep slope with scree at the bottom and conifers dotted on its surface. To the left, a V of open sky. A magical place, made more so by the deep green of the water that gives the loch its name.* We perch on a rock and eat sandwiches. There are no birds here, but it doesn't matter. Given the choice of this and chasing ptarmigan across the windblown Cairngorms, even I have to admit which I'd choose. And maybe there'll be time later to head to the moors and knock off a red grouse or a dotterel.

We continue our ride, trying to interpret the rough map, and reach a stiff climb to the top of a hill from where we'll begin

---

* The Green Loch. Do keep up.

what looks like a precipitous final descent. The forest is more regimented here, sections of clearing giving way to dense and extensive areas of spruce. It's as we're about to start the descent that we hear it. There's anguish in the call, a short high-pitched mew echoing hauntingly across the forest. It's repeated a second later, then again as the bird, a large raptor, enters stage left.

Instinct tells me what it is, but I need to be sure. I go through the process of elimination, surprising myself with the speed and depth of my knowledge.

Not a falcon. Too big.

Not an eagle or kite. Too small.

Not a harrier. The shape's all wrong. And the habitat.

Osprey? Nah. Right size, wrong shape. Ditto the buzzards.

It's the right shape for a sparrowhawk, with a bulky and compact front body, no discernible neck, and a long tail. But it can't be. It's the size of a buzzard. And it can't be a buzzard, for reasons already stated.

My mental database of raptors has sixteen species in it. I've been through fifteen and eliminated them all.

This has to be a goshawk.

It's neither vanishingly rare nor boringly abundant, the goshawk – but I'd deemed the likelihood of seeing one as 'slim to none', its scarcity matched by its elusiveness. Quite apart from the splendour of this single bird in an empty sky, in pure list terms it's a big bonus, such a surprise it almost counts as two ticks.

As the sighting sinks in, I become aware of an unnatural stillness to my right. Oliver has stopped his bike and is watching as the bird glides overhead.

'Goshawk,' I whisper. 'It must be a goshawk.'

He's transfixed, letting out a small 'Wow' under his breath.

Nature programmes spoil us, raising expectations with the brilliance of their execution. When you've seen footage of an osprey catching a fish, talons grasping, wings splayed and straining to control the descent, the splash of the water, the drama of the hit, and then the power of the bird as it lifts off, reaching for the sky with strong wings while clinging to the writhing fish, the reality of a distant bird perched on a post doing nothing but pass the time of day could seem mundane.

But this is what you don't get when you're slumped on your sofa staring goggle-eyed at a peregrine smashing into a pigeon in slow motion. This unexpected encounter lasts about twenty seconds. We don't see the bird in high definition, and it's accompanied by no more pulsating a soundtrack than its own call and the faint rustling of wind in the trees. We couldn't have anticipated it, and if we'd arrived a minute earlier or later we'd have missed it. And we certainly can't catch up with it on iPlayer. But it's ours, a moment shared, and for some reason we feel we've earned it. We can recall it in later weeks, months and years with the simple words 'Remember the goshawk?' – a bond no amount of fancy footage can emulate.

It flies away from us, giving the occasional flap and then gliding levelly over the trees, before, with one last call, in search of something we can't provide, it disappears from view.

And now Oliver's off, catching me unaware and getting a twenty-yard head start before I've got my feet onto the pedals.

'See you at the bottom!' he calls over his shoulder.

I crouch over the handlebars and give chase. Halfway down, by an opening in the trees that gives out onto a broad expanse of loch, I nearly catch him. But then I glimpse a flotilla of birds on the water and screech to a halt, allowing him to sail to the finishing line unchallenged while I indulge myself. They're mallards, coots, a couple of little grebes. The usual rubbish. But obscurely satisfying. And as I look at them, my mind replays the goshawk's journey across our sightline.

I could have insisted. I could have dragged Oliver onto the slopes to look at a bird imitating a rock.

Virtue has its reward.

The goshawk, for all its emotional impact, is just one tick. It doesn't make up for the grouse, capercaillie, Slavonian grebe, black guillemot, ptarmigan, dotterel, eagles, goldeneye and crossbill, all of them on the 'might see in Scotland' list, and now moved in bulk to another, entitled 'didn't see in Scotland'.

The truth is, we were there at the wrong time of year. I knew this. I knew about black grouse and capercaillie leks – the courtship displays of these extraordinary birds, which take place in spring; I knew that ptarmigan inhabit only the higher peaks and that access is limited in summer; and I knew that, whatever the season, you can't just turn up with a pair of binoculars and a hopeful smile and expect eagles to appear out of thin air.

Except that sometimes, with some birds, you can.

I didn't see a dipper as a child. The stream at the bottom of our garden was more a muddy trickle, good for building dams and dirtying trousers, but not for dippers. The nearest river, a tributary of the Thames, was just half a mile away, but it, in turn, was too wide and slow. A visit to friends, who lived in a converted water mill with a resident pair, furnished nothing but a peaceful hour sitting on the riverbank and a complete absence of dippers.

This year, after two failures, it's high on my list of must-sees. The first, back in May, was an early-morning foray from the Dorset glampsite to a local spot known for their presence. It was an entirely pleasant experience, yielding a close encounter with two deer which eyed me warily from a safe distance across a wildflower-filled meadow, but the dipper was absent. And our impromptu bike ride on Skye took us past several fast-flowing streams, the bird's favoured habitat. But again, the telltale whirring of wings, flash of white on the breast and bobbing action that gives the bird its name evaded my scrutiny.

Now I'm in Edinburgh, licking my wounds after failing to find so much as an eagle feather on Skye, and juggling birding with a busy conducting schedule on an orchestral summer course in the shadow of Edinburgh Castle. Tomorrow we go to Bass Rock in search of seabirds, but my dipper research suggests they can be found nearby on the Water of Leith, which flows through the north part of central Edinburgh and intersects with my daily walk to rehearsals. Apart from anything else, this stretch of the river is dramatically picturesque, running through a deep ravine in the middle of Scotland's first city.

All birds have something special about them. Whether it's the nuthatch's capacity for downwards tree-walks, the blue tit's knack for hanging upside-down from a fat ball, the spoonbill's fabulously comedic hooter, the eye-boggling sexual habits of the dunnock,* or the ring-necked parakeet's remarkable ability to be an utter bastard – you'll find barely a species that can't proclaim with some justification that they're unique in some small way.

It's the dipper's aquatic skills that set it apart. Not content with sitting on rocks waiting for prey to jump out of the water into its mouth, it adopts a more dynamic approach to hunting. Short, strong wings, solid bones, an oversized preen gland producing copious amounts of oils to coat its dense plumage – all contribute to the dipper's ability to propel itself to the riverbed to catch its prey. This activity is described by nearly all the guides as 'flying underwater', but I've decided, more correctly but less glamorously, to call it 'swimming'. It's an impressive and unique trick for a songbird, as is the dipper's supplementary ability, once on the riverbed, to walk along it.

I'm prepared to search for this bird, and have allowed an extra hour on my morning walk to rehearsal. The journey from

* Google it. It's not a story for a family show.

our digs in Stockbridge to the rehearsal hall in the shadow of the castle takes about forty-five minutes, and I use this time to go through the music in my head, anticipating possible problems and planning the course of the morning's activities. Edinburgh isn't flat, and the physical exercise means I arrive energised and ready to go. I'm hoping the mood of quiet contemplation engendered by the waterside walk will enhance this positivity and give the rehearsal an extra zing, rather than completely knackering me and leaving me good for nothing except sitting with a thousand-mile stare nursing a flat white and a cardamom bun.

I drop down the steps onto the riverside path, hopeful rather than confident I'm on the right track. The Water of Leith is twenty-five miles long. The odds against there being a dipper on this short stretch must be ooh look, there's a dipper.

The unexpectedness of the sight and the stillness of the bird make me think it must be plastic, placed there for reasons unknown by some ornithological prankster. But then it shifts slightly, blinks, and gives a flick of its tail. In four days, Usain Bolt will win the Olympic 100-metres title in 9.81 seconds. It's taken me about that long to find this dipper, an unprecedentedly quick success. But having seen it, I yearn for more. I want it to perform. Its unwillingness to do so is disappointing, but does at least save me the usual ducking and diving while I try to catch sight of it. It sits on a rock in the middle of the stream, white breast gleaming in the early-morning sun, a beacon of stillness in the shushing tumble of the water around it. Suddenly, with another flick of the tail, it's off, its low whirring flight just above the water making it clear why in some circles it's known as the water wren.

Without haste I follow it along the river. It stays a distance ahead of me, always in sight, finally alighting on another rock, where it resumes its impersonation of one of those street artists who don't move until you put a coin in the hat and whose deductible expenses presumably comprise gallons of gold paint and little else.

I can see why this is prime dipper territory. The terrain is rocky, the water fast-flowing. It's the kind of place you might also find grey wagtails. These small and slim birds, grey above and yellow below, often betray their presence with a constant energetic pumping of their long tails. Unlike the dipper, they mostly stay out of the water, the extent of their derring-do the occasional foray into the shallows for insects and small invertebrates. They've eluded me all year, and my pessimistic side sees no reason why today should be any ooh look, there's a grey wagtail.

Here's the world-famous birder, seeing all the birds before breakfast.

Watching these contrasting birds, with their different approaches to survival in the same habitat, occupies me long enough that I'm not ridiculously early for my rehearsal, and puts me in optimistic mood for the next day's family boat trip to Bass Rock.

Look out over the Firth of Forth from the Scottish Seabird Centre at North Berwick and there is Bass Rock rising from the sea, a 100-metre high lump of volcanic rock which seems, at first sight, to be covered in bird shit. Only as you approach it on the surprisingly non-seasick-making boat ride does it become clear that the white mantle draped over the island is in fact made up of thousands of birds, each little white pixel attaining its own identity as you get closer.

The island is home to the world's largest gannet colony, 150,000 of them at its peak, and while I've already seen gannets this year, it was a relatively undramatic spectacle, four birds gamely loping low across the sea off the Isle of Wight back in May. The colony at Bass Rock is significant enough to give the bird its scientific name, *Morus bassanus*, and there's something perversely alluring about the sight, sound and smell of thousands of seabirds. Until, that is, you get to within a nostril's length of the island and are assaulted by the ammoniac tang of tons of guano.

But even before that they've made their presence felt. As we approach the island there's an intensification of activity around us. A lone gannet falls in behind the boat and accompanies it, as if checking we know the way. It flies easily, with shallow beats of its slender, black-tipped wings, a flying cigar with a dagger bill and tapered wedge of a tail. Behind it more birds circle high above the water, scouting for hunting opportunities. And now, as I look to the front of the boat, I realise these are just the outliers. Up ahead the air is dense with them, swooping and gliding, tens, scores, hundreds. Juveniles learning to fish, adults showing them how. They shear upwards, gaining height, knowing that below the surface there's an abundance of fish just waiting to be harvested. When they're high enough they enter the dive with a little roll, like a Red Arrow peeling off from formation, and plunge towards the surface at a slight angle. At the last second they tuck their wings in so they enter the water smoothly. It's up there with the osprey's as the most dramatic fishing method of all British birds. A heron stalking the shallows ready to impale a trout on its long dagger of a bill; a storm petrel pattering across the surface of the sea, scooping up tiddlers as it goes; a puffin diving deep and coming up with a mouthful of sand eels; a great skua, the bastard, harrying other birds into giving up their catch – all fascinating spectacles, and each in its own way an excellent example of the variety afforded by adaptive evolution. But a gannet plunge-diving into the sea from a height of thirty metres at a hundred kilometres an hour just yards away from you tops the lot, a stirring enough sight to make even this unwilling seafarer brave the waves.

The boat cruises into the armpit of the island and now we see them at close quarters – can study through binoculars the apricot shading on their bulbous heads, and the bare black patch around the beak that lends them their endearing smiling expression. Some sit quietly, bills tucked under wings, saving energy. Two birds get snuggly, an affectionate jousting of bills followed by an intimate nuzzling, consistent with our anthropomorphic idea of the behaviour of a bird that mates for life. Behind them a downy bundle of fluff looks out to sea, like a mortified teenager willing its parents to stop embarrassing it, or preferably just go away for ever while at the same time providing it with four hot meals a day and a free laundry and taxi service.

In the middle of this swathe of gannets sits a lone great black-backed gull, the darkness of its back and awkward hook of its bill rendering it hopelessly out of place among the smiling faces of the gannets, like a teetotaller wearing a dinner jacket at a toga party. The murderous look on its face is nothing unusual – all great black-backed gulls look as if they're about to peck something to a gory and painful death – but in this context the seething expression has an element of impotence, as if it's somehow entrapped by the gannets and has forgotten it can just fly away.

The boat moves to the other side of the island, where the variety of birds is greater, and thanks to the informative and entertaining commentary, I notch up two quick ticks: shag and kittiwake. Both can be confused with other species – the shag with the cormorant and the kittiwake with the common gull – but are easily separable from those birds by the simple expedient of having someone tell you which is which.

Our host tells us that had we been here a week earlier there would have been many more birds knocking about the place, but sadly all the puffins and Arctic terns have left, the former heading out to the open waters of the North Sea, where they will winter until returning the following May, and the latter making their annual journey to the Antarctic, a round trip of forty-odd thousand miles.*

Just as I'm thinking how sad I am we won't see a puffin, our host draws our attention to a small black bird with white on its flanks, bobbing on the water twenty yards away. Its back is turned to us, but the puffin shape is unmistakable, even without sight of the trademark bill. Its status as one of the top five adorable birds in British culture lulls me into a bout of anthropomorphising, and I construct a scenario in which this poor bird is ostracised by its peers for reasons unknown, abandoned, and is now floating around in a welter of perturbation, hoping against hope they'll realise their mistake and come back to fetch it, perhaps with a cordial, 'Aw Steve, you didn't really think we'd leave withoutcha, didja?' and a playful punch on the shoulder.

Just as I get to the bit where it's giving out a plaintive cry of, 'Guys? Where are you? Guys?', the bird hauls itself off the water and flies away, its little wings whirring, I learn later, at the outrageous speed of 400 beats per minute. Is that a tear I see in its eye as it banks past us and away across the sea?

No it bloody isn't. Get a grip.

The boat delivers us, surprisingly unvomity, to North Berwick, and we begin the return bike ride to Edinburgh. The route takes us to the mouth of the River Esk at Musselburgh, where I've ascertained there's a nature reserve, and therefore another opportunity to leave my family in the lurch. The portents are good, with a cluster of waterfowl huddled on the bank, more

---

* Say it quickly and it doesn't sound like the insane distance it really is.

floating loosely on the water and yet more dotted along the mudflats. Resigned to their fate, Tessa and Oliver bid me farewell and I set about my business.

The yield is initially high. Nearest to me are a couple of dozen goosander, streamlined diving ducks with an intent look and a fetching little downward curl at the end of their long bills. They appear all to be females, with red-brown heads and grey bodies. Ah no, wait a minute. It's August. They're in eclipse.

Ducks do this. They moult their flight feathers all at once and are rendered flightless for a month or so. To offset the resultant vulnerability to predators, the males adopt the females' less ostentatious colouring, only reverting to their colourful garb later in the year when their breeding feathers grow back. So this apparently all-female gaggle has been infiltrated by males in disguise.

It's the same story with the group of a dozen eider, some on the water's edge, some floating benignly a few yards offshore, their wedge-shaped bill the main distinguishing feature. Beyond them, much further out, I see a pair of birds, duckish but somehow different. I struggle to get a good view with the binoculars, but some buried instinct throws a single word into my head and I cling to it.

Scoter.

These sea ducks often hang out some distance from the shore, I know that much. The other thing I know is that there are several varieties, all of them basically black. That's the extent of my knowledge. This is all horribly familiar.

Have you done your homework, Parikian?

Nosirsorrysir.

What are the main features separating the common from the velvet scoter, Parikian?

Don'tknowsirsorrysir.

Elsworth-Beast Major?

The velvet scoter has a thicker neck, sir, and less pointed tail feathers, but a good way to distinguish them at a distance is by looking at the white secondaries, prominent when the bird executes its customary wing-flap. The velvet scoter performs this display with head held high, while the common scoter often ducks its head.

Excellent, Elsworth-Beast.

Slimy swot.

All hail the Collins app, which supplies this information just in time for me to see one of the birds rear in the water. Throwing phone to floor and raising binoculars to eyes with a hitherto unsuspected nimbleness, I catch the distinctive flash of white under the wings before the bird sits back down.

Velvet scoter. Come to papa.

Having notched up this trio of water birds I'm emboldened and make my way inland to the ash lagoons, where open concrete viewing points look out onto a heavily populated scrape.

No sooner have I started my sweep of the assembled multitude, with my usual internal monologue of don't knows and maybes, than I'm joined by a tall man who strides across to the first viewing hole and starts scanning the birds in a no-nonsense way that tells me he knows what he's about.

I continue, slightly subdued. There are lots of birds here I don't recognise. The ones I do know, the lapwings and oystercatchers, I dismiss. Anyone can do those. The others are the problem. They're mostly waders, I know that much. But they're far away, and details are hard to make out. Those little ones scurrying around amongst the lapwings: little stint? Or dunlin? Judging size from a distance is not my strong point.

Within seconds, he's asked the question I dread.

'Got anything?'

'I'm afraid you'll have to tell me. I'm pretty new to this.'

He's not unsympathetic.

'Ah well.' He eyes my binoculars. 'To get really confident

identifying waders you need a year to get used to all the different plumages. And a scope.'

Dissolve to sepia. St Petersburg, 1998. I've been working hard. Or at least I think I have. But I just can't get it. Conducting is difficult and I can't do it. I feel a significantly worse and more confused conductor than I was when I joined the class four months ago. My intention was to come here, learn all about it, go home, take the world by storm. A simple four-step process, the product of a fantasist's mind. I'm stuck on step two, my desperation to be immediately brilliant ensuring I have no chance to be.

Ilya Musin has seen it all before. Many times. I like to think he's sympathetic, but I'm not so sure. His English is hesitant and sparse, but he's learned some key words, which he enunciates clearly, as if speaking to a foreigner. Which indeed he is.

'To do this you need... experience.'

This is reassuring but frustrating. I want ten years of experience in ten minutes. I smile and nod. But here comes the kicker.

'And talent.'

No clue as to whether he thinks I'm endowed in that department.

He reverts to Russian, explaining in detail all my technical failings and how they relate to the passage I've just massacred. Most of it is lost on me, but some words have become familiar from repeated use. Nyedostatochno vyrazeetelnost. Sleeshkom bystro. Ochen slaby.

When he's finished I haul my talentless, expression-free, too fast, very weak, and now utterly depressed butt off the podium. Later, I will remind myself that these are the good lessons. He's taken the trouble to point me in the right direction. More than that, he's done it without cruelty, ensuring, through the translator, that I've understood what I need to do, and dismissing me with a faint smile and a pat on the arm. In the least valuable lessons all you get is a platitudinous 'very good' and a wave of the hand to usher on the next pupil, as if it's all so irredeemably awful that he can't bear to spend any more time on you.

It's been a useful lesson. But right now all I see is the mountain of failings barring my way to progress.

Here, in Musselburgh in 2016, it's the same. Never mind the puffin, shag, kittiwake, goosander, velvet scoter and eider I've added to my list today. What about the ones that got away? They've left a shortfall I'll have to make up at some stage, although I have no idea how or when.

Regardless of the list-building, I brood about the difficulties of learning. Twenty years on, I'm still easily frustrated by my inability to acquire new and difficult skills. And then I get annoyed by how easily I get frustrated, and my inadequacies chase their own tail downwards into a vortex of doomy self-recrimination.

I wonder if my father ever felt this frustration. He never expressed it, or at least not within my hearing. What I saw and heard was a rigorous intellectual approach to the art of the violin. Frustrations, for there must have been some, were dealt with maturely and patiently. Not for him the stamped foot, slammed door, brooding introspection.

The sound of the violin was as much a part of the soundtrack of my childhood as the lilting coo of the woodpigeon, its absence a sure sign that my father was away. I remember just one occasion when it occurred to me, listening to him, just how difficult playing the violin was. We were on holiday in Italy. It could only have been by a prodigious act of willpower that he tore himself away from the view, food, wine, and prevailing holiday atmosphere. But he had a concert immediately after our return, and hadn't picked up his violin for several days. He was, no doubt, no stranger to the adage, attributed to virtuosi from

163

Liszt to Louis Armstrong: 'If I don't practise one day, I know it; two days, the critics know it; three days, the public knows it.'

It was an incongruous sound that rang round the hills that afternoon, not exactly in keeping with the prevailing tranquillity. And it was the first and only time that I didn't want to listen to him playing. The concert was, naturally, superb.

These difficulties – inevitable and necessary hurdles on the path to enlightenment[*] – are common to the learning of any skilled pursuit. I console myself with the thought that twenty years on I'm able to look back at my travails in Musin's conducting class and put them into perspective. He was known to reassure struggling pupils with the words, 'Don't worry – it'll sort itself out in forty years.' And I'm sure my father's response to this comparatively minor glitch in my pursuit of what, after all, is a mere hobby, would be equally philosophical.

'Just keep going. That's all you can do.'

The summer course has gone well. We've dispatched Mahler's *Fifth Symphony* with a swift chop to the pressure point just below the neck, the rest of the repertoire a mere bagatelle compared to that behemoth. Players have declared themselves happy, and there's no reason to disbelieve them. My habit of shoehorning bird references into rehearsals seems not to have upset them unduly. Indeed, a stalwart cellist turns out to be a bird ringer of thirty years' experience, and we have an invigorating conversation on the subject of twitching. He is unequivocal.

'I might cross the road for a rarity, but certainly not the country.'

---

[*]   I'm still looking. It's probably down the back of the sofa.

He's more excited about having avoided injury while ringing a great spotted woodpecker a few days earlier, those birds notorious for digging their claws into their handlers' flesh. I find this uplifting, confirmation of my suspicion that the most visible birders, the ones I see proclaiming their successes and bantering about rarities on Twitter, aren't representative of the thousands of enthusiasts who make their way quietly in the world, their priorities aligned to a different calibration.

But the fact remains that I've set myself this challenge and am committed to it. The evening before we leave for home, I survey the wreckage of my birding year, fiddling with the spreadsheet and making gloomy prognostications about my chances. The most pessimistic appraisal sees me stranded in the mid-180s. The most optimistic nudges me over the line at 202. More realistically, I expect to end somewhere in the high 190s. Damn those Scottish birds.

It's time to go home. We'll be dropping in on Tessa's brother in Chester for a couple of days on the way back. Fourteen spoonbills have decided to spend their summer holidays at Burton Mere. There's a good garden within a couple of miles, and we could easily cycle there along the canal towpath. It's a glimmer of hope, but not enough to lighten my mood. The project seems doomed to honourable failure.

I sleep the fitful sleep of the preoccupied, and dream of eagles and ptarmigan, flying away from me with howls of mocking laughter.

August ticks (13)

RSPB Loch Garten, Glenmore, Isle of Skye, Edinburgh, Musselburgh, Bass Rock, Gullane, RSPB Burton Mere Wetlands

Osprey *Pandion haliaetus*, Crested Tit *Lophophanes cristatus*, Goshawk *Accipiter gentilis*, Hooded Crow *Corvus cornix*,

Grey Wagtail *Motacilla cinerea*, Dipper *Cinclus cinclus*, Shag *Phalacrocorax aristotelis*, Kittiwake *Rissa tridactyla*, Puffin *Fratercula arctica*, Velvet Scoter *Melanitta fusca*, Eider *Somateria mollissima*, Goosander *Mergus merganser*, Spoonbill *Platalea leucorodia*

Year total: 154

SEPTEMBER 2016

I'm not wet, in the same way that cats aren't covered in fur. There are bits of me untouched by water, but I lost contact with them some time ago. The rain started in the middle of the night, hammering down on the roof of the shepherd's hut we've rented for the weekend,* and waking me in good time for my early-morning start. The forecast has it continuing till the early afternoon, and for once the forecast is bang on the money. Tomorrow the sun will shine, but tomorrow is bike ride and garden day. My designated birding slot, impartially assigned by the gods of family togetherness, is Saturday morning. I feel like a real birder. I'm alone on the reserve for most of my walk, only encountering other people as I return to the visitor centre after three hours of soggy tramping. The RSPB guy smiles. He understands, sees nothing extraordinary about it. Who wouldn't want to spend their Saturday morning up to their armpits in sludge, enjoying the full gamut of a varied landscape in five-yard visibility?

My reward? Zero ticks. *Keine Zecken. Nul tiques.*

In fact, not many birds at all. They're hardy, the birds of Poole Harbour, but not stupid. Most of them are under cover, nursing a mug of cocoa and watching a Ginger Rogers movie.† And even

---

* Two glamping trips in a year. I'm a middle-class cliché.
† Some people call them Fred Astaire movies, but she famously did everything he did backwards and in heels, so I reckon it's time to redress the balance.

those birds for whom water is a more natural medium look as if they're suffering. Mallard, shoveler and shelduck variously float, dabble and squelch around the pools and mudflats, apparently unaware that this is supposed to be nice weather for them.

A herring gull moves sideways across the shore, powered more by the wind than its own resources. Far away, just visible through the binoculars, a shape I'm assuming is an osprey sits on top of a tree. Black-tailed godwits perch stolidly on one leg, looking put-upon, as if suffering the company of a tiresome relative while forcing down stale ginger nuts and weak tea in an unheated sitting room.

Believe it or not, I'm having fun. Yes, I'm thinking of learning how to pirouette, and rebranding myself as a sprinkler system; yes, I've just spent fifteen minutes under a tree trying to identify the chipping and whistling noises of a mysterious bird that turned out to be a chaffinch; and no, I haven't furthered my Grand Cause an inch. Nonetheless, I regard this morning at RSPB Arne as an unmitigated triumph. The forty-five birds I still need can wait. Because today is a kingfisher day, and that makes today a good day.

My exaggerated delight at the sighting of any kingfisher has been one of the surprises of the year, not just explained by its undeniable attractiveness. Sure, they're elusive, but what birds aren't?

I have a feeling it's to do with childhood disappointment. Our local kingfisher – or, presumably, a series of them, as their average two-year lifespan is distressingly short – always evaded me. Someone dropping in for a cup of tea, knowing of my interest, might mention they'd seen it. Off I would go, down the shady lane away from the village, right up the dusty path, fields either side, left at the stone bridge by the water mill, and along the river bank, picking my way through the overhang of willows and steering well clear of the edge of anything, according to parental instructions.

The blend of incipient curmudgeonliness and rose-tinted hindsight common to those approaching the arse end of middle age no doubt accounts for my feeling that such an excursion, so routine and welcome back then, is neither available nor desirable to the current batch of tomorrow's adults. It's the kind of walk I took for granted, outdoors a natural place to spend an afternoon doing nothing in particular. But it's not as if I was some sort of feral urchin, staying out from dawn till dusk and returning caked in the blood of wild animals. Other attractions were available. Like many cricket-lovers of my generation, I wasn't averse to drawing the curtains on a sunlit day and watching seven hours of a Test match in total darkness. These marathon sessions were interrupted only by a bacon sarnie and a glass of juice served by my long-suffering mother, or occasionally a boiled egg fastidiously cooked by my father – his attention to detail manifesting itself in every aspect of the cooking down to geometrically sliced toast soldiers and a small pyramid of salt on a side plate. But equally, they seemed happy enough for me to roam the village and surrounding countryside on foot or bike with no more than a 'back by supper time' to send me off. The sense of danger so prevalent today was as absent as the kingfisher.

I would sit on the bank, knees up, feet tilted towards the river, picking idly at the long grass or drawing a pattern in the mud with my finger so that the dirt got nicely entrenched under the nail, and keeping an eagle eye out for the telltale flash of iridescence I'd read about in the books. But always to no avail, the bird either too shy or too canny, somehow knowing when my attention was elsewhere.

This 2016 kingfisher, the fifth of my year, has streaked across my line of sight and is sitting on a fence post ten yards away. It stays there, its vivid plumage enlivening the surrounding gloom. The unfairness of this is not lost on me. Pity the small brown birds, dismissed as drab and uninteresting, getting on with life unadmired while all the attention goes to the flashy and flamboyant, our shallow human sensibilities attracted to the blur of colour streaking across the water.

Do they care? Aren't they just concerned with survival and procreation, feeding and breeding?

Maybe.

Nonetheless, always rooting for the underdog, I make a point of studying and admiring those birds whose colour palette is limited to shades of dun, as well as those whose plumage has evolved to catch the eye.

Dabbling in front of the hide are a couple of gadwall, the bird so many people have told me is underrated it's in danger of becoming overrated. They're having a barney, the female chasing away the male, nipping at his backside. The male retreats to a safe distance, then has another go. She's not having any of it. This tussle engages my attention briefly, but I'm aware throughout of the kingfisher on its post. In the end its glamorous allure is too strong. I break away from the gadwall fracas and turn my binoculars on the kingfisher. Even in the dull light it would make a decent photo, so I swap binoculars for camera, make the adjustments and press the shutter just as the kingfisher decides it wants to be elsewhere. The result is a pleasing photograph, against a backdrop of grey water and cloud, of an empty post. Very artistic, and a decent metaphor for my year. Here is the post that until recently boasted a colourful and fascinating bird. If you squeeze your eyes together you can just discern the remains of its aura. I can almost feel the karma winging its way towards me from the Isle of Wight six weeks earlier and draping itself round my shoulders.

The kingfisher is the zenith of my visit. I call it a day and squelch my way back to the visitor centre for a vat of coffee and a slice of chocolate cake the size of Bournemouth.

The weekend hasn't been a total washout, list-wise. No sooner had we unpacked after the long Friday evening drive to Dorset than we were greeted by a congratulatory 'woo-hoo' from a tawny owl in the neighbouring copse. After the woo-hoos – easily mimicked by anyone capable of blowing into their cupped hands and prepared to put in the hours of practice – it gives a couple of calls, a sharp attention-grabbing upwards squiggle (hee-yip!) to prove it's the real thing. My overarching rule – that heard birds count as surely as seen ones – has only come into force once, with the grasshopper warbler back in April. And the memory of Oliver's barn owl in May is still strong. I'm behind on my owls, so this is a welcome addition. I ditch the idea of trailing around the local woods in search of a brief glimpse, retire to bed and update my total: 155.

It's time to begin honing the list. The loss of the Scottish birds* has dented my confidence, but my hopes of reaching 200 are far from forlorn. I've lost a couple of quick wickets to the second new ball, that's all. It's 2–1 with twenty minutes to play. A quick break of serve, a nine-dart finish and a converted try in the last quarter and I'm set for a ninth-inning comeback.†

I list the birds I'm counting on: eight waders, about fifteen duck-geese-swans-divers-grebes-and-so-forth, four owls, up to eight perching flitters, and two raptors. That takes me into the low 190s, with the rest to come from I know not where.

The more I've learned, the more I've realised that instead of footling around stroking robins in my back garden during February and March, I should have been freezing my nadgers off in the wilds of north Kent looking for wintering wildfowl and waders. But not to worry, because winter will bring at least twenty I'll be hard pushed to avoid. And even in September I

---

*   Like a superstitious actor I've decided never to refer to them again by name.
†   Other sporting metaphors are available.

should be able to mop up a few easily enough. And so it proves. Another day devoted to the holy trinity of biking, birding and garden-visiting takes us to Fingringhoe Wick, just south of Colchester, and a conveniently flat and medium-distance bike ride from the Beth Chatto Gardens. Hobbies-wise, we're Mr and Mrs Sprat and Son.

For me the trip is a small slice of nostalgia, Fingringhoe imprinted on my memory as the home of my great aunt. It's thirty-five years since I've been there, but I'm sure if we drive around the area for a bit we'll as good as trip over the place. It was a house, as I recall. Walls, chimney, windows, that kind of thing. And the lane it was on had a hedge running down it. Should be unmissable.

My memories of her and the house are impressions rather than vivid recollections. A quietly formidable lady, awarded the CBE for her contribution to the WAAF in the war. Thin,* with bright eyes and a 'you can't fool me' expression hiding strong inner warmth. Tea in bone china cups. Hens at the bottom of the garden. A narrow winding staircase up to a low-ceilinged spare room. Outside, the lane leading down to the marsh, forbidden territory when the red MoD flag was flying.

One specific memory lingers. A walk, when my mother and great aunt were otherwise occupied. I was old enough to roam alone, and the red flag wasn't flying. So I wandered down the lane to the marsh, feeling terribly grown-up, returning an hour later with earnest reports of numerous sightings. Reed warbler, sedge warbler, marsh tit, willow tit, spotted flycatcher, redstart, wood warbler, lesser spotted woodpecker – you name it, I said I'd seen it.

Let's give me the benefit of the doubt. Maybe I did see those

---

* I might even say 'bird-like' if my idea of what that means hadn't been overturned during recent months.

birds.* Certainly the house was well placed for them, right on the edge of the marsh and with woodland nearby. But more likely I thought I should have seen them, that I felt reports of a robin, a song thrush and a couple of blackbirds would somehow disappoint. Maybe I heard twitterings and saw flutterings, and made the natural leap from 'This is the kind of place I might see a reed warbler' via 'That was a small brown fluttery thing' to 'Yay! Reed warbler!'

I want to find the house, partly to pay homage to a lady who was part of my childhood without being physically present – my parents' evident esteem for her ensuring she was mentioned in dispatches far more often than I met her. Perhaps she was significant because she was the only familial link I had with the generation above my parents'. Three of my grandparents died before I was born. My maternal grandmother lived in Australia. Here was a woman born in the nineteenth century, who lived through two world wars – wasted on the twelve-year-old me, but if she were around now, wouldn't I want to talk to her all evening?

The detour is also to mark the place where one of the great lies of my birding childhood was perpetrated, a symbolic exorcism of past misdemeanours.

As we drive towards the reserve, I get an overwhelming feeling of nearly déjà-vu. The landscape feels familiar, hedges and fields all around but with an underlying hint of being on the edge of something larger. Round every turn I think, 'Here it'll be,' but there it isn't. There's no moment of recognition, no sense of homecoming, no feeling of wonder at how much larger, smaller, broader or narrower everything seems in comparison to my memories. For there's nothing to compare. While the

---

*   I didn't.

landscape feels intangibly familiar, the specifics – the shape of the lane curving away from us, or the outline of a wall or roof – remain elusive.

My faith in my own instinctive powers of recollection is fatally undermined, and after twenty minutes of fruitless meandering, I call off the search and Tessa drops us and the bikes off at the nature reserve.

In the first hide, brand new and overlooking the Colne Estuary, good water management has allowed the high tide to push the birds close, and there are a lot of them, but after fifteen minutes I'm assailed by an unfamiliar feeling. Ennui.*

I don't know where it's come from. Maybe it's the other occupants. There are four of them, in two pairs, their common ground a stolid demeanour which somehow announces, 'We're going to watch the hell out of these birds, whether we like it or not.' I may have read it wrong, but there's something joyless about them I haven't yet encountered on my travels.

They're not impolite, just secretive. A glance towards us, a hint of suspicion, something intangible in the air, possibly carrying a whiff of my own paranoia. Nonetheless I feel, for the first time in the year, that I've stumbled in on a meeting of a club that the members don't want me to join.

Or maybe I'm just having one of those off days when you're assailed with an inexplicable sense of whatchamacallit and everything feels ever so slightly drungly, the kind of day that's only salvaged, if at all, at its end, with the help of a bathtub of pistachios and a schooner of cheap booze.

Perhaps it's the fault of the black-tailed godwits. Yes, OK, let's blame them. There are dozens of the blighters, huddled on an island rapidly shrinking with the rising tide. Their backs are

* Ennui the First.

defiantly turned towards me, and they appear determined, every one of them, and with a barefaced cheek that fair takes the breath away, not to be the bar-tailed variety I so avidly crave. Nothing against black-tailed godwits. Fine, upstanding birds. Sublime, in the right circumstances, but today they fall some way short of filling my trug with raspberries.

And so it goes. Half a dozen avocets cavorting in the middle distance. Meh. Ringed plovers, pecking about on the foreshore then up with a flurry and banking round the island in formation. Whevs. Even a distant glimpse of a marsh harrier doesn't stir me. I'm feeling so disaffected you could pull my trousers halfway down my legs and call me a teenager.

After fifteen minutes of this, I catch Oliver's eye and we exchange slightly raised eyebrows, a tacit agreement to leave. He's taken some photos but is now showing every sign of sharing my apathy.

We visit the second hide without optimism. It's a smaller and more ramshackle affair overlooking a small pool with reed beds all around. But here it's a different story. Released from the oppressive shackles of joyless Tupperware, we join another party of four, their mood as carefree as the other hide's was downbeat. Gentlemen of a certain age,* they're squeezed together on the narrow bench. As we arrive, one of them vacates his seat, muttering, 'Twenty minutes – time for a fag,' by way of explanation. He beckons us to take his place, and offers an apologetic rundown of what's on offer as he leaves.

'Not much, but there's a spotted redshank and a grey plover near the back.' He eyes the camera round Oliver's neck. 'Maybe the young man can get some photographs.'

And with a smile he's gone, leaving us to the ministrations

* Old. They're old.

of his equally friendly companions. Despite the bareness of the hide, there's warmth in the air, and we leave twenty minutes later, nourished by two unexpected ticks and the full-fat milk of human friendliness.

As we return to the visitor centre, there to collect our bikes for the ride to the gardens, I reflect on the strange infectiousness of other people's demeanours. Then, with exaggerated good humour, I chase my son across the flat Essex countryside.

The passage of time plays tricks. It seems only a week ago that I had the idea to see 200 birds in a year, and just a couple of days earlier I was standing by the bird table as an obsessive ten-year-old, hoping to lure a chaffinch into a moment of intimacy.

The bird table at my childhood home wasn't a table but a disused water tank, conveniently placed in direct view of the kitchen window, and covered with a large piece of plywood. I watched the usual smaller birds come and go, their smash-and-grab tactics inevitably meaning sightings were short, sharp and frequent. If I watched carefully I could see them flitting about in the overhanging branches, waiting for their opportunity. While these views were satisfactory, I yearned to see the birds up close, and became convinced it would be possible if only I could find the ideal vantage point. The table was wedged against a wall. Perhaps if I waited by it, close by but quiet and unthreatening, they would be irresistibly drawn to me.

It was a hopeful plan, undermined by some fundamental flaws.

I had a red sweatshirt. It was nice. I wore it a lot. In retrospect it might not have been the ideal camouflage.

Nonetheless, things might have been fine had I kept absolutely still. This I failed to do, checking every thirty seconds that my mother was still at the kitchen window in rapt admiration of my stillness and blending-in-itude.

After a lengthy three-minute vigil, I lost patience with the birds' unwillingness to cooperate and went off to play Scalextric.*

I think of those birds and their understandable wariness as I stand by the side of the road on the heat-baked flats of Oare Marshes in north Kent one afternoon in mid-September. There are several hundred birds here, the nearest of them no more than five yards away. But unlike the garden birds of my childhood, this lot seem unperturbed by my presence. I could re-enact the 1977 Silverstone Grand Prix and they wouldn't bat an eyelid. If I were a bird of prey it would be a different story, but they can tell from my benevolent demeanour that I'm not a threat, so they stay put.

On the left are black-headed gulls and lapwings, familiar birds made more fascinating by proximity. The variations of dark greens and purples on the lapwings' backs are particularly attractive, bearing detailed examination as they patiently submit themselves to our scrutiny.

There are three of us. Ten yards away to my left, a burly man who seems to consist entirely of flesh and sweat has his scope trained on a distant group of birds, a hundred or more, lining a spit of land, and it's to them that I now turn my gaze. As I do so, they take off, spooked by something or other, dainty wingbeats belying the urgency of their action. In this light the fine notching of their burnished plumage glimmers with understated warmth, and you can see how they got their name. Golden plover. The quiet satisfaction of another new bird is eclipsed by the sight of these elegant creatures scattering

---

*   A word, incidentally, that to this day has me throwing things at walls when grown people who should bally well know better pronounce it 'Scalectrix'. Seriously, how hard can it be?

against the cobalt sky. Another snapshot for the memory bank. They fly up and around, closely grouped in a long flat line, then wheel away from us and back round to the spit, some collective instinct telling them it's safe to return. As they settle, I look again towards the birds nearer to hand, and it's now that the third of our little group addresses me.

He's lean of body, keen of intent. He has an air of expertise, and the focus of his expression is matched only by the rapidity of his speech and its utter incomprehensibility to me.

'Youlkinfrboparscull?'

There are those who talk, and those who gabble. He's in the second group, and executes his skills with the ease of a professional gabbler.

He looks at me as if the fate of galaxies hangs on my response.

I have to say something. If only I knew what. I feel like a contestant on *University Challenge*, the one at the end who goes through the whole programme in silence, losing the thread of half the questions after five words and, on the rare occasions they have some idea, unable to catch the attention of their captain.

Before I can ask him to repeat himself, he's pointing at the black-headed gulls.

'Js'there. Je'blag.'

Right then. There's something there, but I don't know what. It's probably masquerading as a black-headed gull, which would explain the 'scull' bit. All I need to do is work out what 'bopar' means. It doesn't resemble the name of any of the regular gulls, but if it were regular he wouldn't be pointing it out. So it must be a rarity. I scour my memory for irregular gulls. My knowledge is scant. I've put gull recognition on the 'deal with later, preferably never' pile. I know a few, though, and try to mangle names into 'bopar'. Glaucous? Iceland? Caspian? Sabine's?

'I'm so sorry. Say it again?'

'Boparscull. Righ'there. Bla'biw.'

Black bill. It's a start. I scan again, and there, looking every bit like a black-headed gull that's dipped its hooter into a cup of tar, is the bird in question.

So now I have the bird. I take a photo of it, just in case. I can always work it out later with the help of bird guides. But part of me thinks that's cheating. I want to pass this test.

At its best, birding is a happy combination of *Where's Wally?*, *Guess Who?*, and *The Krypton Factor*.* This endeavour lacks the physical challenge of the latter, but is laden with fraught intellectual hurdles. The possibility of asking him to repeat himself yet again is too humiliating, as well as rude, so I'm on my own, in the rare position of having seen a bird I know isn't on my list, but lacking the resources to define it.

I hide myself behind my binoculars, and slow down what he said, filling in syllables.

Brogue paths gull?

Bone palms gull?

Below par gull?

Blown apart gull?

Aha.

Deep in the recesses of my sun-and-motorway-addled brain stirs a memory, the residue of idle scrolling through the 'gulls' section of the Collins app.

Bonaparte's Gull. Pretty rare, an American bird that has for reasons best known to itself made its way across the expanse of water separating our continents. I don't, in truth, have much idea what it looks like, but I'd be willing to bet it has a bla'biw.

I turn to thank my mysterious companion, but he's disappeared, replaced by a newcomer, an amiable cove with steel-rimmed spectacles and a bland smile.

* Younger readers: ask your parents.

'Anything about?'

'Well, apparently that bird there is a Bonaparte's gull.'

As I speak, pointing confidently towards the bird, there's a flurry of activity, as of a hundred gulls and lapwings flying away from an approaching predator. The sparrowhawk appears seconds later. It's too late. They've all gone.

Story of my life. I offer my bespectacled friend an apologetic grimace and move on.

'Seen it yet?'

There are three possible answers: 'Yes,' 'No,' and 'Seen what exactly?' There's an assumption there, as if the only reason you could be where you are is to see one particular thing. If this were one of those twitches that occur from time to time when a rare bird randomly plops itself down in someone's back garden, then yes, you'd be safe in assuming that a person with an intent look and a telescope wouldn't be there by accident. But we're on a bird reserve. 'It' could be almost anything.

Clearly I've missed something. My afternoon of birding has got in the way of my obsessive checking of reported sightings.

I have, as the end of the year hurtles towards me, succumbed and downloaded the BirdGuides app, which places news of unusual sightings in my pocket. It's not that I'm planning to charter a plane and fly to Shetland at a moment's notice should news trickle in of Britain's first record of a Siberian accentor. It's more a sign of a peculiar fascination with people who have a peculiar fascination with rarities. I wonder how twitchers plan their lives, what it feels like to be dominated by birds in that particular way.

But my surroundings this afternoon, at RSPB Titchwell Marsh in Norfolk, have been so serenely agreeable, and the bird activity so varied and interesting, I haven't given rarities a second's thought. The abundance of birdlife, the warmth of the autumn sun, the breadth of the beach, the firmness of the sand and the salt tang of sea air on the tongue – all combine to render things oojah-cum-spiff in my birding universe.

It's not even as if I've racked up mountains of ticks. Once again I've found myself less motivated by the acquisition of new species than by the general oohness of the experience, but I have, almost incidentally, added two birds to my list.

On the reserve are hundreds of dunlin, the default small wader, and just a couple of curlew sandpipers. The latter is similar enough to the former to make identification tricky, but I regard it as a challenge to my burgeoning skills, and after a few false starts manage to nail one of them down on the freshwater lagoon. Flushed with success, I reward myself with a walk on the beach, never a chore in Norfolk. It brings me to a flock of small waders whose behaviour betrays their identity as surely as any aspect of plumage or build.

Your sanderling, see, is a scuttler. Pitter-pattering their way up and down the sand like so many wind-up toys, the rhythm of their wanderings dictated by the ebb and flow of the waves, they nuzzle their short bills into the sand in search of tiny crustaceans. Their window of opportunity is short. As the water recedes, their prey burrow back down and out of their grasp, and they have to wait a few seconds before trying again.

It's a hypnotic sight. Scuttle, nuzzle, retreat, wait. Scuttle, nuzzle, retreat, wait. They must be successful some of the time, but the impression they give is of constant and narrow failure, doomed to an unending ten-second cycle, like Sisyphus on fast-forward.

I could, and nearly do, watch them all afternoon, but time is getting on, and I'm keen to assemble myself near the salt marshes for marsh harriers returning to roost. The day is, incredibly, getting more pleasant as it wears on, and there's a particular September late-afternoon warmth to the light which imparts a quality of just-rightness that would have Goldilocks purring.

As I saunter past the striking Parrinder Hide, with its luxury views across the reserve, a friendly birder stops me. Have I seen it?

'It' turns out to be a pectoral sandpiper, showing well. The hide is just there, ten yards away. It would be rude not to. I allow myself five minutes out of the sunshine to find it.

The Collins app lists no fewer than twenty birds with the word 'sandpiper' in their name, enough to turn my brain to mush. The majority are irregular or rare vagrants to Europe, and it's into this category that the pectoral sandpiper falls. My hasty research reveals it to be distressingly similar to the ruff. The text doesn't help much more. Bird guides do this. A typical entry might be reinterpreted thus: 'Brown. Medium-sized. Similar to that other bird you never recognise, but with a minutely distinguishing feature you won't be able to see under most conditions.'

The good thing about a twitch, though, as I've gathered from the more cynical members of the fraternity, is you don't even have to identify the bird. You just follow the direction of the scopes, ask someone to show it to you, tick it and leave.

I like to think I have a bit more moral fibre than that. But then we all like to think that, don't we?

It's crowded enough in the hide to call to mind a twitching version, complete with spotting scopes on tripods, of the cabin scene from the Marx Brothers' *A Night At The Opera*. There are seven of them, all trained on one distant spot across the water. Low murmuring is the order of the day. I duck between the scopes and position myself as well as I can. A kindly birder with an exorbitant-looking Swarovski scope is explaining to his companion where to find the elusive bird.

'Got it?'

'No.'

'OK, it's just gone behind the snipe.'

'Where's that?'

'See the third bush from the left, just in front of the gap in the trees in the far distance?'

'No, hold on.'

'Go fifteen yards to the right of that. No wait, it's moved.'

'Hang on, I think I've got the wrong snipe.'

'Well, anyway, it's not there any more. Gone behind that bush.'

'Which one?'

'The one to the left of... you found the snipe yet?'

'I think so. Is it standing on the little spit on the left?'

'Which one?'

'The, hold on, first, second, third one in from those lapwings.'

'Hang on... no, not that one. The snipe I'm looking at is to the right of them, further back.'

'Oh, that one. Right.'

'Well, the pectoral sandpiper is just behind, no hang on, it's moved again.'

In my head I convert these lines into the drawling delivery of vintage-era Peter Cook and Dudley Moore, and have to suppress a snort of laughter. But I also know how difficult it is to describe the exact position of a bird in a landscape of similarities. And I too am keen to see it, if only to discover what all the fuss is about. I log in to the directions being offered behind me. They've managed to settle the seething issue of which snipe the sandpiper is hiding behind, and just as I find it, a small grey-brown bird with a lightly streaked breast and white belly pops out into view. Obligingly enough, the snipe continues to the right and I have an uninterrupted view of the pectoral sandpiper. I barely knew what one was three minutes ago, but now I'm an expert, just like everyone else in the hide, whose excited little exclamations confirm that this is the pectoral sandpiper I'm looking for.

Honestly, though, and without any disrespect to the vibrant pectoral sandpiper community, it looks like a ruff. There's a ruff, just there, about twenty yards away, riffling around in the mud. This bird looks like that, but much further away. Its attraction lies in its rarity. I get that, but objectively, given the choice of admiring the ruff or the pectoral sandpiper, the ruff would win, and not just because it's closer. There's a freshness to the ruff, the light edges of its individual wing and back feathers forming a strong and crisp scalloped pattern. The pectoral sandpiper looks knackered, as is its right, having flown all the way from America. And what of the snipe, the bird everyone was hoping would budge over so they could look at something more interesting? Or any of the shoveler, teal, wigeon, herons, kestrels, pheasants, jays, swallows, chiffchaffs, blackbirds, robins, lapwings, pied wagtails, little egrets, mallards, goldfinches, woodpigeon, rooks, carrion crows, oystercatchers, cormorants, ringed plovers, redshanks, grey plover, turnstone, bearded tits, moorhens, coots and gadwall (underrated bird) I've seen on the reserve that day?

Well, they're lovely too.

Most of all, they're outside, which is where I want to be, the hide's lack of air and light, on this bright and sunny day, discouraging an extended stay. That anyone would willingly spend more than ten minutes in here on a day like this, when there's so much to enjoy in the glowing late afternoon sunshine outside, seems to me little short of lunacy. But who am I to judge? I did, after all, opt to nip in there just for the tick.

I retrace my steps from earlier, keen to make the most of the remains of the day and enjoying the warm sunlight as it slants across the beach.

Just below the dune, a flash of movement. A small, upright bird, black eye-stripe prominent, hopping across the sand. It's a wheatear. Clearly in the mood for company, it remains within viewing distance, leading me across the flat sands and hopping up onto the ruins of a WWII bunker to enable striking photos of it silhouetted against the sea and the offshore wind farm in the hazy distance.

It won't be here much longer, off to central Africa for the winter in the next few weeks. These journeys, so casually referred to, remain one of the wonders of the birding year. I try to get my head round it by visualising it taking off from the beach, tracing its journey in fast-forward across land and sea, over mountain and valley, guided by an internal satnav that makes Google Earth seem like a crumpled, sixteenth-century chart with *Hic sunt dracones* written on it.

It's as if I decided to walk to the moon and back.*

I think of this and millions of journeys like it, encircling the globe in an annual web of miracles. As if summoned by these thoughts, and determined to blow my mind even further out of its skull, a butterfly, pale cream against the deep blue sky, flutters over my shoulder and heads out to sea. I watch it avidly, fixing on its flickering traces with the naked eye and then the binoculars until it's an etch-a-sketch dot, then a speck, then gone completely. Go well, frail creature. Try not to get eaten by a skua.

September ticks (11)

Fingringhoe Wick, Oare Marshes, Beddington Farmlands, RSPB Titchwell Marsh, RSPB Frampton Marsh, Compton Abbas

Spotted Redshank *Tringa erythropus*, Grey Plover *Pluvialis squatarola*, Golden Plover *Pluvialis apricaria*, Little Stint *Calidris minuta*, Bonaparte's Gull *Chroicocephalus philadelphia*, Spotted Flycatcher *Muscicapa striata*, Sanderling *Calidris alba*, Curlew

---

* I haven't done the maths, or at least I have tried to do the maths, but my mind can't deal with more than four zeros. Anyway, that's what it *feels* like.

Sandpiper *Calidris ferruginea*, Pectoral Sandpiper *Calidris melanotos*, Brent Goose *Branta bernicla*, Tawny Owl *Strix aluco* (heard)

Year total: 165

OCTOBER 2016

I should be at home, writing programme notes, devising concert series, planning rehearsal schedules, replying to emails, doing the laundry. Anything but driving down the M2 to Dungeness.

But if I'm a feckless employee I'm an even more lenient boss – the ideal small office task force in a handy one-person bundle. So when boss me gives employee me the day off, employee me hands over all the admin to secretary me, who instantly makes the executive decision to do it later. Because when fourteen great white egrets assemble in one place, and you don't know how long they're going to stick around, you want to get there as soon as possible. It's not a twitch, I tell myself. I was going birding today anyway. My reply is swift and withering: say that often enough and you might start believing it.

It's the latest in a mini-series of snatched opportunities. I'd love to get fifteen birds in October, and the more I can accumulate before the pivotal trip to Northumberland in half-term, the better.

The egrets are worth the visit. Snow-white herons with S-bend necks, they stand in plain view of the hide, and I admire them for longer than strictly necessary, drinking in their purity and profoundly grateful I'm not subjected to an attack from the lethal orange bayonets adorning their slender heads. 166.

Closer to home, I embrace a local site, previously neglected. South Norwood Country Park is no more glamorous than it sounds, but it's a good size, with varied habitats and a well-populated lake. There I see a water rail early one Sunday morning. Evasive bird, the water rail, the moorhen's reclusive cousin, appearing in its grey and brown suit only for feast days and funerals. It's like an apparition, the briefest glimpse in the shadows as I scan the fringes of the lake. When I look back five seconds later, it's gone. I bow in obeisance to it for even that fleeting audience. I've looked for one every time I've been near a reed bed, which has been often. They've been notable only for their absence. The glamour spots, your Minsmeres, your Dungenesses, your Rainhams, have yielded nothing in the way of railery. I thought I heard one at Titchwell, but, unsure and bound by my infrangible code of honour, didn't list it. Now I've seen one on my doorstep. 167.

Rainham, deficient in the water rail department, does at least give me a ring ouzel. It's a generous gift, as befits my birding epicentre. Similar to the blackbird, but with a distinctive white crescent bib, it's a mountain breeder, but drops in on the lowlands during migration. This one, maybe inspired by the vibrant architecture of the visitor centre, cavorts in a bush with a brazen cockiness, as if to say, 'You've come to see *me*, haven't you? *Me me me.*'

I agree, doff my imaginary cap and move on. 168.

The growing urgency of my quest has led to intensified surveillance of rare bird sightings. When a yellow-legged gull is reported on Regent's Park lake, I utter a sound, half exultant whoop and half hollow groan. The whoop because, you know, ticks, and the groan because, you know, gulls.

For four years in my youth Regent's Park was home turf, round the corner from the Royal Academy of Music, where I was studying beer and kebabs, with music as a second subject. Whenever my musical workload became too much I'd take myself off for a walk round the park. I went there a lot. And now the power of geographical association means whenever I'm near the area my mind is flooded with a jumble of memories. Today is no different, but this memory is very specific.

My first week as a music student. This new world is big, bewildering. Everyone else is confident; everyone else is good; everyone else is grown-up. Next to them I am a child. It's all a bit much.

We are in a rehearsal. The conductor is from the 'hail fellow well met' school, revelling in his status as guru to the next generation, and keen to establish his credentials as our favourite uncle. He is making a point of addressing us by name. Compared to the mind-boggling feat facing any primary-school head teacher every September, memorising the names of an orchestra of thirty is small beer, but conductors like to do it as a matter of courtesy.

He looks up, surveys the six of us in the percussion section.

'Which one of you is the Parikian boy?'

And there I was, hoping to lie low and not draw attention to myself. Great. Thanks.

I raise a tentative and mildly resentful hand.

'Ah yes. I know your father very well.'

I suppose I should have expected it. My father is eminent in the classical music world. He's a regular on Radio 3, where presenters, keen to show they can pronounce his name, mangle it atrociously, turning Manoug Parikian into something that rhymes with Nanook Tricky-barn.* He is also a professor at this very institution. It's nice that people want to know him. But this public demonstration of credentials is embarrassing for me, and comes across as self-serving and otherwise pointless.

The rehearsal goes, the way rehearsals do; we play, he corrects,

---

* The trick, incidentally, is not to add letters that aren't there and not to make a big deal of how foreign it all looks. Stress the 'Man' and then the 'rik' and you won't be a million miles away.

we play again. He knows the music well, but his brisk demeanour and angular conducting style, reminiscent at times of a gull trying to lift itself from the water, do little to endear him to any of us, least of all me.

Afterwards I meet my father, on one of his rare forays into the Great Institution, in the foyer. Enter conductor, walking embodiment of effusion. As he bombards my father with misplaced bonhomie, I smile a quiet internal smile. I recognise the look on my father's face. It's one of bland resignation, a quarter smile accompanied by an occasional nod and the merest hint of a laugh. It's an expression that leads those meeting him for the first time to call him 'charming'; for those close to him it screams 'take me from this person before I kill'.

The conductor warms to his subject; my father's smile grows ever blander. Finally the effusiveness dribbles to a halt, and with a cheery wave the conductor takes his leave, striding into the night. I realise he has spent the last five minutes hoping to be included in whatever social activity we have planned.

My father turns to me.

'I hate to say it, Lev, but I have no idea who that was.'

If this life lesson warned me off pretence of acquaintanceship, pretence of musical knowledge remained a trap I fell into all too easily, lulled into the illusion that conductors must be omniscient, and trying too hard to impress people with expertise I barely possessed.

But when it comes to birds, there can be no pretending. I could easily claim to have seen this yellow-legged gull, but the idea is anathema. What would be the point?

As I walk towards Regent's Park I cram the distinguishing features of the bird into my head. It's basically a herring gull with, predictably enough, yellow legs. But it's not that simple. Lesser black-backed gulls also have yellow legs, so an idiot could easily get them confused. And if you can't see the eponymous appendages, the bird is so close to a herring gull as to be almost indistinguishable, especially to the aforementioned idiot.

I'm in luck. Someone has uploaded a photograph of the bird in question, so all I have to do is turn up and gather all the gulls on the boating lake for an impromptu identity parade.

I find it in minutes. It's bobbing on the water, away from the others, as if ostracised because of its leg colour, which is invisible in the murk of the lake. I will it to take off so I can verify the identification. No sooner wished than done. Up it gets, yellow legs trailing, and in every other respect matching the photograph on my phone. No need to pretend. 169.

Four random ticks, accumulated through a mixture of happenstance and endeavour. I roll up my sleeves and plan the big trip.

In my childhood Lindisfarne meant beards and mandolins and the kind of twangy music I suffered on *Top of the Pops* while waiting for T-Rex to come on.* I only discovered years later that they were named after a place, and years later again that the place was also called something else.

The name Holy Island, in turn, was off-putting to one whose natural stance towards religion has always been somewhere between worldly cynicism and confused ignorance. Why would I want to visit somewhere whose name implied a duty to devotion as a condition of entry?

Birds, it turns out, are reason enough.

The east coast is a magnet during migration seasons for birds travelling south in search of milder weather, and Lindisfarne,

---

* It was 1974. Give me a break.

sticking out just enough to be a first port of call, is known as a hotspot, just as it was for invading Vikings at the end of the eighth century. It's a good time to visit, although had I been organised and savvy enough, I would also have come earlier in the year and gone to the Farne Islands so I could be physically assaulted by Arctic terns defending their nesting grounds.*

Nonetheless, I'm optimistic I'll get a good portion of the remaining birds. In truth, I'm pinning my hopes on it. With two months left, all I can see are small beacons of opportunity. There will be days out, for sure, and another few days earmarked for Norfolk just before Christmas, but a lot of the heavy lifting needs to be done here and now.

My fears that the trip would be hard to smuggle past a family ideologically neutral on the subject of birding proved unfounded. Northumberland, with its hiking, biking and Vikings, turns out to be a pleasing prospect for us all.

And so we find ourselves in the shadow of Bamburgh Castle on the Thursday evening of half-term, exhausted by the drive but refreshed by the heady mix of sea air and the fleeting freedom of the mini-break.

I've drawn up a list of target birds for the visit. Of course I have. This whole thing has merely been an excuse for fiddling around with spreadsheets. The list comprises twenty names, about fifteen of them realistic. I'm hoping for twelve, would settle for nine, and any less would have me crying into my flat white.

Before we visit the island, I'm keen to explore what the mainland has to offer, so the next morning I'm up before dawn, walking down the middle of the Bamburgh–Budle road in the dark, listening to *Test Match Special* and mentally reciting a list of bird names.

---

* Visitors to the Farne islands in breeding season are recommended to wear a sturdy hat. Seriously.

Eccentric? Me?

I hear the birds before I see them. These sounds, the piping of waders, squawking of gulls, whistles and snorts of wigeon and teal, with a background of the alarm calls of robins and chackings of corvids, make up an unconventional, autumnal dawn chorus of the coast. I let the sound envelop me, no single feature predominant. It's a relief to shun the tyranny of identification, to listen without thinking, 'That's a curlew, there's a redshank, oystercatcher in the distance' – to let the sounds blend into a unity that can only be Budle Bay at dawn on this specific October morning. Tomorrow it will be similar but the balance subtly different. And there's music to be found in it. I've read that it's possible to identify certain places by their soundprint, their unique blend of background noise. Budle Bay's soundprint, enhanced by the dawn-nibbled darkness, and free of mechanical noises, has an eerie melancholy all its own. As I lose myself in it, I notice a slight shift, new voices. I pick out flickerings of activity, and six, no, seven, no, eight shapes. They lift off, hugging the ground as dawn begins to break. Then they wheel round and fly past in formation, and suddenly my head is full of Sibelius.

There was a time when I would have dismissed Sibelius in favour of his contemporary Mahler. Where Mahler's canvas is huge, encapsulating the drama and despair of the human condition with sweeping gestures, a broad colour palette and outrageous mood swings, Sibelius distils symphonies to their essentials. His late symphonies have the musical density of a black hole; Mahler's are more like galaxies. And it takes just as long to travel through them.

I make the comparison not just because their approaches were so contrasting. They were friends, and their conversation about 'The Symphony' has passed into musical folklore. Sibelius's view included the phrases 'severity of form' and 'profound logic'; Mahler's rejoinder was abrupt.

'No. The symphony must be like the world. It must contain everything.'

The vast scale of his compositions, both in duration and forces, bears testament to his dedication to this ideal.*

Sibelius may not have put the world into his symphonies, but he did include, in his most famous example of the genre, one important element of it.

Swans.

Boy, did he love swans. He loved cranes, too ('Their cries echo throughout my being'), but it's swans who feature more overtly, from the mystical *Swan of Tuonela* to the birds which, in his *Fifth Symphony*, do pretty much what these ones are doing right now in front of me.

These aren't the familiar park birds, the inappropriately named mute swan.† These are whooper swans. They're the same size as their cousins, but their slender necks and more delicate facial features – their bills have a pattern of pale yellow and black, and lack the distinctive 'knob' of the mute swan – set them apart.

It's 101 years, six months and a week since Jean Sibelius saw sixteen whooper swans and made an entry in his diary.

'One of the great experiences of my life! They circled over me for a long time. Disappeared into the solar haze like a gleaming ribbon. Their call the same woodwind type as that of the crane, but without tremolo.'

---

* I do, despite my protestations, love Mahler. But, like his contemporary Strauss, he was a bit of a show-off. The story goes that while on a day's walking in the mountains, his friend Bruno Walter stopped to admire the view of the Höllengebirge. Mahler swept on, throwing over his shoulder the dismissive comment, 'Don't bother looking. I've put it all in my Third Symphony.'

† Mute swans have a repertoire of hisses, snorts and clicks that quite strike terror into the human heart, petrified as we are that they will rise up and break our arm under the full protection of the Queen. And the sound of their wingbeats as they fly past in formation counts as one of the top five non-vocal nature sounds I've experienced.

In the symphony he represented them as a simple rocking motif that now inhabits my head as these eight birds – a half-Sibelius – rise from the early-morning mud and disappear over the horizon, suffused in the pink glow of the rising sun.

It's three minutes after sunrise. I could go back to bed right now and call the day a success.

Even after the swans have left, the mudflats are a hubbub of birds, like a winter market, constant activity everywhere. Curlews, their gurgling calls haunting in the early-morning gloom; oystercatchers, teal and wigeon scrabbling around in the shallows; a flock of gulls, four species bundled together in a sprawling clump, bickering amongst themselves; redshank piping noisily, just wanting everyone to know they're around and doing fine.

But no pink-footed geese.

It's a momentary disappointment. From everything I've read, they should be here. When autumn comes they arrive in their thousands from breeding grounds norther and colder, commuting inland from coastal roosts to feed on leftover crops in muddy fields, and Budle Bay is one of their favoured sites. But not, apparently, this morning.

I scan the mudflats again, looking for anything resembling a goose. The closest I find are some shelduck, but these are not the geese I'm looking for. They can't have gone already. I was here before dawn. Another desperate scan. Nothing.

The first sign is a distant disembodied squabbling. Before I can locate it, I see a flicker in the distance. Five seconds ago it was a dark surface, muddy sand on the broad estuary. Now I can see a clump of dots, wriggling and rising to form ragged arrowheads against the sky.

They fly over my head, their steady approach allowing me to attempt a head count. Doing it bird by bird is impractical, so the thing to do is count in manageable bunches. If you know roughly what ten geese look like, you go through the group counting bunches of ten. For larger groups you use the same process, but with units of a hundred or even a thousand. Using this method I arrive at a total of 240. Then, recounting as they get closer, I make it 360. Split the difference. Call it 300.

Three hundred geese make enough noise to qualify as at least half a racket, but their calls seem to me less hectoring than the cries of the more familiar greylag. They pass overhead, an asymmetrical, straggling, join-the-dots puzzle on the move, the steady crescendo of their calls peaking at a strong *mezzo forte* before they disappear over the hills behind me. What a sight. The frisson I feel might be the cold reaching the back of my neck, but I doubt it.

On the way back I follow the contours of the coast, Budle Water at low tide giving me the run of the enormous expanse of sand. Within ten minutes, prodding their long bills into the runnels of water that irrigate the sands, five birds stop me in my tracks. Five sought-after and desirable birds, within easy reach of my optical equipment, conveniently located for immediate viewing, and fully furnished with streaked plumage on the back and wings, long, slightly upturned bills, and light barring on the tail.

Bar-tailed godwits. At last. Thirty-eight years after I chased a flock of them off the Forth estuary, here are my bar-bloody-tailed god-sodding-wits. I mutter an apology to their breed on behalf of my younger self, give them the widest possible berth to ensure I don't flush them, and make my way onwards, buoyed by this connection with the past and the partial repayment of my debt to the species.

If a young person setting out in life chose, for reasons best known to themselves, to ask my advice, high on the list of crucial nuggets – sandwiched between 'Don't accidentally elect fascists' and 'Avoid desiccated coconut except as an insulating material' –

would be: 'Walk along broad, deserted beaches as often as possible.'

It's a spectacular stretch of coast, rendered more memorable by a clutch of three female red-breasted mergansers cruising on a broad stream a few hundred yards further on. I'm four ticks to the good and it's not even breakfast.

A thin layer of sand eddies away from me on the expanse of beach ahead, like snow on the Arctic tundra. The sea on the left is distant and unthreatening, a thin silver wedge separating broad sheets of sand and sky. Two sets of footprints, duo of man and dog, lay a trail to low dunes on the right. I scan them for a hunting short-eared owl, or even a merlin. But I'm not holding my breath.

I come to rocks, dark and low, blocking my path. Even from afar I can tell they're slippery, exuding the malevolent gloss of evil, like Darth Vader's helmet. They're prime concussion territory for anyone, let alone a flappy-footed clumsybundle like me. I've been wary of shiny surfaces ever since the unfortunate* incident of the ice hockey game on the frozen field when I was nineteen. Easy to say now[†] that oversized wellingtons weren't the ideal choice of footwear for the endeavour. Always at the forefront of fashion, I took my tumble within three minutes of the start. The game was abandoned to get me off the ice and into hospital, so our side won by one unconscious idiot to nil. I came round in the back of a pickup truck, exhaust fumes in my nostrils, half an hour lost to my memory for ever, and with the percussion section of the London Symphony Orchestra playing the famous 11/4 bar from *The Rite of Spring* on a loop in my head. Miraculously, I suffered no lasting ill effects, unless you count an irrepressible desire to stand in front of musicians and wave my arms in the hope that music will appear.

---

*   Moronic.
†   And, to be fair, quite easy at the time.

I give the rocks a wide berth, scrambling over the dunes and onto the road, from where there is a spectacular view of Bamburgh Castle and the Farne Islands beyond.

The question springs into my head unbidden, as so often when exploring the more peaceful corners of the country. Why exactly do I live in London?

Because I'd most likely be unemployed anywhere else. You can't heave a brick in central London without hitting an amateur orchestra, a situation unrivalled anywhere else in the world, and since those fine institutions provide the bulk of my employment, to move away would be perverse.

I knew there was a reason.

I breathe in lungfuls of clean air. I'll be needing reserves of it when I get back.

No matter how many times I consult the tide tables, there remains the nagging doubt that halfway across the causeway linking the mainland to Lindisfarne the sea will pounce and leave us embarrassedly awaiting the emergency services. According to the timetable, we can cross between 5 a.m. and noon, and will then be trapped on the island – like characters in an Agatha Christie play – until drinkies time. Mid-morning seems safe enough, and so it proves, although driving across a narrow strip of tarmac in the knowledge that it will shortly be covered in water is a slightly uncanny experience.

Birdwise, the early signs aren't good. We park, unstrap the bikes and cycle around the village, then on towards the castle and harbour. There's a ghostly quality to the place, human activity bordering on zero, avian barely better. I'm hoping for red-throated divers, Slavonian grebes, goldeneye, short-eared owl, merlin. I get a couple of herring gulls and a cormorant.

Excessive reading can give unrealistic expectations. A summary of any location's sightings will necessarily include the highlights, and the unwary will be gulled into thinking that these birds, seen over a period of years or even decades, will be crowding round them the moment they arrive. The reality is inevitably more prosaic.

Even allowing for this, I'm disappointed by the island's first offerings.

There's been a slew of rarities there in recent weeks. Isabelline shrike, Pallas's warbler, White's thrush, red-breasted flycatcher – names to conjure with. But the pinnacle was a mega rarity, a Siberian accentor, the very first record of which in the history of everything British had occurred a couple of weeks earlier on Shetland.

My awareness of this profusion is tempered by the balancing knowledge that no sooner had these birds arrived than they either scarpered or died. But I'm not discouraged. Something is clearly afoot. Anything could turn up.

Anything, in this case, turns out to be starlings. There are small groups of them everywhere. A couple of dozen tear about the village, streetwise youths up to no good. By the limekilns below the castle, six more forage on the path ahead of us, scattering as we pass and regrouping behind us. As we walk along the east coast of the island, buffeted by a bracing North Sea wind, starlings pop up everywhere, like the bowler-hatted men in *The Thomas Crown Affair*. One perches on a grazing sheep. Just as I'm beginning to suspect that some bewitchment has turned all the island's birds into starlings, I spot a flicker of movement on the rocks ahead of us. It's so fleeting there's no time for an identification beyond the habitual 'some sort of small brown bird', but I somehow know it's different, worth pursuing. It could, from that glimpse, be anything from a house sparrow to a Siberian accentor. My instinct is it's somewhere in between.

More movement, and there, on the fringes of the path, playing hide-and-seek among the mottled pebbles and thin, scrubby grass, is some sort of small brown bird.

Then it's gone.

I inch forward. It pops up again, well camouflaged but discernible. Definitely not a house sparrow. This bird has a demure look to it, with a fetching hazel blush on its cheek. There's black and white on the outer wing feathers, and a stout yellow bill.

This, unless I'm mistaken, is a snow bunting. Sweet, mobile, tickable.

We establish a pattern. It moves, I follow. I get close, it moves again. Repeat until fed up and begging the bird to sit still, dammit. At last I pin it down, and it poses long enough for a couple of photos so I can check its identity later. This is frowned upon by the old school, who will be heard to complain that birders nowadays are more like photographers. Get a bird book, do your homework, don't mumble, pull your trousers up, tuck your shirt in, turn that racket down, young people today, I'll have a tea with three sugars and one of those biscuits, been birding 140 years man and boy, and I've never needed to take one of those newfangled photographs.

I ignore these objections, viewing the photography as both a learning aid and a harmless pastime, and snap away to my heart's content. Later, I look at a bird book and confirm its identity, and now I really do know what a snow bunting looks like, so yah boo sucks to the old school.

The snow bunting marks the geographical and emotional peak of our morning. We head back to the village, lunch on sandwiches and crisps, and part ways, Tessa and Oliver exploring the island by bike, me striking out on foot. I don't want to be stopping them every five minutes to look at something that might be a Pallas's warbler but will inevitably turn out to be a dunnock. But I also want to make the most of my time here. They seem happy with the arrangement, so we agree to meet at dusk back in the village.

The heartiness engendered by a long walk in wild scenery lasts as long as you let it. Bolstered by the snow bunting, there's a spring in my stride. It sees me all the way up Straight Lonnen, the path that leads towards the northernmost tip of the island. It sustains me over the dunes and up to the cliffs at Nessend, then along to the spectacular viewpoint at Castlehead Rocks. It's still in full flow as I scan a small flock of waders on the beach at Sandham and find yet more starlings noodling around in the seaweed. I rest for five minutes on a considerate bench at the white pyramidal beacon at Emmanuel Head, the heartiness showing no sign of abating. It only subsides as I trudge back towards the village, coming to terms with the realisation that I'm done for the day. As I pick my way through some patient cattle in the gathering dusk, I become aware of a distant hubbub. It's a mild hubbub, no more than a high-pitched chattering carried to me on the light wind, and gone as soon as I hear it. I plough on, my legs reminding me I've walked nearly twenty miles today.

A hundred yards further on, another hubbub, louder, persistent. Or maybe it's the same one and I'm closer to it. As I try to get a handle on its source, a visual commotion sneaks into my eyeline from the right. Twenty birds. Fifty. A hundred. Arrowheads in the sky, birds with a purpose, converging on an agreed destination. More come in from the left, their collective shape billowing slightly as they approach a reed bed a hundred yards away.

Starlings.

I've stumbled on a murmuration and now nothing else matters, the paucity of sightings on the island instantly forgotten and the tiredness in my legs evaporating. I change tack and head towards the hubbub, which morphs into a downright hullabaloo as I approach.

By the standards we've come to expect, it's not a huge gathering. Not long ago these astonishingly fluid skydances, thousands strong, were commonplace, but the decline in the native starling population means they're now sought-after events, with the displays at Brighton, Aberystwyth and the Somerset Levels attracting crowds throughout winter.

I text Tessa.

–*Can you get to the east side easily and quickly?*

–*Not really. We're near the village. Why?*

–*Starling murmuration.*

–*Oh. Bugger.*

I take that as a 'no', and realise on reflection that cycling across rough and squelchy terrain on road bikes wouldn't be the best use of their time and resources, no matter what the incentive. I'm also heartened by what seems to be her genuine regret at missing the spectacle. No matter how many times they reassure me that my idiotic project isn't causing them perturbation and despair, I'm nonetheless beset by the worry that I'm going to be 'that' guy, the one who makes his family do the things he wants to do without consideration of their preferences. Accordingly I pounce on any display of even moderate enthusiasm as validation.

My attention is drawn back to the starlings by another group joining from the west. I'm at a loss to know how many birds there are here. More than a thousand. Less than a million. Somewhere in that ball park. The 'counting bunches' technique works less well when the birds are closely grouped and moving fast and unpredictably, and I lack the experience to make an educated guess at what a thousand starlings look like. I'm reminded of the family legend about my brother's first efforts at counting. 'One, two, lots and lots.' That'll do me.

More birds arrive, from all compass points. A smallish group, let's say a hundred birds, swoops in low and fast, sashays round the reed bed and then goes down, joining the multitudinous chatter, adding a decibel to the noise, an extra level of shading to the dense mass of birds already assembled. Now, from the south, comes the biggest group yet. I'm going to say 400. Enough to catch the eye from a distance and for me to follow their progress as they approach. They come in from higher than the last group, sweeping round to the west, bunching closely, then ballooning before shape-shifting over the reed beds no more than twenty yards away, as smooth as if thoroughly rehearsed. There are no stragglers. It's easy to think of them as a single entity, so fluid is their morphing from shape to shape, their reactions too fast for the human brain to comprehend. As they perform this everyday miracle, I become aware of a voice above the white noise of the birds' ceaseless chatter. A human voice, coming towards me on the path.

'Yeah, we said thirty, no more. Yeah. Uh huh. Yeah. Inbox me.'

He hangs up and walks past, looking neither at me nor the birds, seemingly oblivious to his surroundings. Thirty what, I wonder? Thirty pounds? Thirty Ferraris? Thirty large bags of John Innes No. 2 potting compost?

Ten yards behind him come his presumably wife and presumably daughter. They stop, look at the starlings for a few seconds without comment or expression, then scuttle off.

I stay, watching the birds settle in for the roost. The hullabaloo dies down until it's a hubbub again, and then a mere commotion, the sight and sound staying with me all the way back to the village and beyond, battling for attention in my head with the desire to kill the person who first made a verb out of the word 'inbox'.

Our almost barren day on Lindisfarne leaves me disappointed but unbowed. We still have a day and a bit.

I consult local knowledge, thanking the gods of ornithology for dedicated people who share information on the internet. As I browse, I realise I missed a trick on my pre-dawn excursion. At Stag Rocks near Bamburgh there should be a flock of turnstone, and with them purple sandpipers, one of the birds I haven't looked into. They're the suspect in the murder case who doesn't get investigated because the detective's always distracted by something else, but who turns out to be the killer.

There's only one thing that gives me pause. I know Stag Rocks. I avoided them yesterday. I call them Vader Rocks. Flat, shiny, slippery. To see these purple sandpipers I'll have to put myself into physical danger. Never the best start to a weekend.

There are moments, the next morning, when I doubt the wisdom of my decision. Moments when I feel my foot slide on the rock, the balance of my body shift, my heart race as I try to rearrange my weight forwards. I've seen birds from the safety of the dunes, but all I can tell is that they're waders. I need to get closer, and that means picking a way across the rocks. There are patches of seaweed and the occasional encrustation of barnacles, both offering a more stable footing, and if it came to it I could go down on hands and knees, and to hell with dignity. But mostly it's the glossy mirror of Darth Vader's face.

We all have to go one day. Charming and enticing as the purple sandpiper is, do I really want to risk it all in pursuit of one?

Apparently so.

Inch by inch I shuffle forward, feeling increasingly like a Galapagos turtle. Quite how I'm going to manoeuvre binoculars to eyes without coming a cropper is a mystery, but as I get closer the terrain becomes more reliable, my footing firmer, and I find I can sidle across to a ledge, park my bottom and reassess. The birds are within range now, but hopping up and down off the rocks, dodging the spray, showing an uncanny ability to know when they're about to swept out to sea, and moving out of the way at the last second. A dozen of them are turnstone, stout tortoiseshell-plumaged birds named, like wagtails and woodpeckers, after their defining activity rather than their appearance. Where others recoil from the wriggling life forms found under rocks, turnstone seek and devour them. My first of the year was at Minsmere back in spring. I pounced on it, not knowing whether I'd see another, not understanding that they're relatively common birds at the right time of year and in the right place. Now I've seen enough of them to be blasé, and turn my attention to the darker, less eye-catching birds dotted amongst them. I find one standing helpfully still, wrestling with a clump of seaweed, and tick off its distinguishing features. Dark grey upper body – check; whitish underneath – check; orangey-yellow legs – check.

Purple sandpiper, consider yourself ticked.

After this life-or-death struggle, a relaxing beach walk in the afternoon is in order. The beach in question, Ross Back Sands, is just to the south of Lindisfarne, and subject to the same tides, so there's a bunch of beach at our disposal. It's a lazy afternoon of strolling through the dunes, experimenting with camera settings, and wishing we'd brought a ball or Frisbee. The bird activity is equally lethargic. Distant blobs on the sea, wafting in and out of view, are gradually brought close enough by the tide for an attempt at identification. A couple of eider bobbing up and down, some low-flying cormorants, the usual gulls, and a pair of non-specific grebes with flattish heads. They're enough to quicken the pulse a fraction. I walk as close as I can to the tide, forgetting that some waves come further in than others. But wet feet will dry, and these birds might disappear at any moment. An instinct tells me they're not the run-of-the-mill little or great crested varieties. Even at this distance there's something about their shape and size, the flatness of the head, but they remain frustratingly on the cusp. Too close to give up on completely, too distant for certainty.

Providence, in the shape of a young man with better binoculars and more knowledge than me, comes to the rescue. He knows grebes all right. I wonder out loud if they might be Slavonian, and when they drift close enough he confirms the identification with a crisp nod and a muttered comment about head shape, and we part ways.

They're a boost, those birds, but the trip still isn't meeting expectations. I need two more ticks to fend off coffee-related lachrymosity. It's the longest of long shots, but desperation is my spur, so I leave my sleeping family for another pre-dawn start the next morning, the last of our visit, and drive to Lindisfarne once more. We go home in four hours. No sooner have I made my way to the east of the island than I waste 2 per cent of that time admiring the sunrise.

In my defence, it's spectacular. Rendered in paint it would have critics berating its lurid vulgarity. Thin, low cloud heightens the drama, battleship grey against light blue underpinned with the burning coral of refracted sunlight. As the sea turns orange, a black-headed gull, standing on a rock on the shore, is silhouetted against it. It would make a fantastic photograph, except it doesn't, the gull drowned by the brightness of the light, which changes so quickly I'm unable to adjust the settings in time to capture the splendour of the sight. Perhaps that's for the best. Maybe it's healthier to have the memory of it rather than add it to the unceasing digital parade of our minutely recorded lives.

Three minutes later, both gull and light are gone, and the morning can continue as normal. I walk, hoping against hope that something will turn up. Flocks of starlings pass me, dispersing from the night roost to their constituencies.

After twenty minutes I turn round. My time here is limited, and this excursion has the cloak of futility around its shoulders. Maybe there'll be something around the harbour, I tell myself, unconvincing and unconvinced.

The tide around the harbour is at its lowest, transforming the landscape. It's now possible to walk across to St Cuthbert's Isle, where two days ago swimming would have been the only option. This tiny island just off the harbour, pinpointed with a plain wooden cross, is where the eponymous saint gave hermiting a try-out before undertaking the real thing on Inner Farne just down the coast. The isolation he sought from human company in both places would have been more than compensated for by the presence of birds, and I'm hoping for plenty of the same. His name is enshrined for birders in the local nickname for the eider: cuddy duck. I see at least a dozen cuddy ducks on the surrounding mudflats as I pick my way across to the islet. It's not the easiest of going, ragged rocks combining with seaweed to make it almost as treacherous as Stag Rocks.

I spend as long as I can there, scanning the mudflats for unfamiliar shapes to no avail. The thought that six months ago I wouldn't have been able to identify half these birds is scant consolation. There's no single moment in this enterprise when hope disappears completely, just a gradual erosion of expectations until you realise the run rate is too high and all you're left with are tailenders. But here, on this little island, surrounded by all the wrong birds, I can feel it slip out of my grasp.

For the first time I begin to hate the birds. I'm tired, I've got up at stupid o'clock, and we've got a five-year drive home. The birds in front of me are unwitting recipients of my ire. Those brent geese, standing around brazenly not being bean geese. Bastards. That great crested grebe, resisting my efforts to will it into the shape of a red-throated diver. Selfish git. That duck over there, floating away from me, would it kill it to be a goldeneye?

It's a goldeneye. A female, its distinctive head shape conveniently silhouetted to help me.

All right then. As you were.

You're gorgeous, every last one of you. I want to marry you all.

Paranoia about incoming tides sends me off Lindisfarne earlier than strictly necessary, and I drive back to Bamburgh, there to scoop up the others before heading home.

As I park, a text comes through.

–*Gone to castle. See you car park 12ish?*

It's 11.15. Extra time. I can walk along the top road, scan the fields for grey partridge, or maybe there'll be a brambling hanging around with the chaffinches. Or perhaps a Rüppell's vulture will decide today's the day, after a lifetime in the Sahara, for a jaunt to colder climes.

The truth is more mundane, but equally welcome. A small bird of prey, agile and nippy, on the chase low over the field, its size, slate-coloured upperparts and pointed wings giving me the clues I need.

Merlin. The smallest British raptor, and my new favourite bird.

It does a couple of passes across the field then dips over a low hedge. I look at my watch. It's 11.53. My work here is done. I'm still, just about, in the game.

October ticks (13)

RSPB Dungeness, South Norwood Country Park, RSPB Rainham Marshes, Regent's Park, Budle Bay, Bamburgh, Lindisfarne

Great White Egret *Ardea alba*, Water Rail *Rallus aquaticus*, Ring Ouzel *Turdus torquatus*, Yellow-legged Gull *Larus michahellis*, Whooper Swan *Cygnus cygnus*, Pink-footed Goose *Anser brachyrhynchus*, Bar-tailed Godwit *Limosa lapponica*, Red-breasted Merganser *Mergus serrator*, Snow Bunting *Plectrophenax nivalis*, Purple Sandpiper *Calidris maritima*, Slavonian Grebe *Podiceps auritus*, Goldeneye *Bucephala clangula*, Merlin *Falco columbarius*

Year total: 178

NOVEMBER 2016

When life gives you lemons, summon barn owls.

There are two of them, in broad daylight, perched in a tree at Rainham. They are, of course, oblivious to world events. They don't even know who Donald Trump is.

Lucky them.

It's two days after the US presidential election, and I've felt the need to get away from it all. With concerts piling up this month, I have work to do, music to prepare. This distracts me for a bit, but my concentration levels are low. Birds, as they were back in June, are the obvious answer. The score of Elgar's *Violin Concerto*, sitting accusingly on my desk, can wait just one more day.

There's been significant rain since my last visit to Rainham a couple of weeks ago, dried pools refilling and wetland birds showing signs of returning. It's been a dry summer.

I chat with Howard, RSPB rep, fount of knowledge, and all-round good bloke, at the visitor centre.

'Do you know when we last had measurable rain here?'

'Go on.'

'June twenty-third. Brexit day.'

'Must be a sign.'

'Definitely a sign.'

The barn owls, distant daytime ghosts, give me a boost. They're a long-awaited tick, but I'm also taking them, based on nothing but ignorance and superstition, as a good omen. Where one species of owl is seen, the second must surely follow. Today is definitely going to be short-eared owl day.

The short-eared owl is an almost absurdly fascinating bird. Its disk of a face, mascara smudge around the eyes, broad, floppy wingbeats and a non-owly propensity to hunt during the day would make it unmistakable, if only it would come out to play. I missed repeated opportunities to see one in the spring, and now, with winter approaching, we're entering high season. Pity the voles of the Thames estuary.

I hang around the most likely area of the reserve. One was seen this morning, two yesterday. I wait for twenty, thirty, forty minutes. A front of turbulent air moves in from the river, bringing with it moderate to heavy westerly winds and a light drenching.

I've never been more grateful for extra layers.

A sparrowhawk puts the wind up a flock of lapwings. It's a handsome sight, 200 birds getting up and circling, and gives me an opportunity to indulge my most recent obsession, attempting to count large flocks of birds. I say 200; it was probably 400 or more. Or maybe just seventy-five.

Counting the short-eared owls is more straightforward.

I'm momentarily distracted by a water pipit, its pale streaked plumage and 'look at me' restlessness catching the eye. It lands on the water's edge and fidgets around, pecking at the mud, tail flicking.

It's on my list of must-gets, one of those scarce but common winter visitors, and renders the trip officially a success, so I call it a day. I'm two ticks to the good, and have seen some memorable sights, but somehow feel as if I've missed out because of short-you-know-whatted you-know-who.

Inevitably, as I inch towards the target, new ticks have been harder to come by, and my trips have become ever more focused. I'm still content I'm not breaking my 'no twitching' rule. I designate birding days, then choose a place to go. There are no frenzied dashes across the country, no desertion of the family to go and stare at a muddy field in Norfolk for six hours, hoping to see a goose that looks very slightly different from another goose.

Faced with a tight work schedule, I've mapped out the rest of the year, blocking off eleven days of birding, sacrosanct and immune to intrusions. The Berlin Philharmonic calls to ask me to stand in for Sir Simon Rattle at short notice? Ask my friend Toby. I'm birding.

Eleven days. Twenty-two birds.

The first day, a visit to Cliffe Pools in north Kent, gave me a distant sighting of a black-necked grebe and a deeper understanding of the true nature of cold and wet. I haven't had a harder-earned tick all year. But it was only one. Somehow, somewhere, I need to compensate for falling behind the required rate.

Today I come away from Rainham cherishing the barn owls and water pipit, but cursing the short-eared owls, who, as I walk back to the station, are doubtless emerging from their hiding places with cheeky grins and exchanging the strigine equivalent of a high five.

Two of my eleven days have gone. I have three ticks. Nineteen to get in nine.

It's so tempting to cram another day in, to leave the desk, to think I can get away with it. Apart from anything else, the gentle rhythms of birding offer a pleasing antidote to the energies expended while conducting. But the process of absorbing music is gradual, like learning a language, and while I'm comfortable with my knowledge of some of this month's repertoire – the music's contours embedded through years of revisiting and regular performances – there's enough unfamiliar stuff coming up to keep me tethered to the desk. I need to build strata of familiarity, to reach the stage when I can stand in front of the orchestra, lift my head from the score and engage with the players, rather than flap around in the hope that I'm not making things worse.

That's the challenge. Stand in front of a group of musicians and make them play better. How hard can it be?

It can be impossible.

Even before you start, you have to decide what you mean by 'better'. Music, like all art, is subjective. I might insist till I'm blue in the face that Beethoven's *Missa Solemnis* is 'better' than Led Zeppelin's 'Whole Lotta Love', but it's not going to cut much ice with the average heavy-rock fan. And while one person might be pleased enough with a performance of either in which the notes are in the right place – neatly lined up like toy soldiers – another might say, 'Who cares about the odd mistake? Let's hear the passion.'

Nonetheless, the notes on the page are a good place to start. And assuming that by 'better' we mean 'more together', 'more in tune', 'more rhythmic' and so on, then the rehearsal process is often a matter of listening to what's being played, comparing it with your internalised ideal, and trying to make the former sound as much like the latter as possible. If you can do that without saying a word, so much the better. There are rare conductors who stand almost without moving as the music flows around them, a twitch on the thread enough to summon angels.

Then there are those who, heady with power, fondly imagine that the glorious sound conjured with an elegant swirl of their baton is entirely of their own making.

This is a dangerous illusion.

To the unenlightened public, the conductor's role is often seen as mysterious, a situation reinforced by an innocent question from an audience member after a concert: 'So, your movements, do they have, like, some kind of meaning?'

Touché.

The conductor makes no sound, yet everything appears to revolve around them. It's an enticing image, and one enhanced by the cult of personality that has arisen around conductors over the years. No wonder, then, that the downtrodden professional orchestral musician – underpaid, underappreciated and under-valued – can grow to hate the conductor on sight.

In the musical world that is my stock-in-trade, the amateur orchestra, I like to think this hatred is at least diluted by the relative infrequency of rehearsals. If I stood in front of them every day, no doubt resentment would fester. But I can get away with once a week. Just about. And no matter how often I do it, it's best to be prepared.

So work comes first, and those nine days are, to my mind, the absolute limit of what I can afford. I intend to use as much of them as possible. The following Thursday I get up at half past ridiculous, aiming to reach Dungeness before dawn. Heavy rain and high winds are forecast, but they're not due till lunchtime. By then I'm hoping to have seen four new birds, a haul which would bring me below the asking rate of two per trip.

I clamber up the shingle bank by the power station, pretending to myself and the world that what I really fancy in this turbulent weather is a short burst of seawatching. It's an exercise in futility, but it feels like a ritual now, undergone every visit I make. There is, as usual, a swirling mass of gulls around the foaming waters of the area known as The Patch. Its proximity to a nuclear power station has me asking all sorts of questions to which I'm pretty certain I don't want to know the answers – but whatever the reasons, the birds seem happy enough to feed there. If I had the patience, and, more pertinently, if I were able to stand upright in the teeth of the wind blowing steadily from the south-east, I'd stick around and test my gull-identification skills. As it is, I pay no more than lip service to the exercise and am soon walking round the perimeter fence on my way back to the car, with half an eye out for the mythical black redstart. Four rock pipits form a guard of honour along the fence. I like rock pipits, the memory of my first, chased along the cliff edge at Portland Bill five months and several aeons ago, still fresh in my mind. But the wind makes me restless, and no matter which way you slice it, a rock pipit isn't a black redstart.

I never quite know how long to devote to a bird vigil. I don't want to spend too much of the visit waiting on a bird that might or might not show its face. On the other hand, it would be perverse not to give it half a chance.

There's also the issue of where to concentrate the effort. The power station isn't small, and the bird could turn up anywhere in the surrounding area of scrubby land. Or it might be hunkered down behind one of the outbuildings in the restricted zone. Whether staying in one place or roaming, you run the risk of the bird playing silly buggers, dogging your every move behind your back while carrying a placard bearing the legend 'This idiot couldn't spot an ostrich in a shoebox'.

After twenty minutes I call it off, traipsing dejectedly back to the car and driving the short distance inland to the RSPB reserve in search of kindlier birds.

There are three, in particular, I'm counting on. All have been knocking about the place for a while, displaying various degrees of spotability. The first, the ring-necked duck, is the most straightforward. In one of those confusing quirks of the birding world, identification can be secured not by a ring around its neck, but around its bill. This bird has been hanging around for weeks with the coots and tufted ducks on the pond by the entrance to the reserve, and showing no sign of leaving.

I pull in, get out, binocular up, and there it is. Literally a sitting duck, similar to but easily distinguishable from the dozen or so tufties surrounding it.

This is more like it.

Half an hour later, I'm back in the slough of despond without even a teaspoon to dig me out. This is very much less like it again.

It's not the steady wind, nor the flurries of rain, nor even the gradual loss of feeling in my gloved fingers. It's the dastardly game of 'Still You Don't See Me' that I'm playing with a long-eared owl. This isn't one of those desperate searches across swathes of countryside, or a patient vigil in a hide waiting for a bird that isn't there. Reliable witnesses have reported this owl. It's roosting in bushes across the pond by the visitor centre, disguising itself superbly as a collection of leaves. I'm beginning to wish I'd warmed up by doing a 10,000-piece jigsaw puzzle of the Sahara. With the wind whipping around my neck, and gusty showers beginning to develop, it's becoming increasingly difficult to focus on the task, but it won't do to give up now. The bird is there.

There comes a moment, after hours of not finding Wally, when you do find him, and you then wonder why the hell it took you so long, I mean he's *there*, just look at his unmissable hat and his goofy grin. So it is with the long-eared owl. A blink, a slight shift of the head, a movement just different enough from the rustling of the leaves for me to notice it, and now my binoculars are drawn to it like a magnet and there it is, deep in the bush, dozing the day away, oblivious to my burst of happiness. I would break into a celebratory song and dance routine, but I've just been joined by two other birders, and I don't want to scare them or the bird away. Also my tongue is frozen to the roof of my mouth and I can't feel my feet.

The nearest hide is just yards away, and I dive in there, if only to shelter from the growing weather.

I exchange hellos with the single occupant, a burly man who, hunched over his telescope, dwarfs it as if it were a toy. Normally we'd leave it at that, but over the next couple of minutes he seems continually on the point of saying something, several times half-turning towards me but then apparently thinking better of it. Eventually it spills out of him in a welter of frustration.

'I've had this bird in front of me for forty-five minutes, and I can't work it out. Is it a Caspian gull?'

His faith is touching. I issue due warning about my lack of expertise, but offer to help in any way I can, and fire up the trusty Collins app. It's the Minsmere Mediterranean gull all over again, except this time I'm in the game, not a hapless bystander.

The app has several illustrations of Caspian gulls in different plumages. I examine them while he talks me through the salient features of the bird in front of us, and then I study the bird itself. It's standing up to its knees in water in a group of a dozen birds, all of which seem to be herring gulls in various stages of development. They act as handy comparison.

I try hard to avoid my habitual brain meltdown when confronted with a mess of confusing plumages. The bird's not going anywhere. We can take our time.

What we're looking for is a slightly flatter forehead, a more upright posture, a less hooky bill and an absence of streaking about the head. In all four categories our bird scores about seven out of ten. As far as I can tell you could argue it either way, but seriously, what do I know? I can understand why my companion was all of a twitter.

As we masticate our findings, the door opens and we're joined by a third man. He bustles into the hide with a faintly proprietorial air.

'Morning. Caspian still around?'

Bench guy and I exchange a look.

'We think so,' I offer, 'but any help appreciated.'

He sits next to me, raises binoculars. The logo on his binoculars is worn from years of use. He smells slightly of peppermint. We describe the bird in question, and he falls silent, concentrating.

We wait. And wait. After an age, he lowers the bins.

'Yup. Third-winter male. Not the one I saw earlier, either.'

Strange, the trickle of euphoria on hearing the news. I'm at a loss to explain it. It's just a bird. More, it's a bloody gull.

But it's also a tick. Three today. I'm back on level terms.

Rainham.

Nothing.

Bastards.

I say 'nothing'. I've seen fifty species. Six months ago this would have represented untold riches. Today, in the universe of 'just going out to do some birding', that's still the case. But in the parallel 'must see sixteen more birds otherwise I'll bally well explode' universe, they're far from satisfactory. I nurse my grievance and a coffee in the visitor centre.

Howard, freed from duties around the reserve, is in chatty form. He raises his head from the scope set up overlooking the river.

'Anyone want to see a common scoter?'

Yes please.

I join him by the scope, as casual as a Boden catalogue.

'Hold on, it's gone.'

Bloody hell.

'Ah, there it is again.'

Even through the telescope it's dim and shady, sitting in the middle of the river far away. As I watch, it relocates about twenty yards downstream, clearly recognisable as a female common scoter because of its shape, white on the head and the speed of its wingbeats.

That's what Howard says, anyway.

Melanitta nigra, you are my 185th bird of the year. You can stay.

I'm pinning a lot on the Isle of Sheppey. It's a heavy burden, but I know it can take it. From everything I've read and heard, in winter on Sheppey you can barely move for birds.

Some months ago, with remarkable and unaccustomed foresight, I enlisted the help of a professional. Somehow I knew that come the end of November I would need someone who could tell me where to go and when, and once there, could help me pinpoint exactly what I was looking for and at.

David lives for birds. He thinks nothing of ten hours on a freezing hillside surveying bird numbers. That is, after all, his job. It also helps that he clearly loves it, the enthusiasm bubbling out of him like water out of an alpine spring.

Within minutes of our meeting it's clear I'm in safe hands. He's already pointed out three species I wouldn't have recognised, based on staccato chipping sounds and a disappearing shadow. I'm aware that my admiration is at least partly the natural regard of any apprentice for the master, but have never been more grateful for outside help. There's something reassuring about being in the company of a really good birder. You feel you can relax, safe in the knowledge that if a blue tit sneezes half a mile away you won't miss it.

In this case, though, it's not blue tits I'm after.

David has formulated a plan for the day, revolving around the late-morning high tide at Shellness, on the eastern tip of the island. If all goes to plan I'll be several ticks to the good by the time we return to the raptor viewpoint for dusk, when birds of prey will be as good as swooping out of the sky and taking the hats off our heads.

The thing about plans is they sometimes come off. Almost.

The day is grey, cold, windy, cold and cold. I'm wearing five layers. It feels a couple short. The birds, however, seem immune, and if David is inconvenienced by it, he doesn't let it show. Just me, then.

As we tour the island it becomes even clearer how indispensable David is to my plans. By myself I might have driven past the field that contains the bush that contains forty corn buntings, but he sees them a mile off and we stop awhile to watch them, busy as all get out, a hive of jabbering and flitting.

A story often told is of the decline of bird populations, and the corn bunting is a prime example, its former abundance curtailed by the denuding of the farmland on which it thrives. These ones seem happy enough, but it's a comment on the bird's decline that it's taken me this long to see one.

I like to think that, even if I'd missed the corn buntings, the white-fronted geese would have caught my eye. They're mingling with a flock of greylags, grazing in a field. These winter visitors from Siberia, at first glance similar to the greylags, are quickly recognisable by size, the streaky black patches on their underbellies, and the eponymous white front, this in fact being the forehead rather than the chest. My confusion over the different kinds of geese is gradually beginning to sort itself out, and looking at them through David's scope, I'm confident I'd know this bird again.

I wish I could say the same about the red-throated divers, but even armed with the most powerful optics and all the field guides at my disposal, these birds, flying over the sea in the far distance, would have gone unidentified, added to the pile of 'don't knows' that litters my year. David draws my attention to them with succinct directions.

'Four red-throated diver, flying right to left, just below the horizon.'

He moves out of the way, I look through the scope, and there they are, exactly as he says. I would have described them as minuscule dots rather than red-throated divers, but as he explains the identification points, I can indeed discern the low-slung head that helps set them apart from their close cousins.

This ability he has to conjure birds from thin air feels a bit like witchcraft, but that's how the combination of experience, knowledge and skill often looks to the uninitiated. I think again of my father's ability to draw the sweetest tone from any violin or Ilya Musin's extraordinary grasp of orchestral sound – hard-won talents, earned over decades.

It's not all plain sailing. Brilliant though he is, David is unable to summon a Richard's pipit out of thin cold air, the single bird that winters in a specific area of the nature reserve staying stubbornly out of sight. And everywhere we go we seem to encounter birders who have just seen a short-eared owl, without any evidence of the birds themselves. But the huge flocks of waders, whether assembled in close-knit groups on the shore or making the sky sing as they fly round in mobile swirling flocks, are ample compensation, and with a species total nudging eighty for the day, three of them welcome ticks, it's in high spirits that we return to the raptor viewpoint for our dusky vigil.

This viewpoint, a platform by the side of the road with panoramic views over marsh and farmland, with their wealth of small scurrying mammals, is fertile hunting ground for raptors. From reading about it I get the impression we'll be fending the birds off from all points of the compass.

Reality couldn't possibly live up to expectations. I'm delighted to see a barn owl quartering the reed beds in the middle distance, of course I am. The roosting birds at Rainham were gorgeous, but there's nothing to compare with the wraith-like figure of a barn owl on the hunt, silent of wing, stealthy of attack. And the graceful choreography of a dozen marsh harriers, switchback swoops and languid glides intersecting for a mesmerising crepuscular ballet, never fails to take the breath away.

But where's my hen harrier?

Hen harriers have been in the news this year. There are people who pay other people to kill them, the hen harriers, because they, the hen harriers, kill other birds that they, the other people, are paid to keep alive so that they, the first people, can charge a third set of people wads of cash to kill the other birds.

That sentence, by the way, makes more sense than the thinking behind the illegal killing of hen harriers.

Because of the aforementioned killiness, the hen harrier is now almost non-existent as a breeding bird in England, but they still come here from northern Europe for the winter, and dusk on Sheppey is as good a time to find them as any.

Half a dozen people gather at the viewpoint, wringing the last drops from the day. As I try to control my binoculars with arms that have reached the 'shuddering uncontrollably' stage of hypothermia, I almost suggest we huddle together for shared bodily warmth.

Watching the marsh harriers, I hear David's voice, my cold-numbed brain taking a second to register and process the words.

'Hen! Ringtail, below horizon, flying right to left.'

He has it in the scope, beckons me across, and I follow it closely as it quarters the marsh, disappearing behind some trees here, a building there, low over the ground. Its build and plumage are noticeably lighter than the marsh harriers behind it, the difference visible even in the gathering gloom.

A ringtail is a female or young hen harrier, predominantly brown and white where the male is blue-grey, the name deriving from the dark rings across the upper tail. More easily visible is the white band across the rump, and it's this I now see, prominent against the brown of the bird's body and the murk of the background.

The light has almost disappeared. I can no longer feel my head. Time to call it a day.

As I take my leave from David, trying to express through chattering teeth my gratitude for his time and expertise, one of the other birders turns to us and smiles.

'Shame you didn't get here five minutes earlier. There was a short-eared owl.'

Of course there was.

November ticks (11)

RSPB Cliffe Pools, RSPB Rainham Marshes, RSPB Dungeness, Isle of Sheppey

Black-necked Grebe *Podiceps nigricollis*, Water Pipit *Anthus spinoletta*, Barn Owl *Tyto alba*, Long-eared Owl *Asio otus*, Caspian Gull *Larus cachinnans*, Ring-necked Duck *Aythya collaris*, Common Scoter *Melanitta nigra*, Corn Bunting *Emberiza calandra*, White-fronted Goose *Anser albifrons*, Red-throated Diver *Gavia stellata*, Hen Harrier *Circus cyaneus*

Year total: 189

DECEMBER 2016

21 December 1987. I'm a second-year student at the Royal Academy of Music, home for the holidays. London is great, but it's good to be back. Clean air, open spaces, good food, all the comforts of the family home allowing a brief retreat to childhood amid the turmoil of student life.

I'm listening to the radio. Bach. *Brandenburg Concerto No. 3*. There's a short passage in it, an extended goosebump moment, the simplicity and perfection of which never fail to make me wonder. A series of descending scales in the bass, that's all. Dry analysis fails to capture its heart; therein lies its genius. It's coming up in about fifteen seconds.

My father, erranding about the place, pops his head in.

'There's the most marvellous bit coming up, Lev.'

We stand together for a minute, listening. Words aren't necessary. That's the thing about music – it picks up where words leave off.

The moment passes, the movement ends, and he goes about his business.

He has, did we but know it, three days to live.

The birds fill the sky, black as death, floating shadows against a backdrop of mist and winter half-light. They sweep up from the roost, describing a large arc across the reserve, their chacking calls spreading through the flock like snooker balls at the break. The light is draining rapidly, frost on the buds sharpening. In a few minutes these jackdaws, four, five hundred of them, will settle, like the rooks already at their posts in the trees in front of me. The fading light, the spiny fingers of winter trees reaching for the sky and the calls of a thousand birds combine for a simultaneously thrilling and sinister spectacle. I try not to think of Tippi Hedren.

The Bewick's swans were easy. They come to Slimbridge every winter and show themselves willingly by the Peng Observatory, not fifty yards from the entrance, tame as pets. I think of the dangers they face on their long journey from the Russian tundra, the decline in their population thanks to the familiar combination of hunting, habitat loss and climate change, and I reckon they're entitled to a bit of cosseting.

The swans are the point of this diversion, a cheap tick in a growing maelstrom of uncertainty; the jackdaws, and a bittern, slopping around in the reeds for twenty minutes while I keep my binoculars trained on it with the tenacity of a limpet, are a bonus. Such moments further my quest not an inch, but are bound to it with hoops of steel, encapsulating the reason for its existence.

I stay till closing time, milking the reserve for everything it's got. Then I head for Somerset, where tomorrow I'm pledged to succumb to the romantic allure of the glossy ibis.

Striking and elegant large waders with a curlew-like decurved bill, the ibis have been at RSPB Ham Wall for a while – strays from southern Europe. But they're wilful blighters, taunting twitchers with their mobility, and often lying low for days at a time. I might see them. I might not. It's a happy coincidence that Ham Wall is home to one of the largest starling murmurations in the country, so at least I'll have that if all else fails, my appetite whetted by the accidental experience on Lindisfarne. And beyond that, who knows what may turn up?

As it happens, nothing. Or as close to nothing as makes no difference.

The barren scene from the new hide at WWT Steart Marshes is almost comical. A lone curlew patrolling the frozen mud isn't just the highlight – it's the only bird there.

Richard, my host for the trip, couldn't be more apologetic. With the generous instinct that leads people to apologise for things they can't control, he feels responsible for the dearth of Somerset birdlife, as if, had he been a proper host, he would somehow have been able to lay on a sumptuous array of sightings carefully curated to tally with my wish list. But I'm not worried. He's good company. That's all that matters.

We walk round the reserve, talking about our birding experiences, his far more extensive than mine. Sixty-five years of birding is a lot to draw on, but even that can't conjure up a brambling in a flock of chaffinches. We scan them anyway, looking for the telltale flash of orange among the pale pinks and browns of the commoner bird, but without avail.

Steart on the coast and Avalon Marshes inland are linked by the lack of birds. It raises a simple question: where do they disappear to?

I get that it's cold here. Maybe they don't like it cold. But it's cold everywhere else within easy reach, too. I've read that swifts sometimes take day trips as far as Germany if the British summer gets a bit chilly for their liking. Do wildfowl and waders do the same in the winter? Have they all trotted off to the Bay of Biscay for a romantic mini-break? Or are they hunkered down in the depths of the reed beds with a *West Wing* box set and a tub of cheesy nachos?

Ham Wall, in the afternoon, is better. There are herons and cormorants. There are teal and wigeon. There are great white egrets.

There are no ibis.

The volunteer assures me they've been seen on the reserve that morning. They won't have gone far.

'Try the Avalon hide.'

We try the Avalon hide. Ninety minutes later we've seen six juvenile 'mule swats' and a shoveler. If I were alone I'd be grumpy, muttering, railing against the iniquities of life. But I owe my host the courtesy of a cheerful but resigned demeanour, so that's what I try to give him. When it becomes absolutely clear that the ibis are to remain memorable for their absence, we assemble our optics and leave.

And that, ladies and gentlemen, concludes your entertainment for the afternoon. Please kindly follow the stench of starling shit and make your way to the reed bed for the evening show. Those of you seeking 200 birds in a year, please ensure you take your shattered hopes with you.

Starlings and people alike trickle in. These gatherings have become spectator events, and even though it's not yet prime murmurating season, the spectacle is enticing enough for there to be a steady stream coming in as I stroll back to the car, against the flow of traffic, to fetch an extra jumper.

I'll never know what makes me look up. I'm the only one who does.

Two birds, in close formation, coming in to roost, silhouettes with decurved bills.

My first thought is, 'That's strange, those are the first curlews I've seen here.' My second thought, on seeing the broad wings and trailing legs, is hauntingly similar to a line delivered by Steve Martin in *Planes, Trains and Automobiles*.

Those aren't curlews.

The ibis, may the Lord bless their glossy purple plumage, go down within seconds, behind the reed bed, hidden from sight. They won't get up again tonight. It was the briefest window of opportunity, and I flatter myself it's only thanks to my developing birder's instinct that I saw them.

Forty-five minutes and a quarter of a million starlings later, I'm on my way home, cherishing the memory of those two cagey but temporarily cooperative birds.

The starlings weren't bad either.

Dungeness. Again.

It's a long way to go not to see a cattle egret. If I want not to see a cattle egret, I can do so from the comfort of my own home.

The day is saved by the smew. Any day would be saved by a smew, that foxy little saw-billed diving duck fresh in from its breeding grounds in the north European taiga. Here there are two. Two smew, Barney McGrew, Cuthbert, Dibble, Grub.

I spend some time honouring my tradition of looking for black redstart around the power station.

We all know how that turns out.

Stupid birds.

Eight birds to get. Three birding days left. Squeaky bum time.

I scour the diary, but in all conscience I can't squeeze anything more in and still call myself either a professional musician or a dutiful parent.

There's the remote possibility something will turn up on the Isle of Wight, where we're pledged to spend the last few days of the year. But I have the BirdGuides alert set to 'Tell me the moment anything with a feather lands on the island', and it's been ominously quiet.

I consult Andrew, and we concoct a plan for a 'mopping up'

day in north Kent. It's an ambitious schedule. Waxwings in Strood at 9.00, cattle egret at Marshside around 10.30, Oare Marshes for the great northern diver at lunchtime, leaving the remaining short hours of daylight for Sheppey and short-eared owl. Oh, go on then, let's have Richard's pipit there as well.

Andrew's well up for it. If the birds behave, it'll be straightforward. If not, I'm depending on Norfolk to deliver.

A waxwing is a bird to put a smile on your face. Punky hairdo, pastel plumage, red flashes resembling sealing wax on the wings, and a narrow yellow bar on the tail. A waxwing winter will see an irruption of the birds from Scandinavia, driven by poor conditions at home to search for red berries further afield. This is a waxwing winter. I've been following their progress, the first sightings in Scotland followed by a trickle southwards. According to reports, the three we're after have occupied a tree near a pub in Strood, conveniently close to the M2, for a couple of weeks.

The reports aren't lying. They're perching on a TV aerial on a house opposite the pub, basking in our attention. Damn fine birds, even in the murk of the early morning. I feel the easing of a tension I wasn't aware of. 193.

Two men hanging around a residential area with binoculars at nine in the morning are bound to arouse comment, but nobody beats us up or reports us to the police, so we regard it as a win and make our escape.

The cattle egret is a different matter. Descriptions of its location are vague, citing merely a field beside a road not far from Canterbury. I've looked the road up. It looks rather longer than I'd like. All we can do is drive up and down it, examining the fields on either side. It bears the hallmark of a fruitless mission.

But the finger of fate, as fickle as a cat in search of a lap, is pointed firmly in our direction. No sooner have we arrived at Marshside and started up the road than we see two skulking figures, Persil-white, in the first field. They're either egrets or members of the north Kent division of the KKK.

The pair, one cattle, one little, seem in no hurry to go anywhere. It's interesting to see them side by side, the familiar little egret standing more upright, its cousin slouched in a way that is crying out for a remedial Alexander Technique course.

We admire them for a while, then remind ourselves of our strict schedule. We're running late already, delayed by an inconvenient desire to spend time looking at the birds we've gone to such lengths to find.

Oare Marshes next, scene of my encounter with the boparscull a few months earlier. But where that day was bright and warm and the marshes filled with birds, today is dull and grey and empty.

Our mission: a great northern diver, reported with irritating lack of precision as 'on the water'.

It's a marsh. By the sea. Water is all there is.

Nonetheless we plump for the seawatching hide as an opening bid.

There's something strangely soothing about sitting in a wooden hut looking at an empty expanse of water. But soothing isn't what I'm after. Not today.

The required frisson is added when we realise the water isn't completely devoid of life.

It's too distant to make out any markings with the naked eye, but even from afar the flat-bottomed boat shape and heavy head are visible, and when it dives with barely a ripple, Andrew gives a little nod.

'Divers are so smooth going down.'

He prepares the scope while I play a couple of rounds of 'Guess where the bird will surface', and then we have good views of it as it floats around, diving occasionally, fishing grounds all to itself. Its markings and general demeanour confirm it as the bird we're after. I only twig as I see it that this is the realisation of a forty-year ambition, the romance of the Arthur Ransome book *Great Northern?* implanting the idea that this bird is impossibly rare and to be sought out if at all possible.

I have a sudden desire to hear its call, familiar from any film wanting to establish a scene of lonely wilderness in the forests and lakes of North America. It's a pipe dream, of course. It's deep winter in southern England. Wrong time, wrong place.

Our thirst for the diver slaked, we take a moment to consider our next move. It's 2.00. We have two hours of daylight.

A single long-tailed duck has been reported on the estuary on the way to Sheppey. Looking for it will take valuable time out of our day, but it might also be worth it if we can find it quickly. Andrew contacts a birding acquaintance for inside knowledge. The reply is swift.

'Interesting area. Probably best not to stop. If you do, take all your valuables with you, including the car.'

We decide against the long-tailed duck.

Oare to Shellness is no more than five miles if you're a bird, but twenty-three by road. It takes nearly an hour. Sheppey seems to have grown. Traffic lights refuse to change. All the slow drivers in north Kent decide they want nothing more than a pootle along the A2500. We pass the turn to the raptor viewpoint. For a moment I want to suggest we go there instead, but Shellness, ten minutes further on, offers the options of both short-eared owl and the fabled Richard's pipit.

The approach road to Shellness is 80 per cent suspension-breaking potholes, 20 per cent road. It's 3.15. Sunset is at 3.51.

We park. The path is along a raised bank between marshes and open ground. If we don't see anything near the car park, it could turn into a trek, and time isn't on our side. There's still the possibility of a dash to the raptor viewpoint if all else fails, but we'd need to take that option sooner rather than later. We set off, scanning for the Richard's pipit while also keeping the antennae a-twitch for owl action.

In the pipit's favour is its striking upright posture and propensity to call when flying overhead; against it is my suspicion that, despite regular reports to the contrary, no such bird exists.

In the owl's favour is Andrew's assertion that he's never visited Sheppey without seeing one. I'd hate to be the one to break his winning streak.

As we walk, I grapple with conflicting inner thoughts. Sensible me is happy with the day's haul, happy to be out birding, happy to call it a day; impatient, irritable me would gladly kill for a confirmed sighting of a short-eared owl, and tells sensible me to do one.

When it does appear, we both, for an instant, think it's a kestrel, a shrouded shape rising from beside the path far ahead. Then it opens its wings further and flollops over the path and onto the scrubby ground beyond, and we know.

I want to say something pithy, a memorable quote for a memorable moment.

All I can dredge up is, 'About bloody time too.'

We catch up with it and watch it hunting low over the grass. It's every bit as handsome as I'd hoped. At one point it lands, turns its head and looks directly towards us, the white disc of its face almost glowing in the twilight. Then it's up again, its loping wingbeats manoeuvring it easily over its hunting ground and out of our lives.

It's ten minutes before dusk on 13 December, and I finally have my short-eared owl. 196.

The Richard's pipit? I don't believe such a bird exists.

Long-tailed duck. Black-throated diver. Scaup. Shore lark. Brambling. Twite. Perm any four from six.

North Norfolk is grand for birding. It's also grand for pre-Christmas family mini-breaks, Tessa and Oliver accompanying me on this final leg so as not to miss out on the making of history. Also possibly to temper any potential adverse reaction when the dim-witted avians fail to show their faces.

Plan A: Titchwell. No leisurely strolls along sunlit beaches today. It's the shortest day of the year and the wind is bracing underneath slate-grey skies. It's exactly twenty-nine years since I stood in my childhood home listening to Bach with my father. I hum a series of descending scales in his honour.

Long-tailed duck, black-throated diver and scaup are around, but I'm ill-equipped to find them. They're not going to be floating conveniently within binocular range on the freshwater lagoon. Without a scope I, like them, will be all at sea.

What I need is an RSPB volunteer who is about to go round the reserve, preferably armed with a scope and a willingness to help.

Hello Richard.

He's my second helpful Richard of the month. There must be something about Richards. He's heading for the beach specifically to count the long-tailed ducks. There are dozens of them, the biggest haul the reserve has had in years.

It's so simple. We walk to the dunes, Richard sets up his scope, trains it on a group of birds bobbing on the waves, and invites me to have a look.

I accept.

I could have pursued a long-tailed duck into the dodgier parts of north Kent. If ever I needed vindication for the decision not to, here it is. Why chase one when you can have forty without risking injury?

I thank Richard and relinquish the scope. He's assailed by other visitors wanting to pick his brains, so I bask in my glory for a few minutes while buying telescopes in my imagination.

Richard beckons me over. He has something.

'What do you think?'

A test.

It sits low in the water, far away, bill very slightly raised. Mostly black and grey, with white flashes on foreneck and rear flank.

I'm not certain, but guess anyway.

'Black-throated diver?'

He knows, wanted me to work it out.

'See the white patch near the rear? Diagnostic.'

Two to go. My goal is so close I can tickle it behind the ear and listen to it purr.

It's been almost too easy. All we need now is for the scaup to emerge and then a brambling to be sitting on the bonnet of the car, and our work will be done.

Not so fast, man cub.

Brambling and Scaup, a quirky TV comedy-drama just crying out to be made, are absent from RSPB Titchwell.

Time for Plan B. I'm hoping we won't need Plans C, D or E.

It takes time to drive to Holkham, a few miles along the coast, where about twenty shore larks have been hanging out for days. It takes time to park and get our things together. And it takes time to work out exactly where the birds are supposed to be. It's a big beach, and we don't want to waste valuable minutes striking out in the wrong direction.

Holkham beach is gloomier and colder than when Gwyneth Paltrow walked across it in the closing credits for *Shakespeare in Love*. There's a broad area before you get to the beach proper, an expanse of firm mud interspersed with patches of scrubby grass.

We're greeted by a flurry of twittering finchy doo-dahs, quick to fright and flight, lifting off in a rush and landing a safe distance away.

Hang on.

Were those twite? They're finchy. And twittery. The more I think about it, the more they fit the bill. It's the flight call that clinches it. Twittery. Finchy.

I tick them in a state of heightened excitement. If we see the shore larks we'll be done. You can keep your scaup, your brambling. Shore lark would be a perfect way to finish it off. Foaming pints all round.

There's a tall, rangy figure in the middle distance, next to a telescope on a tripod, looking dunewards. He's either an incompetent spy or a birder.

He's a birder. And the couple of dozen little brown jobs with patches of yellow on their heads, snuffling around in the grass thirty yards beyond him, are shore larks.

200.

A rush of euphoria overtakes me. I approach the rangy gentleman. He has a long beard, a friendly smile, bad teeth.

'Gorgeous, eh?'

His accent is proper Norfolk, not the half-baked version people do that sounds like bad West Country and we think is Norfolk-y because they've added 'm'beauty' to the end of every sentence.

I agree. They're gorgeous.

From nowhere, I'm overwhelmed by doubt. It's not the kind of doubt that creeps up on you. It arrives in my head fully formed. And once it's there, I have to know.

'Any twite around today?'

'Well, there's a flock of linnets back by the boardwalk. Probably a couple of twite in there, but good luck picking them out.'

Ah, knackers.

Classic confirmation bias. I knew twite were around, saw a flock of twitterfinches, jumped to the conclusion. For those two minutes, so desperate was I for the 200, I expunged the linnet's existence from my mind.

Even if there were twite in that flock, I can't count them. That would be wronger than a desiccated coconut omelette.

199.

Knackers.

I resist the urge to bean my temporary companion over the topknot with my binoculars, and snarl at my family instead.

Stupid stupid birds. What a ridiculous way to spend your time.

We return to Titchwell. Marsh harriers come in to roost, five, ten, fifteen of them, gliding and swooping over the reed beds. They hold centre stage, but there are additional attractions all around. Golden plover – 300? I can't count, don't, on this occasion, want to – head in from the east; lapwings circle, wingbeats more languid than their cousins'; off to the right, starlings, silhouettes unmistakable against the darkening sky – three groups, maybe a couple of thousand in total, conjoining for a mini-murmuration, a teasing glimpse of impossible geometry before they flop down into the beds, miraculously unanimous.

They're magnificent, every last one of them. Tessa and Oliver, despite the cold, despite the wind, despite the creeping darkness, stay and watch to the end, transfixed.

Would it be too much to ask for the scaup as well?

Yes it would.

Tessa's birthday is 22 December. My present to her is not dragging her out birding. It's the least I can do.

It's the perfect winter's day. Sun. Sky. Frost. A walk is obligatory. So is hot chocolate. The walk takes us to Felbrigg Hall, twenty minutes from the rented cottage. Big house, big grounds, big lake.

I take the binoculars, just in case. Plan C. A little owl is known to live there. Brambling have been seen.

Not by me.

It's not a good ball. India are on their way to their highest ever score in Tests and a crushing victory, but that's by the by. At any stage of the game it would be a bad ball. But bad balls sometimes take wickets.

K. L. Rahul, the Indian batsman, scoops it tamely to the fielder at cover point. His innings is over. He squats on his haunches, bereft. After an age, he creeps like snail unwillingly to the pavilion, shrouded in anguish and disbelief. He has scored 199 runs. It's been a superb performance, the highest score of his young career, a pinnacle of achievement. Yet he reacts as if he's just accidentally shot his beloved pet canary.

If he'd scored nineteen, say, or forty, such a dramatic reaction would be considered over the top. But everyone watching understands.

It's uniquely cricketing, this logic, that having done so well you're still deemed in some obscure way to have failed. It's the allure of the landmark.

The possibility that I will, after a twelve-month of blood, sweat and feathers, be left stranded one short of my target, is agonising.

Maybe it's not just a cricketing thing.

No matter that I've regained contact with the sights, sounds and smells of the natural world, discovered new parts of the country, and been for more family mini-breaks in a year than in the whole of the previous decade. No matter that I've become fitter, lost weight, met new people and relearned how to learn. No matter that I've revisited my youth, made myself soggy with nostalgia, and found new perspective on the meaning of parenthood, as well as the importance of carpe-ing the diem.

Just one more. Please.

I consider emergency backup plans. There's a rose-coloured starling loitering in Crawley. We're spending Christmas Day in Brighton. Crawley is on the way to Brighton.

It would definitely be Plan Z.

I can't. Can I?

No.

Maybe?

No. What kind of person would do that?

But…

No.

I check the BirdGuides app obsessively. Plan E is still a possibility, but it reeks of desperation.

And what's so bad about that?

Reports of a black redstart on Culver Down on the Isle of Wight. Yes, that'll work, because I've been so successful at finding them everywhere else. I'm not going to get the last one on the Isle of Wight. I can feel it. It has to be here in Norfolk, and it has to be now.

Last day, last chance.

Plan D. A return to Felbrigg Hall, hoping to catch the beggars unawares while they're still rubbing sleep from their eyes. I set out on my own, Tessa and Oliver understandably having little appetite for a pre-dawn start followed by a cold and fruitless traipse around the Norfolk countryside with an increasingly irritable me.

I can picture the little owl, perching on a fence post then darting across the shallow grass in search of a mouse.

But picturing it isn't enough. I need to see it.

Some days, you just know you're doomed to failure. There's something in the air. It dawns on me as I skirt the big house that this is merely an early-morning walk, good for exercise and nothing else. But I carry on anyway, willing an owl to appear from behind a wall, trying to conjure a brambling from the thin December air.

I find a bench overlooking the grounds and sit, summoning the patience I lacked as a child, hoping my stillness will draw them out. As I wait, I allow the memories of the year to drape over me like a blanket. From Dungeness to Skye I've sought the birds, Clouseau-like in my doggedness and, at first, incompetence – but graduating through Rebus and Frost to achieve the very occasional Sherlock moment.

The thought bludgeons me around the head, as it has done repeatedly throughout the year: what the hell was I doing for those thirty-five years? How could I have gone so long without this simple pleasure in my life? What was I thinking?

At some point in the early 1980s I laid aside my binoculars. I don't remember exactly when. It was a gradual tailing off rather than a sudden renunciation. Perhaps I was finding it too difficult to hold them at the same time as a cricket bat. Perhaps the torpor that enveloped me during my teenage years buried any interest in birds so deeply that it took another three decades to resurface. Perhaps I just moved on to other things.

At times this year I've wanted to go back in time, revisit my younger self and urge him not to give it up, not to yield to whatever repressing influence it was that pushed birds into the sidelines. But even if time travel were possible, and laying aside the inherent space-time paradox that would arise from meeting myself, a paradox likely to cause the universe to collapse in on itself or indeed never to have existed at all, what would it achieve? And what exactly would I say, anyway?

Hello.

Who are you?

I'm you in 2016.

What happened to my hair? And my clothes? And... well, everything?

Never mind that. I've come to tell you something very important.

Have you?

I have. It's this: don't forget about birdwatching.

Umm... OK. Are you sure you want to waste time travel on that? Because, you know, Hitler...

Pretty much. Also, do your piano practice, don't pretend you like smoking when you're in your twenties – you're not fooling anyone – and when you meet Douglas Adams in 1987, try not to stand there drivelling like an imbecile, and don't get smart with him about time travel. Oh, and I've got this bit of paper for you.

What is it?

It's a list of all the girls who aren't interested in kissing you.

Ew.

Believe me, it will save you a lot of time and energy.

OK.

Oh, and this is the most important thing...

What?

Make absolutely certain you watch every minute of the Ashes series in 1981 and 2005.

I would have done anyway.

Yeah, but it can't be said too often. Where are you going?

Sorry, but Tomorrow's World *is about to come on.*

Can't you watch it later on iPlayer? No, hang on, cancel that. Wasn't thinking.

What's eye player?

Never mind.

Look, is that all? I really want to watch it. They've got a thing about wireless telephones you can carry around the house. They sound amazing.

You just wait. Anyway, yes, we're done here. There's other stuff, but it's too big to go into at this stage.

OK.

Oh, but... one last thing.

What?

Just in case you do give up birding in the next few years, could you put a tick against black redstart first? You won't regret it.

A memory arrives, as it does most years at this time. Welcome. I've been expecting you.

He was sixty-seven. No age, but at least spared the slow decline of passing years. Our memories of him will always be of a man cut off while still at the peak of mental and musical acuity. His suffering was intense, short-lived; mine lingered, cast a shadow over the early years of what I came to understand wasn't really adulthood but an extended adolescence.

It's two days before the funeral, early evening. Christmas and New Year have come and gone in a fog of numbness. They will remain hurdles for many years to come, the innocent memories of childhood Christmases obliterated by the timing of bereavement. Family and friends have gathered, the rallying-round process continuing for weeks, solidarity and friendship united to ease the burden.

A meal is being prepared, the atmosphere in the kitchen one of strangely social conviviality. I've taken myself into another room to watch television. Four channels are plenty, especially when one of them is broadcasting Schubert. *The Trout Quintet*. I watch, listen, relax.

And now I'm walking down the corridor to the kitchen, and there are sirens, but they're not sirens, they're me, my whole being erupting in a keening howl of grief, all the shock and emotion coming out for the first time, exploding in one anguished non-human wail. And I can't hear myself. To me, the walk is conducted in total silence. But they hear me above the sound of conversation in the kitchen, and when I get there it's full of cooking steam and warmth and love, and, I'm later told, great relief. At last. About time. Now it can begin.

I hear honking. A flock of pink-footed geese approach from the west, high, haunting, taunting, bringing me back to the present. They remind me of Plan E. There's no alternative. I check the BirdGuides app one last time. It's still there.

I go back to the cottage, make Tessa a cup of tea, thank her for doing all the packing in my absence, put on my best winning smile, and ask if it might be possible to go home via the scenic route.

If you were driving to London from Cromer, you might go via Docking, but only if you'd never read a map before. It's not completely in the opposite direction, but completely in the opposite direction is the sea, and even I'm not mad enough to go that way.

In a field about half a mile outside Docking is, apparently, a red-breasted goose. It's been there for several days, showing no signs of moving. They breed on the Arctic tundra, migrating to the Black Sea in autumn. This one is as off-course as I am.

There's no doubt about it. This is a twitch.

The snag isn't that the bird's in a large field all by itself. The snag is that it's in a large field with 6,000 pink-footed geese. That's a lot of geese. But the red-breasted, its striking plumage reminiscent of an anatomical diagram, is bound to stand out.

Such misguided certainty.

The field isn't hard to find. It's the one with all the geese in it. We park in the nearest convenient spot, about 200 yards down the road, and I leave Tessa and Oliver in the car with their good wishes ringing in my ears. No time limit has been set, but I know the rules of engagement.

Here's the world famous birder, hunting down his 200th bird of the year.

Arriving at the field, I feel my heart sink. Until you're face to face with 6,000 geese, it's difficult to imagine the space they occupy. Quite a number are on the edge of my binoculars' range, mere silhouettes on the brow of the hill. There might be some on the other side. Fearing the worst, I start scanning. The wind whips up so strongly I can't hold the binoculars still. The hood of my coat and my wild flyaway hair combine for a perfect storm of annoyance.

I find wind unsettling, even at the best of times. Now it acts as a tap into my inner seam of sweariness. I hurl a tirade of championship-quality invective at a pile of sugar beet. My mother would be proud.

Trying to bring both binoculars and temper under control, and failing, I do a quick scan of the field, hoping the red-breasted goose will leap out at me. It doesn't. Then I do a slower scan, taking in clumps of geese but not examining each one, just looking for the standout bird. Again no luck. The geese stretch as far as I can see, and beyond, the hedge getting in the way. On the other side of the hedge, the long pile of sugar beet offers another obstruction. How long will it take me to work my way along the field?

Stupid bloody birds. What am I doing here? I should just leave. No shame in 199.

Tell that to K. L. Rahul.

I stay, doggedly scanning, examining, hoping.

It's about setting goals, achieving them, seeing the job through. It's about cashing in, at long last, the investment your parents made with their unobtrusive interest in nature. It's about acquiring new skills, learning and caring about yourself, other people and the world around you. Without this urge in its many and varied forms, from the trivial to the important, where would we be?

Falling at the last hurdle is not an option.

A cheerful younger man strides up, scope over his shoulder. I see that he's parked his car on the verge, almost in the ditch, a hundred yards up the road. I try to bring my inner toddler under control, reassemble toys in pram, and plaster an unconvincing smile onto my face.

'Any sign?'

'Afraid not. I'm not best equipped, though.' I nod towards his scope.

'It's definitely there,' he replies, assembling the tripod. 'Saw it from the other side of the field, took a bearing from the end of this pile of beet, thought I'd come round to see if it's visible. But it's down in this dip here. Just got to wait for it to wander out, I suppose.'

I'm relieved it's not just through incompetence that I couldn't find the darned thing. But I'm also frustrated. It's within touching distance. Now I know how Tantalus must have felt.

Hungry-looking men with telescopes, full of intent, are beginning to assemble. My frustration is shared by another, younger man standing shivering next to me.

'My family's in the car,' he says. 'I've only got fifteen minutes.'

'Me too. But I don't have a time limit. In theory, anyway.'

He grimaces. 'I'm still being punished for last Christmas Day.'

'What happened last Christmas Day?' I ask, half wanting to know, half already knowing.

'I took a slight diversion to see a pallid harrier on the way to the in-laws.'

'Slight diversion?'

'About an hour. Didn't even see the bloody thing.'

I don't say so, but my sympathy is entirely with his wife, who is probably even now sitting in a car quarter of a mile away trying to stave off family meltdown.

I, of course, have left my wife and son in a car quarter of a mile away, but that's entirely different.

I've asked myself to what lengths I'd go to get my 200 birds, and now I have my answer. I'm no paragon of virtue, and there have been times when I've felt my obsession impinging on family harmony, but Christmas Day? Really?

I grunt a non-committal, non-judgemental answer. Conversation trickles. Time, as it tends to, passes.

I've been away from the car half an hour, maybe more. I really can't stay much longer. There are limits. But these geese aren't for shifting. The twitchers, about a dozen of them now, are ranged along the verge, showing no sign of impatience. They're used to much longer vigils. For them this is a mere blip.

Five minutes. Then I have to go.

The five minutes pass. Loads of geese, but no goose. I briefly consider storming the field, clambering over the sugar beet and flushing the damn thing.

Maybe not.

Two more minutes, then I really have to go.

I wonder how I'd feel if I'd been left in the car for forty-five minutes before a long journey home.

I think of my exchange with pallid harrier guy, and all that revealed. It was mild, but there was still about it a jokey, blokey

244

chumminess that makes me cringe – family a thing to be escaped and then moaned about over just one more pint. She's only doing the ironing, maybe she'll have finished and started on the hoovering. Eh? Eh? The little lady. 'Er indoors. The ball and chain.

No.

The red-breasted goose is a fine bird, but it's just a bird. There will be others. Some things are more important.

With leaden legs I trudge along the verge. I reach the end of the twitching line, where the cheerful man who first joined me on the scene is looking through his scope. It's pointing away from the supposed location of the alleged red-breasted goose. I wonder what he's looking at. I stop beside him. He notices me, flicks his head.

'I've got a couple of tundra bean goose in the scope if you want.'

He says it casually, as if they're not the most important fourteen words he's said all year. The bean goose are nothing to him, everything to me. I amble across to the scope, nonchalance personified.

Parikian?

Sir?

Have you done your homework?

Yes sir.

What are the distinguishing features of the tundra bean goose, Parikian?

Tundra bean goose, sir. Anser fabalis rossicus. *Similar to the pink-footed goose* Anser brachyrhynchus, *but with orange legs rather than pink, heavier head, and a small orange patch on the bill.*

Very good, Parikian. You may go.

Sirthankyousir.

As I drink them in, in all their bean-goosey magnificence, I'm flooded with inner calm. I nudge the ball off my hips down to fine leg, and stroll through for an easy single.

200.

I thank him, make my excuses, and return to the car, humming Bach's *Brandenburg Concerto No. 3* under my breath.

December ticks (11)

WWT Slimbridge, RSPB Ham Wall, RSPB Dungeness, Strood (Kent), Marshside (Kent), Oare Marshes, Shellness NNR, RSPB Titchwell, Holkham Gap (Norfolk), Docking (Norfolk)

Bewick's Swan *Cygnus columbianus*, Glossy Ibis *Plegadis falcinellus*, Smew *Mergellus albellus*, Waxwing *Bombycilla garrulus*, Cattle Egret *Bubulcus ibis*, Great Northern Diver *Gavia immer*, Short-eared Owl *Asio flammeus*, Long-tailed Duck *Clangula hyemalis*, Black-throated Diver *Gavia arctica*, Shore Lark *Eremophila alpestris*, Bean Goose *Anser fabalis*

Year total: 200

JANUARY 2017

I wake early, memories of *Jools Holland's Hootenanny* ringing in my head. It was Roy Wood who did for me in the end. I survived the mountains of food and the flagons of wine. Several rounds of board games couldn't finish me off. But the sight and sound of the hirsute 1970s pop idol sent me scurrying off to bed like a squirrel being chased off the bird feeder.

I feel surprisingly fresh.

New Year. New hope. New plans.

I spring out of bed and hobble across to the window.

A blue tit hops up from the wall to the branches of the sycamore on the other side, flits around for a few seconds, and bounces off on a secret blue tit mission.

One.

ACKNOWLEDGEMENTS

Firstly, all praise and huzzahs to the supporters of this book – people who stumped up their hard-earned (I assume) cash to support an idea without really knowing if or when it would appear. It simply wouldn't exist without your generosity.

The process of writing and producing the book has been pure pleasure from beginning to end. I send a beribboned thank you to everyone at Unbound for making it such a delight, and especially to Scott Pack – without his unceasing support, from commission to delivery, it would never have got off the ground. And without DeAndra Lupu's calm and seamless guidance, the production phase would have been far more stressful.

In the birding arena I have magpied information from many people. They all deserve my gratitude, but particular thanks go to: Andrew McCafferty, who guided me from robin song to short-eared owl, and kindly checked the manuscript for ornithological idiocies – if any remain, they are mine, not his; Chris and the boys for letting me in; Richard Montagu, who was blameless in the matter of the empty mudflats; David Darrell-Lambert, Peter Alfrey, Alastair Whitelaw and Howard Vaughan, who shared their expertise unstintingly; and the tribe of anonymous birders who provided me with entertainment, enlightenment and arcane snippets of knowledge throughout 2016.

Any writer relies on the support of a network of like-minded individuals, so to my fellow authors, who have given me inspiration and support over the years, I say thank you. There are loads of you, and any attempt at a list would be both long and incomplete. But specifically, I must say thank you to Laura Pritchard. She read this book more than once and guided me gently towards the righteous path – without her patience, generosity and eye for detail it would be much longer and much worse.

Thanks, as always, to Tessa, for her love and support and for letting me do it in the first place; and to Oliver, for all of the above and the pochard to boot.

And finally, to my parents, who, possibly without realising it, got me interested in the first place.

If you would like to support Britain's wildlife you can find out more from these organisations.

The Wildlife Trusts: wildlifetrusts.org

The Royal Society for the Protection of Birds: rspb.org.uk

The Wildfowl & Wetlands Trust: wwt.org.uk

The British Trust for Ornithology: bto.org

A NOTE ABOUT THE TYPEFACES

Berling

The Berling font family was designed in Sweden in 1951 by Karl-Erik Forsberg, a Swedish calligrapher, typographer, type designer and artist. It was designed for the Berling Type Foundry in Lund, Sweden, which cast foundry type from 1837 to 1980. Berling is an example of modern typeface art in Sweden in the 1950s, greatly influenced by the Neorenaissance. It is an old-style roman with classic features, such as ascenders that exceed the height of the capital letters.

Waters Titling

Waters Titling, used here for the chapter titles, is an all-caps typeface that looks best at larger sizes. With a high weight contrast between the thick and thin character elements, this typeface is an elegant way to add personality and flair to all-caps text. It was designed in 1997 by Hampshire-born calligrapher and type designer Julian Waters, an artist known for his classical calligraphic roman capitals.

Unbound is the world's first crowdfunding publisher, established in 2011.

We believe that wonderful things can happen when you clear a path for people who share a passion. That's why we've built a platform that brings together readers and authors to crowdfund books they believe in – and give fresh ideas that don't fit the traditional mould the chance they deserve.

This book is in your hands because readers made it possible. Everyone who pledged their support is listed below. Join them by visiting unbound.com and supporting a book today.

Rhodri Britton
John Bryant
Lynne Bulmer
Kate Bulpitt
Guy Burkill QC
Geoff Burton
Jonathan Burton and
    Diana Bickley
Stephanie Butland
David Butler
Janina Byrne
Rachel Calderon
Simon Callaghan
Giles Cambray
Jo Cannon
Car722
George Carbutt
Mallory Carroll
Meriel Cartwright
Barry Caruth
Helen Castley
Rosanna & Estella Charlesworth
Robert Chatley
Levon Chilingirian
Lady Ciara
Adrian Clark
Therese Clark
Wing-Commander Clark
Paul Coleman
Mike Collins
Laurence Collyer
Lesley Cookman
Jeff Cox
Julia Croyden
Charlotte Cunningham
Harriet Cunningham
Nigel Dant
Amanda Davidson
Steve Dawes
Simon de Souza

Alison Deane
Philly Desai
Miranda Dickinson
Angela Dickson
David Divitt
George Dobell
Hans Dols
Maureen Dominey
Marc Dooley
Edgar Dorman
Robert Philip Douglas
Richard Dryer
Jessica Duchen
Steve Dyson
T & R Eaton
Joanna Eberhardt
Hilary Edgcombe
Marti Eller
Ric Elsworth
Tom Elwin
June Emerson
Paul Emmett
Gareth Fairweather
Virginia Fassnidge
Gordon Faultless
Peter Fender
Paul Ferguson
Barry Douglas Fisher
Marion Fleming
Margaret Ford and John Stewart
Lucy Foss
Chris Foster
Tom Frederikse
Katie Fuller
Mark Galtrey
Andy Gardiner
Viviane and Roger Garland
Lewis Gaston
Gavin Geary
Josie George

Martha Gifford
Matthew Gilbert
Christopher Gillett
Marian Givens
David Goddard
Marcus Goddard
Alan Grant
Lulu Guinness
Francesca Hall
Lauren Hamer
Nathan Hamer
Dan Hamm
Stuart Hancock
Matthew Harries
Meirion and Susie Harries
Milo Harries
Mike Harrison
Lisa Hart
James Harvey
Sheila Hayman
James Heal
Alison Henry
Josh Hillman
John Holland
Samantha Holland
Steph Hovey
Philip Howard
Jacob Howe
Justin Hulford
Alastair Hume
Nick Hely Hutchinson
John & Sally Isaacs
Karen Izod
Sebastian James
Mike Jarman
Nicholas Jenkinson
Paul Jeorrett
Rita Jepsen
Rosie Johnson
Outi Jokiharju

Shirley Judd
Andres Kabel
Christina Kennedy
Dan Kieran
Matt Kingston
Andrew Kirby
Stephanie Kirschke
Amanda Knight
Francesca Knowles
Susan Knowles
Lord & Lady Knucketts
Richard Kuper
Adele Lapwood
Catherine Lee
Chris Lewis
Gwenllian Lewis
Jeremy Limb
Iain Lindsay
Matthew Longhurst
Ellie Loveknickers
Kathryn Lowe
David Lydon
Hugh Lydon
Kiera Lyness
Jane MacArthur
Harriet Mackenzie
Roxanna Macklow-Smith
Stephen Macklow-Smith
Nick Maingot
Robert Maniura
Richard and Helen Mansfield
Fenella Mappin
Quentin Maxwell-Jackson
Andrew McCafferty
Carol B McCollough
Eileen McManus
Julie Meikle
Deborah Metters
Tim Milford
Amos Miller

Kelly Millington

Sarah Milnes

Kay Minchington

John Mitchinson

Jon Mizler

Andrew Money-Kyrle

Richard Montagu

Nicola Morgan

Nessa Muir-Smith

Sarah Munby

Charles Mutter

Emma-Louisa Mutter

Carlo Navato

Robert Nichols

Ian Noonan

Anne-Marie Norman

Sanchia Norman

Mark Oppe

Andrew Osborne

Emily, Jon and Axl Owen

Vicky Owen

Scott Pack

Oliver Parikian

Step Parikian

Jane Park

Geoff Patterson

David Perchard

David Perry

Tara Persaud

Claire Pettitt

Caroline Phillips

Jonathan Pinnock

Sophie Plowden

Justin Pollard

Callum Porritt

Dudley Pritchard

In memory of Barbara Pritchard

Laura Pritchard

Peter Pritchard

Tessa Pritchard

Toby Purser

Jo Quail

Josephine Quealy

Lisa Rajan

Lynne Ramsden

Susannah Rang

Liz Rantzen

Dominic Redfern

Alison Rees

Emmanuella Reiter

Denis Ribeiro

Jane Richards

Richard Robbins

Andrew Roberts

Elizabeth Roberts

Keith Roberts

Alison Robinson

David Robson

Isabel Rogers

Johanna Romberg

Andrew Ross

Peter Rowe

Alison Rowley

Ken Saberi

Antje Saunders

Bronwen Scott

Rachel Scott

Thomas Search

Anne Sedgwick

Debbie Shipton

Sarah Siese

Alastair Simpson

Peter Sive

Kate Skeet

Michael Slater

Alex Smith

David Smith

Lydia Smith

Martin Smith

Anna & Ed Snow

Sylvia Snowden
Jackie and Dom Steinitz
David Stelling
Katherine Stephen
Andrew Steven
Sonia Stevenson
Dan Stinson
Alexander Stockler
Lisa Stonham
Alice Stringer
Richard Studt
Martin Sullivan
Annie Sun
Masayuki Tayama
Andrew Taylor
James Taylor
Christopher Tew
Eric Thomas
Robin H.L. Thomas
Helen Thompson
Christine Till
Tithers
Paul Tomkins
Sarah Too

Edward Tricklebank
Justin Tunstall
Salima Virji
Richard Vodden
Kate Waddington
Giles Wade
Adele Wagstaff
Bryn Walters
Samantha Ward
Charlotte Warner
Mark Welling
Tony Whelpton
John White
Alastair Whitelaw
Catherine Williams
Elly Williamson
Nicole Wilson
Frances Winstone
Louise WJ
Ken Woods
Jacqueline Woolf
Laura Wright
Charles Wroth
Alice Yelf

Observing nature as part of my daily routine has changed my life. You might want to use the remaining pages of this book to note down your own sightings. Or maybe you'd prefer to draw pictures of geese. Up to you.

MY BIRD SIGHTINGS...